W9-DFH-729

CRADLE OF ISLAM

Cradle of Islam:
The Hijaz and the Quest
for an Arabian Identity

MAI YAMANI

I.B. TAURIS

LONDON · NEW YORK

Published in 2004 by I. B. Tauris & Co Ltd
6 Salem Road, London W2 4BU
www.ibtauris.com

ISBN 1 85043 710 6
EAN 978 1 85043 710 9

A full CIP record for this book is available from the British Library

Typeset in Palatino by JCS Publishing Services
Printed and bound in Great Britain by
TJ International Ltd, Padstow, Cornwall

14096966

PLO

Contents

v

Contents

Contents

◆

To my father,
AHMED ZAKI YAMANI,
who travels with me
in my heart.

◆

Acknowledgements

I WANT FIRST OF ALL to acknowledge a great debt to Peter Leinhardt, my late supervisor at Oxford and his brother Godfrey Leinhardt, who 'inherited me'. Both gave me tremendous encouragement and guidance and this book is a tribute to their memory. Baroness Daphne Park, formerly Principal of Somerville College also offered unstinting support. I also want to thank Ahmed Al-Shahi, my DPhil examiner for his meticulous criticism, Nick Hostettler, Michaela Prokop, Jonathan Stein and Rosemary Hollis. I would like to acknowledge the work of those at I.B. Tauris who helped to bring this book to publication. Needless to say there are many Hijazis whom I cannot thank by name, but they are aware of my appreciation. The only two I thank publicly are my daughters Zain and Fatima.

Prologue:
Returning to the Cradle

F ATIMA WAS WELL INTO her eighties when I went to see her on a bright winter's day in Jeddah. She was sitting on her bed, dressed as always in full Hijazi clothing. That meant the impeccably starched white head cover, the high collar with the seven buttons, and the close-fitting pale dress, embroidered with tiny flowers. Born at the start of the twentieth century, she never compromised her standards, or the elegance, style and manners of her people. That, she said, was what distinguished the Hijazis from others in the Arabian heartland. As we talked, a Hijazi man entered the room—she had no compunctions about meeting men or women—seeking advice about the way he had tied his own headdress ('umama).

'My son,' she said in her clear Hijazi dialect, 'I approve.'

Fatima was always dispensing advice, right up until the day she died at the age of 104. Her expertise was in the rituals of the Hijazi people and culture, belonging as they do to the holy cities of Mecca and Medina.

Her conversation that day ranged wide over the days of pilgrimage, to trips made on the back of camels from Mecca to Medina, to the wedding ceremonies she witnessed and the invasion of Mecca by the Al Saud. What seemed to horrify her most was that the invading warriors had been only 'half dressed in underwear', with their feet encased in 'strange slippers'. She refused to learn, or understand, their dialect and professed herself mystified by everything they said. Her defiance of the new culture managed to embrace both pain and humour.

That day, as she recounted her stories, she became the inspiration for this book. It is the story of the people closest to the holiest sites of Islam, of their alienation and subjugation at the hands of the Saudi state, at the attempts to extinguish their pride and their culture. It is in every sense, therefore, a story of modern Saudi Arabia.

In 1926 the Hijazi kingdom was conquered by the Al Saud and six years later forcibly incorporated into Saudi Arabia. The Hashemite royal family were dispersed and the Hijazis became a people without a country. And yet they still retained a separate cultural consciousness, continuing to draw identity and stability from their sense of belonging to the cradle of Islam: Mecca and Medina. These cities of Hijazi origin lay claim to a distinctive history dating back over 1,400 years, to the days of the Prophet Muhammed and the leaders of the Muslim dynasties that the Hijaz exported. Everything else might change, but not the Hijazis' relationship with Islam's holiest sites. The fact remains for them that the Hijaz is the cradle of Islam.

Throughout the 1970s and 1980s, I began to hear references to a cluster of terms: *'adat* (customs), *tagalid* (traditions), *usul* (propriety), *tajammul* (adding honour or lustre to one's image) and related words and expressions. It seemed to me that, over the years, such language and behaviour was becoming increasingly widespread and significant, for both men and women. Despite pressure to conform to the dominant culture of the Najdis of central Arabia who now rule the country, Hijazis seemed to grow more aware of their own conventions, distinctive rules of conduct and unique religious or social ceremonies.

I was sure that Hijazi rituals and customs were gaining in importance, and I wanted to understand why. I also wanted to observe their rules of conduct and to explain their increasingly central role in defining the identity of urban Hijazis and their place in preserving a unique heritage from the threat of extinction. Throughout my research I was regarded as any Hijazi woman of similar age and status. But I was also expected to comply with the rules of propriety, which gave rise to some restrictions. As a native woman, I could not attend most of the formal male gatherings. I had to accept the fixed place in the seating hierarchy and adopt appropriate modes of speech and conduct.

Before formal events I was instructed what to wear, what to say and what kind of gift to offer. I naturally made mistakes. And yet I was soon viewed as a 'considerate' person, someone with *hawas* (sensitivity and consideration). I knew when to keep quiet during elaborate cultural rituals, and how not to miss any important detail. Perhaps my most important advantage was speaking the Hijazi dialect.

Of course there were risks for the people I interviewed. In the modern Saudi state, with its huge security apparatus, how could it be otherwise? And yet most of the Hijazis expressed their acceptance, even enthusiasm, for my project. Many were proud of their rules of good conduct and their 'traditions', and they wanted the world to know about them.

I have, however, respected their desire for personal anonymity, in the hope that one day they will be able to speak more freely.

Mai Yamani
London
2004

1 Defining the Hijaz: The Roots of Cultural Resistance

◆ THE CRADLE OF ISLAM

T HE AREA OF THE Arabian Peninsula known as the Hijaz takes its name—and its character—from *al-Hijaz*, the 'barrier' formed by the great escarpment that rises to the south like a wall behind Mecca and runs parallel to the coast as far as Yemen. Historically both nomadic and settled communities inhabited the area, but the Hijaz's urban centres—the Islamic holy cities of Mecca and Medina, as well as Jeddah and Taif—have dominated its development during the past fourteen centuries. Looking not inland but towards the sea, the Hijaz gained an international reputation for trade and as the focus of the Islamic *hajj* (pilgrimage), which contributed to its relative economic prosperity and enhanced its political significance.

Following the establishment of Saudi Arabia in 1932, the Hijaz came to form the westernmost of the kingdom's four regions, together with Asir in the south, the central Najd region, and Ahsa in the east. Each of these territories had been politically separate domains and culturally distinct prior to unification under the Najdi Al Saud royal family. Najdi standards of economic, political and religious behaviour were imposed throughout Saudi Arabia, and the autonomous political and religious leaderships of the other regions were displaced, as power and authority became centralised in the Najd.

1

However, at the outset Hijazi bureaucrats ran the new state apparatus. When Mecca fell to Abdul Aziz Al Saud's forces in 1924, effectively ending nearly 1,000 years of Hashemite rule in the Hijaz, the Najdi rulers found themselves in control of the most sophisticated administrative system in the Arabian Peninsula. A unified political structure had existed for centuries, with the *majlis al-shura* (consultative council) sitting atop a central administration whose annual budget provided for secondary schools, a regular army and a police force. The more elaborate administration of the ousted Hashemites' rule provided a model for Abdul Aziz Al Saud.[1] Whereas the Najdis were mainly tribal, nomadic, illiterate and subject to almost no foreign influence, the Hijaz had newspapers and several large public libraries. The official gazette, *Al-Qibla* (the direction in which all Muslims pray), published articles about developments outside Arabia and covered European events widely.[2] Another Hijazi newspaper in this period, the *Sawt al Hijaz* (The Voice of the Hijaz), became *Al-Bilad* (The State) after unification.

In the Najd, by contrast, there were no newspapers prior to the formation of the kingdom. The first Najdi newspaper, *Al-Yamama* (Dove of Good Omen), was founded in the 1950s. Similarly, a number of secular elementary schools operated in the Hijaz at the turn of the century. In Mecca there was Al-Madrasa al Ragiya (The Refined School), Al-Madrasa al Fakhriyya (The Honorary School), Al-Madrasa al-Sultania (The Sultani School); and in Jeddah the Falah (Success) school opened in 1903, with a branch established in Mecca in 1905. Meanwhile, no secular education was introduced in the Najd until 1938.[3] Indeed, reflecting and reinforcing the Hijaz's cosmopolitan, outward-looking character, Saudi Arabia's diplomatic corps, along with many government agencies, were based in Jeddah as recently as 1985, when they were finally moved to the capital, Riyadh.

The Hijaz's relative prosperity and the Hijazi elites' political influence reflected the high status derived from historical guardianship of Islam's holy cities. From 961, Mecca came under the rule of the *Ashraf* ('the honourable', singular:

Sharif), who were descendants of the Prophet Muhammed. The *Ashraf* trace their lineage from Muhammed's daughter, Fatima, and his first cousin, Ali ibn Abi Talib. All *Ashraf* claim descent from Hashim ibn 'Abd Monaf, the founder of the Banu Hashim clan of the Quraysh, the dominant tribe of Mecca during Muhammed's lifetime. Fatima's two sons, Hussain and Hasan, founded the two main branches of Sharifian descent, known as the Husaynids and Hasanids. From 961 until the Al Saud take-over in 1924, the Hasanid *Ashraf* asserted control over Mecca, while the Husaynids often controlled Medina.

In 1517 Sharif Barakat of Mecca acknowledged the Sultan of Turkey as Caliph. An Ottoman pasha was appointed to Jeddah, and small garrisons were stationed there and in Mecca, Medina, and other towns. Throughout most of their rule, the Ottomans allowed the Sharif a free hand in the management of Mecca and Medina, while the residents of the Hijaz received subsides from the Sultan and were exempt from taxation and military conscription. The Sultan was honoured with the title of Servant of the *Haramayn* (the two mosques), while the Grand Sharif earned money and prestige as the head of the entire *hajj*. His power depended partly on his ability to manoeuvre vis-à-vis the Ottoman government, but the *Ashraf*'s descent from Muhammed gave the Sharif high standing in the Muslim world—so high that the Sultans maintained an outward show of regard and circumspection.[4]

◆ THE RISE OF SAUDI POWER

The first Saudi state emerged from an alliance between Muhammed Bin Abdul Wahhab (1703–92), a Najdi preacher and theologian, and Muhammed Bin Saud, the ruler of Dir'aiyah in southern Najd. Wahhabism, a unitarian movement advocating God's oneness and undivided almightiness proved to be a potent force in the expansion of Al Saud rule, providing religious legitimisation for the conquest of the Arabian Peninsula while inculcating the population with a unifying belief system. Abdul Wahhab's aim was to abolish all *bid'a* (innovation) following the third Islamic century. His teachings are based on the idea that Islam has sunk into impiety, and a return to its supposed former purity remains Wahhabism's basic tenet. Anything that departs from the oneness of God as defined by the Wahhabis is *shirk* (idolatry), and implies *kufr* (disbelief). From its earliest appearance, Wahhabism has thus viewed many Hijazi customs and rituals—especially those that involve rituals honouring the Prophet Muhammed or his companions, particularly celebrations of the Prophet's birthday, visiting of shrines, reverence of the dead, dreams and visions, the sanctity of sites or shrines and especially Sufi practices—as superstitious, if not heretical. For the early Wahhabis, the Hijaz, with its versatile religious traditions and cosmopolitan outlook, was rife with impurity and heresy.

Relations between the Hijaz's Hashemite *Ashraf* and the Al Saud nonetheless remained moderately friendly for a long period. The Al Saud were preoccupied with conquering the Najdi tribes, converting them to Wahhabism and expanding their realm to the Ahsa in the east, which they finally conquered in 1795. But Al Saud-led forces started raiding the area between the Najd and the Hijaz—and attacking oases and tribes under the *Ashraf*'s indirect rule—after crushing a military expedition sent by the Sharif of Mecca in 1790–1. Then in the conquest of Taif in 1802, the Wahhabis killed every woman, man and child they saw; the streets were flooded with blood. The Wahhabis then set about destroying all the holy tombs and burial grounds of the city, followed by the mosques and *madrasa*s (Islamic schools).[5] In 1802–3 the Al Saud-led forces entered Mecca, and in 1805 Medina surrendered. The Wahhabis destroyed all mausoleums, domed mosques and other buildings considered un-Islamic, and obliged the Hijazis to pray and refrain from wearing silk or smoking in public.[6]

By 1806, Al Saud rule extended over most of contemporary Saudi Arabia and large sections of what is now southern Iraq. The Hijaz was annexed to the Al Saud state, but the Sharif of

Mecca retained most of his independence, and the region continued to be exempt from taxation. But neighbouring rulers viewed the Saudi expansionist drive as a threat—especially the Ottoman Sultan, whose authority and prestige suffered a severe blow from the loss of Mecca and Medina. Ottoman anger at the Wahhabis was heightened as the Wahhabis challenged Ottoman Sunni Islam as impure and heretical. Many inhabitants of the newly conquered territories were also appalled by the atrocities committed by the Wahhabi forces at Karbala and Taif. The number of Ottoman pilgrims dropped sharply, depriving the cities of their main source of revenue and the Bedouin tribes of payments for the safe passage of caravans.

◆ THE RETURN AND DECLINE OF THE OTTOMANS

Ottoman-led expeditions of Egyptian forces dispatched by the Egyptian leader Muhammed Ali managed to drive the Al Saud out of the Hijaz in 1813. In 1818 the Saudi capital Dir'aiyah, surrendered to the Ottomans and Abdullah, the head of the Al Saud, was captured and later executed in Constantinople, while the rest of the family retreated to Riyadh. In 1840 the Ottoman Sultan restored rule to the *Ashraf,* and the Hijaz became a *vilayat* (province), with a *vali* residing in Mecca in winter and in Taif in the summer, his jurisdiction stretching from the *vilayat* of Damascus down to the border of the *vilayat* of Yemen.

The opening of the Suez Canal in 1869 strengthened Turkey's position in Arabia, facilitating transport of military equipment and soldiers to the region. In the 1870s the Ottoman forces managed to reconquer Yemen and Asir. The construction of a railway from Damascus to Medina in 1900 under Sultan Abdul Hamid II provided easy access to Ottoman garrisons in the Hijaz, Asir and Yemen, and made the *hajj* safer and faster.

In 1908 Sharif Hussain Ibn Ali was appointed Grand Sharif of Mecca. His imposition of effective control over the Bedouin tribes at the beginning of his rule ensured economic prosperity and brought temporary peace to pilgrims, who had long suffered raids and levies. Initially he pursued a pro-Ottoman policy, helping to suppress a rebellion against the Ottomans launched in 1910 by the Idrisi ruler in Asir, who was helped by the Yemeni ruler, Imam Yahya, with the assistance of the Italians.

But Sharif Hussain also sought to expand his power vis-à-vis the *vali*, and as the Ottomans' hold on the region weakened he, too, began to rebel against Turkish officials. Struggles emerged over the extension of the Damascus–Medina railway to Mecca and the new administrative reform, which aimed to reduce the Sharif's power. After 1908 the rising influence of the Young Turks, with their emphasis on pan-Turkism, also antagonised many Arabs, leading to the formation of groups advocating Arab subjects' rights and seeking independence for the Arab provinces.

Sharif Hussain's prestige throughout the Muslim world placed him in a category of his own. As lord of Mecca, Islam's metropolis, no devout Muslim—least of all an Arab Muslim—could ignore his voice. On an issue involving the safety of the holy cities, he could challenge the authority of the caliph himself. Sharif Hussain's second son, Sharif Abdullah, was already calling for an autonomous Hijaz that would lead the rest of the Arab provinces to freedom. In 1914 Abdullah approached Lord Kitchener, then British agent in Egypt, and indirectly informed the British of his intentions and inquired about the possibility of assistance.

With the outbreak of war that year, the Turkish Sultan appealed to all Muslims to rise up against British, French and Russian forces in the region. To counter the threat, Britain negotiated an alliance with Hussain, reflecting the Hijaz's strategic position at the centre of Ottoman power in the Arabian Peninsula. Hussain's assistance would cut off the Turkish garrisons in Asir and Yemen. Lord Kitchener in turn promised Hussain that the British government would guarantee his position as Grand Sharif and would defend it against external aggression.[7]

In 1916 Sharif Hussain agreed to lead an Arab revolt against the Turks in exchange for a British promise to make him 'King of the Arab Lands' after the war. Instead, five independent states succeeded the capitulation of the Ottoman Empire in Arabia—Hijaz, Najd, Jabal Shammar, Asir and Yemen. The Versailles Treaty created a system of mandates that gave Britain control over most of the Arab East. Britain juggled conflicting promises, which finally led to the international recognition of Hussain as King of the Hijaz but placed Faisal on the Iraqi throne and his brother, Abdullah, on the throne of Transjordan.

◆ THE END OF HASHEMITE RULE

King Hussain had sought to expand his rule eastwards well before the anti-Turkish Arab Revolt in 1916. His territorial ambition came into conflict with that of the Imam of the Najd, Abdul Aziz Al Saud, as early as 1910, when Hussain attempted to push the Hijaz's borders to the eastern frontier of Qasim. The Najdis organised an army to fight 'the old grey devil in Mecca' from that point on, and while Abdul Aziz Al Saud supported the uprising against the Ottoman Turks, he rejected Hussain's claim to the title of 'King of the Arab Lands'.

Throughout the period after the Arab Revolt, King Hussain paid little heed to mounting tensions with Abdul Aziz Al Saud. Instead he pressed ahead with efforts to expand his rule eastwards, launching several attacks on the Khurmah oasis, an Utaiba settlement. The inhabitants, after beating back Hussain's forces three times, finally called upon Abdul Aziz Al Saud for assistance. In May 1919 Hussain's son, Emir Abdullah, led an army of 4,000 men on a fourth raid against Khurmah, but the Saudi-led forces launched a devastating counterattack from which only Abdullah and 100 of his men escaped. The defeat left Hussain severely weakened, but Al

Saud did not continue his campaign, fearing British intervention.

Even so, relations continued to deteriorate. Abdul Aziz Al Saud sent an armed detachment in May 1920 to seize the town of Abha in northern Asir. He conquered Asir later that year, and, after occupying the formerly pro-Ottoman Rashidi chieftaincy in Hail in 1921, he concentrated his sights firmly on the Hijaz. As the Al Saud consolidated their positions in Asir by 1923, it became clear that a direct military conflict was inevitable. The conquest of Asir was a prelude to a more aggressive military encroachment on Hussain's territories in the heart of the Hijaz. Two reasons are identified for Al Saud's expansionism. First, Al Saud's finances suffered a blow when Britain stopped its monthly subsidy of £5,000 in 1924. He began to look towards the more prosperous region of the Hijaz, where income from pilgrimage tax and custom duties levied in Jeddah would by far exceed his limited income from Najd and Ahsa. Second, Hussain had assumed the caliphate that had been abolished by the Turkish assembly two days earlier. The idea of an Arabian Sharifian caliphate had been in wide circulation since the fifteenth century but became extensively debated in the Arab world in the waning years of the Ottoman Empire.[8] However, the Al Saud regarded the conquest of the Hijaz as a historical mission all along.

In 1924 Saudi forces attacked Taif, and Hussain's soldiers, led by another of Hussain's sons, Ali, retreated to Mecca, leaving Taif's inhabitants undefended; many were subsequently massacred.[9] When Al Saud forces approached Mecca, Ali's troops retreated to Jeddah. Mecca surrendered without a fight in October 1924 and Abdul Aziz Al Saud entered the city in the garb of a pilgrim. King Hussain's position had become untenable, and the Hijazi nobility, the leading merchants and *'ulema* (religious teachers) pressured him to abdicate in favour of Ali. Hussain left the Hijaz for Aqaba and was later taken by the British to Cyprus. Medina surrendered in December 1924 and Jeddah fell later that month. Ali went to Baghdad, ending Hashemite rule over the Hijaz.

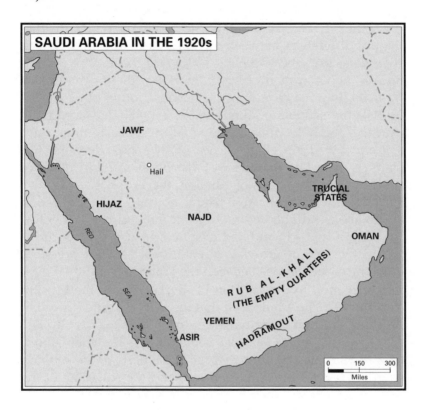

◆ THE LOSS OF HIJAZI INDEPENDENCE

In 1926 Abdul Aziz Al Saud changed the name of the Sultan-ate of Najd to the Kingdom of Najd, but he did not attempt to absorb the Kingdom of Hijaz, realising that it was too complex and sophisticated a state to assimilate in one go. Instead, Abdul Aziz Al Saud adopted a policy of gradual integration, initially preserving most of the administrative structure that had been created by the Hashemite *Ashraf*. He appointed his son Faisal as viceroy of the Hijaz in August 1926 and

9

promulgated the Fundamental Provisions of the Kingdom of Hijaz, similar to a constitution, defining the status of the viceroy, the *majlis al-shura* and the administrative bodies.

Another challenge for Saudi rule was to overcome the theological differences between the Hijazi and the Najdi *'ulema*. In January 1925 the Wahhabi *'ulema* and those of other religious schools met in Mecca, marking the beginning of Wahhabi dominance and the marginalisation of other *madhahib* (Islamic schools of thought). The Wahhabis eventually 'purified' the holy cities as they had in the early nineteenth century: by destroying places of worship deemed un-Islamic—including the shrine of *Mawlid al-Nabi* (birthplace of the Prophet), the house of Khadija, the Prophet's wife, and *Beit Abu-Bakr* (Caliph Abu Bakr's house). Their aspiration was to abolish rituals central to Meccan culture and identity. But Abdul Aziz Al Saud had to soften the drive for purification in the face of growing international Muslim pressure, which included clashes between the Wahhabis and the Egyptian delegation to the *hajj*.[10] In his declaration to the Muslim World in 1925, he announced that the *shari'a* would prevail in the Hijaz, but that no damage would be done to holy shrines.

The turning point came in September 1932, when Abdul Aziz Al Saud decreed 'the merger of the parts of the Arabian Kingdom' under his family's name, and the Kingdom of the Hijaz and Najd and their Dependencies became the Kingdom of Saudi Arabia. In a famous speech in Mecca in 1924 King Abdul Aziz spoke of his wish to see the elite of Hijazi society—including the *'ulema* and merchants—in charge of their own affairs. His use of the formula 'your homeland, your country' was a recognition of the Hijaz's right to local governance free of Najdi interference, and even after the establishment of Saudi Arabia, separate Hijazi institutions continued to function, as set out in the Fundamental Provisions.

But these institutions' authority and effectiveness quickly waned after the consolidation of Saudi rule. Administrative reforms that followed the Al Saud annexation of the Hijaz created a system of regional governance that ultimately became entirely dominated by the Najdi elite, effectively ending the last vestiges of 1,100 years of Sharifian Hashemite rule in the Arabian Peninsula. A Council of Deputies succeeded the Consultative Council in 1931, but it ceased to exist in 1953, and local autonomy was gradually eroded.

Saudi rule over the Hijaz, imposed by force of arms, led to discontent among parts of the population, particularly the local nobility. Soon after the fall of Jeddah, the so-called League for the Protection of the Hijaz was formed in Egypt. Hijazi oppositionists also founded the Hijazi Liberation Party, Hizb al-Tahrir al-Hijazi, advocating the creation of an independent state of Hijaz. Many opposition representatives, particularly members of the *Ashraf*, maintained close ties with Ali's forces. Abdullah also provided the opposition groupings with money and arms in the late 1920s. But in 1932 Abdul Aziz Al Saud banned all political parties in the Hijaz and ordered the arrest of all opposition members.[11]

◆ THE HIJAZI 'STATE OF MIND'

In the years since its annexation and incorporation into the Kingdom of Saudi Arabia, the Hijaz's exact territorial borders have become less significant than its social and cultural boundaries. Despite Saudi political unification and nation-building, the importance of these boundaries has grown in recent decades. On the one hand, the Hijazi elite's deepening ambivalence towards the ruling Al Saud family and their own identity as Saudi Arabians has become apparent; on the other hand, Hijazi elites seek to be acknowledged and accorded respect by their Najdi counterparts, a group they recognise as being politically more powerful. Najdis, who today form almost the entire governing and religious elite, reciprocate this view, perceiving and treating Hijazis as second-class citizens.[12] As a result, Hijazis have also sought to assert their distinctiveness vis-à-vis the Najdi elite, particularly as assimilation into the Najdi ruling elite is virtually impossible.

The Hijaz and its inhabitants have always viewed themselves—and been viewed by others—as a kind of chosen people, whose links with the Muslim Holy Places give them a deep religious significance, while all the time benefiting from relative moderation and a highly developed cosmopolitan sophistication. But as the Kingdom of Saudi Arabia has evolved, urban Hijazi elites have sought not only to preserve but also to accentuate a distinct cultural identity. They have gradually adopted and elaborated a highly selective system of 'traditional' rituals and ceremonies that serves to bolster a sense of cultural superiority and to counter their political and economic subordination to the country's Najdi rulers.

Studies of different social boundaries show that communities living on peripheries have a great awareness of their cultural differences.[13] The Hijazi assertion of a distinctive social identity should thus be viewed as a delayed reaction to political marginalisation under Najdi Saudi rule, facilitated and shaped by social and economic developments accompanying the unification process. Prior to September 1932 there was very little contact between the Hijaz and the other regions in the Arabian Peninsula. Often there were more contacts with other Muslim countries than with local Bedouin tribes. As a result, unification initially stimulated a regional consciousness, as people became more aware of the other Saudi cultures and thus of their own distinctiveness. But this was coupled with the imposition throughout the kingdom of 'organic' Najdi traditions and codes of behaviour, which were presented as the Saudi norm.

Rapid economic change and growth, extending from the 1950s until the 1980s, generated greater exposure and receptivity than ever before to foreign ideas, including educational and commercial opportunities overseas. This produced contradictory pressures on Hijazi identity. On the one hand, oil revenues brought windfall wealth and rapid (economic) modernisation, which contributed to the creation of a shared Saudi identity, however superficial and inauthentic. But these developments also began to reinforce a distinctive Hijazi identity by fuelling greater competition with the Najdi for economic and political influence in the Saudi state. While Hijazis regarded themselves from the outset in the context of Saudi Arabia as a whole, Hijaziness remained a latent but deep layer of social identity, desired or embraced by some and ignored or rejected by others, depending on their political and economic participation in Saudi public life.

◆ THE PROBLEM OF IDENTITY

The Hijaz as an identifiable entity has been removed from contemporary maps of Saudi Arabia and the region has simply become the Western Province. Therefore, the Hijaz must be considered mainly as a social construct, and not as a geographically defined region. Consequently, Hijazi identity must be defined primarily according to shared public perceptions. A difficulty this poses is the fact that other Saudi Arabians, other Arabs and other Muslims observe many forms of behaviour that Hijazis regard as specifically theirs. It is vital, therefore, to determine those areas of cultural life by which the Hijazis recognise themselves, and which are recognised by others as different. When asked, 'What is the Hijaz?' or 'What does the Hijaz mean?' the most typical response from Hijazis would be, 'The Hijaz means Taif, Mecca, Jeddah and Medina. The Hijaz consists of the cities and those who belong to them'.

Indeed, the urban component is reflected in the nomenclature of Hijazi identity. Those who belong to the cities are called *Hijaziyyin*, while those from the nomadic tribes in the region are referred to as *Hujjuz*. One essential difference between urban and tribal Hijazis is that the former identify themselves first with their city and then as Hijazi, while the latter associate themselves first with their tribe, and then with the Hijaz as their tribal territory. The urban–tribal distinction is all the more marked in the Hijaz because of the heterogeneous descent of the urban population. Even urban Hijazis who claim tribal descent are still identified with the city of belonging, whereas both urban and nomadic people in the Najd are

13

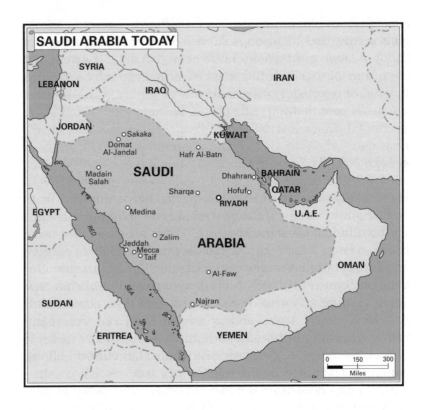

typically identified with tribal groupings. This is because the Najd was mostly nomadic, with only a few towns and villages, and no urban culture until the advent of oil wealth.

The problem of Hijazi identity is made more complex by the political climate in Saudi Arabia, which precludes any overt expression of regional difference. There is no decree that explicitly prohibits the term 'Hijaz', but its use is generally interpreted as contravening the official emphasis on the social and political homogeneity of the Saudi state. This de facto prohibition is keenly felt and transgressions are greeted with a range of more or less punitive sanctions. Any new school with the name *madaris al Hijaz* (school of the Hijaz) would soon face bureaucratic problems. A Hijazi daring to wear traditional clothes consisting of the *jubba* (overcoat) and *'umama* (headdress) rather than Najdi national dress would be considered eccentric at best and would be inviting trouble if employed by the government in any capacity.

Hijazi regional loyalties can thus be expressed only indirectly, through the use of outwardly ambiguous symbols. The result has been an emphasis on the Hijaz's association with the holy cities—and hence to intensify the urban basis of Hijazi identity. The pronouncement 'I am Hijazi' has nearly disappeared from current use. But the statement 'I am Meccan' or 'I am Medinese' recurs constantly. Even for those who have never lived in Mecca, the mere identification of one's family with it conveys a sense of pride. Being 'Meccan' has in itself become a distinct and unique symbol of Hijazi identity. This symbol entails other symbols, of which ethnography furnishes many examples. For instance, Hijazis who live outside Mecca hold 'Meccan evenings' with related themes and objects, some of which are recreated from the past. Since Mecca is the 'Capital of the Muslims', to stress one's Meccan identity cannot be seen as overtly controversial, and thus it can not be challenged by the authorities.

◆ PLACING THE BOUNDARIES

There are, in addition to the fundamental urban–tribal distinction, a number of cultural forms that serve to distinguish Hijazis from other Saudis, and especially from the Najdi. Differences in language are one vehicle for expressing distinctiveness. The Hijazi dialect, *al-lahja al-hijaziyya*, is separated by pronunciation, intonation and usage of terms from the Najdi dialect, which is also spoken in the Eastern Province and is similar to the language used in the tribal areas of some of the Gulf Co-operation Council (GCC) countries. The Hijazi texture of voice and accent are also distinctive, although it shares similarities with Asiri and Yemeni speech.

Religion, too, continues to distinguish the Hijazi from the Najdi. Prior to unification, the Hijaz followed three schools of law: the Shafi'i, the Hanafi and the Maliki, the first two being predominant. Officially there are no longer differing schools of law in Saudi Arabia, with *Al Mazhab* (the school of law) signifying only the Hanbali school and, more specifically, its interpretation and application by the Wahhabi *'ulema*. However, while the official state practice is Wahhabism, Hijazis still do not always view themselves as Wahhabi Muslims, who prefer to call themselves *Muwahhidun* (unitarians) to emphasise their belief in the oneness of God.

Hijazi traditional food and dress are also distinctive. The heterogeneous, prosperous, urban past resulted in the creation of a rich and sophisticated cuisine that continues to be prepared as a reminder of both class and ancient Islamic roots. Although dress has been officially unified, with all Saudi Arabian men wearing the Najdi dress and women wearing a form of 'modest' Western dress in private and a Najdi form of black veil in public, there are subtle differences that local people recognise. These differences are found at the level of choice of fabric, pattern or decorative motif, as well as in the manner in which the dress is worn.

The most obvious and important expression of the persistence of social boundaries is the rarity of intermarriage between Najdis and Hijazis, with obvious implications for cultural assimilation. Hijazi opinion on this matter varies. Some explain that Najdi men fear the consequences of marital alliances with Hijazi families, while others contend that Hijazis are reluctant to allow their daughters to marry Najdis, because of polygamy, ease of divorce and stricter gender segregation among the Najdis. Najdi men—who do not hesitate to take wives from other Arab countries—regard marrying a woman from the same country as a greater commitment, especially when she is from an inferior or less 'pure' lineage in the Najdi grading of tribal descent. Meanwhile, the Hijazis, who claim descent from the Prophet's tribe, the Quraysh, consider themselves the superior ones. Competition in 'purity of blood' in the Arabian Peninsula reaches its apotheosis in the context of intermarriage, and the few instances of it are typically between a Hijazi man and a non-tribal (i.e. 'non-pure blood') Najdi *khadiri*, as a tribal Najdi *gabili* will not marry outside the group. Even in these rare cases, the Najdi *khadiri* family typically makes the marriage procedures very lengthy and costly.

The images that Hijazi and Najdi have of one another and the names they use to describe each other are further indications of social boundaries and the consciousness that sustains them. The Hijazis, for example, call the Najdis *shurug* (Easterners), a derogatory term. Another term, *badu* (Bedouin), carries an even worse connotation—essentially a lack of urban refinement. On the other hand, the Najdis call Hijazis *tarsh al-bahr*, (the flotsam of the sea) and *bagaya hujjaj*, (pilgrimage remnants). Whereas the first term is applied to those from Jeddah and the second to Meccans and Medinese, both allude to the 'impurity' of Hijazis' Arab descent, owing to intermarriage with non-Arab Muslims. While the Najdis pride themselves on their lineage and *asala* (purity of blood), the Hijazis pride themselves on their *zawg* (good taste), *anaga* (elegance), *nazaka* (refinement) and *usul* (knowledge of the rules of propriety). To be sure, Hijazis also place lineage as the first criterion of status and respectability, especially those claiming descent from the Quraysh. But for those from other Muslim countries who settled in Mecca, Medina or Taif, lineage does not imply 'blood purity', but rather three generations of good social standing. As a result, 'Najdis regard Hijazis as degenerate and not quite Arabian'.[14]

◆ THE POLITICISATION OF DIFFERENCE

These internal cultural distinctions and their ramifications are rarely visible to outsiders, or even to expatriates living in the country, for whom everyone appears to be Saudi Arabian. At this level, the distinction between Saudis and non-Saudis is a simple necessity, since Saudi Arabia is full of expatriates: Westerners, Asians, Far Easterners, Africans, other Muslims and other Arabs.[15] Until recently Westerners were called *khawaja*, a Turkish word originally used to denote Europeans. Today more specific terms, such as 'Americans' or 'English', are widely used, although the average Meccan still uses *khawaja*.

This shared terminology reflects a common Saudi feeling of the need to assert their distinctiveness from *ajanib* (outsiders). It is clear that a common 'Saudi' consciousness has resulted from a state-based dimension to conduct and the sharpening of differences with the West, as globalisation poses a further threat to identity and a clash between 'tradition' and 'modernity'.[16]

While cosmopolitan within the context of Islam, Hijazi attitudes towards Western culture are ambivalent. Western lifestyles are enjoyed, but only as a holiday. Even those Hijazis who travel to the West for long periods on vacation or for business will often comment that they are 'just passing through' or 'holidaying', 'not really resident' in those places. Although much of their wealth is transferred abroad and held in banks in Europe and the United States, and they own property there, they do not settle in the West. They believe that they must continue to live in the land of their origin. This attitude is to be found among other Arabs and Arabians too, but is particularly pronounced among Hijazis who are more defensive about 'home'.

The development of leisure travel among wealthy urban Hijazis is an interesting reflection of this. Before the 1930s they went to Taif, the mountain resort, while the *Ashraf* ruling elite also went to Turkey and Europe. After 1950 most Hijazis began taking trips to Egypt and Lebanon, but since the oil boom of the 1970s, they have acquired a taste for the most fashionable Western summer and winter resorts. But foreign travel and strong ties to the West have, paradoxically, resulted in a sense of exclusion from Western elites. This has, in turn, strengthened the need to reassert a Hijazi Arab identity through 'traditional' ceremonies and events. Thus, upon their return to Saudi Arabia they resume their Hijazi gatherings and rituals. By the 1980s a consciousness of their social status as Hijazis—and thus an emphasis on their regional identity—alongside an emphasis on their own national identity, due to rejection of Western culture, further complicated their sense of identity. As they reject Western values they feel closer to other Saudis, but while in the country Hijaziness comes first. Again, non-Hijazis often respond to rejection by Westerners in the same way, but it is among the elite of the Hijaz that these sensitivities run deepest.

It was only at the end of the 1970s that the Hijazi elite began to perceive a need to find an identity closer to home. Hijazi elites say that by the 1980s they finally realised the full implications of what had happened as a result of Al Saud rule since the 1930s, and that their cultural identity—and the political and social privileges to which it entitled them—were at stake. Although the autonomy enjoyed by the Hijaz under Ottoman rule was lost, Hijazis, too, had benefited from the country's oil wealth, especially during the 1970s, giving them a stake in Saudi nation-building. But the recession of the mid-1980s, combined with an increasingly expensive lifestyle and dependence on the patronage system established by the Al Sauds, exposed the weakness of national, as opposed to regional, sentiment. As the country's population grew and political authority became more narrowly centralised in the Najd, the Hijazis' sense of regional affinity increased, a process strengthened in the 1990s by globalisation, on the one hand, and, on the other hand, the attenuation of Saudi identity.

2

The Hijazi *'awa'il* and the Preservation of Hijazi Identity

◆ A MARGINALISED COSMOPOLITAN ELITE

THROUGHOUT THE Islamic world, 'belonging' to the holy cities of Mecca and Medina is recognised as conferring a religious advantage and has thus been a powerful symbol for Hijazis since the beginning of Sharifian rule in 961. Identification with the holy cities—and with the strategic port of Jeddah—has been strongest and most central to the identity of the Hijazi *'awa'il* (the 'families'),[1] the patronymic clans that formed the wealthiest and socially most celebrated elite in the Arabian Peninsula prior to Saudi political unification in 1932. Their position in Hijazi society make the *'awa'il* more sensitive to political and cultural change, and also more likely to respond to it. Moreover, as the representatives of Hijazi urban culture and traditions, the rituals and ceremonies they adopt filter down to the rest of Hijazi society.

Since the beginning of the 1980s Hijazis, and especially the *'awa'il*, have increasingly asserted a regional identity expressed precisely in terms of the prominent urban centres. This is tied to Hijazis' historical identification with a 'Red Sea' culture that is distinct from—but has been overwhelmed by— 'Gulf Arab' culture, particularly after the founding in 1981 of the Gulf Co-operation Council (GCC) with Bahrain, Kuwait, Oman, Qatar and the United Arab Emirates. Official Saudi restrictions on the use of the word 'Hijaz' have reinforced

Hijazis' tendency to identify with 'their' metropolises. For example, Hijazis now often address each other according to paternal city of origin, taking full advantage of the sense of distinctiveness that this can afford—even when the addressee never actually lived there. At a time when Hijazis feel marginalised on the Arabian Peninsula, and hence politically and socially vulnerable, attributing a Hijazi identity to cities—and, above all, to Mecca and Medina—is to claim a unique and inalienable cultural resource.

The urban *'awa'il* have been the central component in this process of cultural assertion, modifying Hijazi ceremonial life by drawing on highly emotional, urban-based traditions of religious mysticism. The official Saudi denial of indigenous religious diversity implies that such 'traditional' activities are frowned upon and even forbidden by the Wahhabi *'ulema*, the official government agents.[2] This makes the rituals defined by the *'awa'il* all the more politically significant. Two Hijazi traditions, in particular, are considered *bid'a* (dangerous innovation): the *mawlid*[3] (the celebration of the Prophet's birthday) and the *hawl* (a memorial ceremony conducted on the anniversary of a family member's death that also involves chanting for the Prophet). Hijazis' frequent invocation of Muhammed, for example during the *mawlid*, is forbidden by thirteen *fatwas* (religious decrees) issued by the Saudi religious authorities, who condemn as *bid'a* any elaborate use of the name and memory of the Prophet.

By reviving the rites of the old society—festivals, merry nights and calendar feasts—the Hijazi *'awa'il* are consciously recalling the pre-Saudi period of Hashemite rule. The apparently innocuous romanticisation of the Hijazi past, therefore, becomes an implicit challenge to the legitimacy of the Saudi state. Such rituals help to distinguish Hijazis from the Najdis, who have themselves adapted ceremonial life to the assertion of a Saudi national identity based on Najdi dominance. These royal state ceremonies portray the ruler's uniqueness, drawing heavily on tribal customs popularly referred to as the 'Saudi way of life', sanctified by the Wahhabi *'ulema* (religious scholars) and transformed into a national ethos.[4] They typically express the 'desert virtues' of strength, chivalry and asceticism, make great play of camels as symbols, and employ displays of horsemanship, sword dances and ceremonies set in desert tents. While the modern architecture of the capital, Riyadh, is unsuitable for staging official ceremonies, the official media help convey an impression of traditional continuity, broadcasting at great length formal greeting rituals—such as bussing hands and noses—that non-Najdis may not practise.

Hijazi rituals, by contrast, are quite literally at home in fine buildings. Certainly, Hijazi ceremonies are confined to the privacy of the home because their observance takes place in defiance of official rules. But the richly decorated houses that conceal these unsanctioned ceremonies also invoke the urban culture of the past, with its sophisticated and flourishing architectural tradition. Indeed, Hijazi architectural heritage was revived during the late 1970s with the boom in oil wealth. Arab and other Muslim architects and interior designers paid by affluent Hijazis built magnificent 'traditional' Hijazi homes mixing some of the original Hashemite styles with old Turkish, Egyptian or Moorish designs.

Above all, the Hijazi system of rituals has in recent decades developed into a mechanism of securing and preserving a measure of social precedence and control. The Hijazi *'awa'il* are conscious of their past as descendants of *tujjar* (merchants), having lost their positions as *'ulema* and *mutawwifin* (guides to the pilgrims) following the unification of Saudi Arabia.[5] The religious sphere is now dominated by the Al Sheikh—the descendants of Wahhabism's founder, Muhammed Bin Abdul Wahhab—who co-founded the Saudi state.[6] At the same time, the established Najdi merchant families, those from the other regions of Saudi Arabia, as well as the Hijazi *nouveaux riches*, threaten the economic pre-eminence of the urban *'awa'il*. The government's dominant role in the economy—since most activities are directly or indirectly related to public spending— has aggravated the pressure on the Hijazi *'awa'il*, as has the absence of anti-trust laws, which has given single families secret control of entire economic sectors and branches.[7]

The Hijazi elite's response to the political, economic and theological pre-eminence of the Al Saud and other leading Najdi patronymic groups—such as the Al Sudeiri and families similarly allied by marriage to the Al Sauds—has necessarily been inward-looking, founded on custodianship of urban refinement and 'good taste'. Because social manners are thought to be within the control of the *'awa'il*, focusing attention on them has come to constitute an effective defensive strategy, used to demonstrate high status and maintain cultural distinctions within today's Saudi Arabia. Indeed, the Hijazi *'awa'il* take it as their task to promote the central role of formal manners in defining Hijazi identity.

Owing to their urban, affluent past, the Hijazi elite has always had an elaborate vocabulary describing *anaga* (elegance), *labaga* (eloquence), and *hawas* (consideration or social awareness, implying a formal set of expressions and compliments). Although many of these words and expressions are derived from classical Arabic and through cultural contact are now used in other Arab countries such as Egypt, the *'awa'il* regard them as proprietary, because they provide a point of contrast with Najdi vocabulary and manners. The *'awa'il* revive old terminology and phrases used before the unification of Saudi Arabia—and hence before contact with the Najd—to stress their regional distinctiveness, which includes historically closer ties with Egyptians, Syrians and Yemenis due to the *hajj*.[8]

◆ TOOLS OF TRADITION

The term *'awa'il* refers to a network of Hijazi patronymic groups who consider themselves a discrete elite and are widely viewed this way by others, with all of the broader practical meanings that this entails. Although the etymology of *'awa'il* is wide-ranging,[9] it is in this deeper sense of cultural recognition that the term is indigenous and hence descriptive of a unique pattern of social relations. The *'awa'il* regard themselves as a stable and coherent group, with origins legitimised by a firm link to the past. Indeed, it is common for *'awa'il* members to claim descent from the Prophet Muhammed's tribe, the Quraysh, as the Hashemite *Ashraf*: points of reference that express past political dominance and a solid sense of Arab identity. Family trees that trace roots back to the Prophet hang on the walls of some *'awa'il* homes.

In reality many urban Hijazis are descendants of pilgrims who settled in Mecca or Medina long after the time of the Prophet and who have no genealogical link to the Quraysh or are not linked to the *Ashraf*. In addition to the Hijaz's intrinsic heterogeneity throughout the centuries, the rapid increase in social mobility due to oil money since the 1950s and especially the 1970s has made group boundaries even more fluid. At any point in time, the *'awa'il* contains those referred to as *minnana wa fina* (established members of the core) and others called *min-awwaltams* (literally 'of the day before yesterday', i.e. new-comers). But the *'awa'il* has not become an open elite. On the contrary, its members' revival and elaboration of formal cere-monial life since the 1980s has not only politicised Hijazi identity; it has also served to prevent easy entry by Hijazi *nou-veaux riches* and *arrivistes*—groups that are most likely to be Najdi clients and loyalists. Hence they are treated with suspi-cion, as potential cultural agents of the Saudi state.

In the urban Hijaz it is generally accepted that there are approximately 25 families which constitute the *'awa'il*. Of these, five or six are generally acknowledged to be *minnana wa fina* and thus leaders among the *'awa'il*.[10] Originally from Mecca, Medina or Jeddah, most now choose to live in Jeddah, the centre of commerce and trade, whose strategic location and cosmopolitan character cater well to the lifestyle of the *'awa'il*. Being from Mecca or Medina remains a source of pride, but only a few remain in these cities, whose economic and political role has been marginalised by the shift to an oil-based economy. Indeed, there is a perception that even the country's religious centre has shifted to Burraidah, the Wahhabis' capital.

The barrier of elite cultural tradition in the Hijaz is erected and supported by *al 'ai'la* (the family), which continues to

serve as the basic unit of loyalty, obligation, friendship, sociali-
sation, moral and economic support. Kinship, based on
patrilineal (descent from the father's line), patrilocal (residence
in the father's locality) and patriarchal (dominance of the
father and other male relatives) patterns, remains the primary
source of individual identity and thus the basis of social classi-
fication and organisation. No other institutions, such as firms,
voluntary associations and clubs — or, indeed, the nation —
have superseded the family and the sacrosanct idiom on
which it is constructed. On the contrary, since the 1980s, the
'awa'il have increasingly relied on this idiom to represent the
Islamic and Hijazi character of their identity.

The reinforcement of kinship's salience in the Hijaz has been
a response to the ruling Al Saud family's power and prestige,
as well as its sheer growth in numbers.[11] It has been suggested
that the meaning of the word *'ai' la* in the Hijaz is the urbanisa-
tion or modernisation of the tribe; this is reflected in the well-
known proverb, *I belong to nothing else but Ghuzaiyya [my tribe].
If Ghuzaiyya goes astray, I go astray. If it returns to the right path, I
will do so.* Whereas the Bedouin's loyalty is to the tribe, for an
urban Hijazi it is to the patronymic group, that is, to all family
members who share a common surname. Any individual's
achievements are, accordingly, secondary to his family's
acquired standing and reputation, although this depends, *inter
alia*, upon the achievements of its individual members. If a
family member achieves an unusually high position or
acquires great wealth, the status of the entire patronymic
group is raised both directly, through the patronage he is now
able to extend, and indirectly, through his own status, owing
to the prevalence in Saudi Arabia of *wasta* (family
connections).

The identification with the patrilineal family is even
stronger for women. When a woman introduces herself in
public, she will always say that she is 'of the family of …' without mentioning her first name. This is for the sake of
respectability; using the first name implies exposing her personal identity to male strangers and endangering their
honour through familiarity. A married woman gives the name

of her husband, because he is her official guardian. But her fundamental sense of identity continues to be that of her patrilineal kin, reflecting the civil—and hence terminable—nature of the marriage contract in Islam. Women demonstrate solidarity with the patronymic group at times of birth, marriage and death.

As in other societies the Arab concept of family is closely linked to that of female honour.[12] In the Arabian Peninsula the urban Hijazis have historically been viewed as more lax or lenient in such matters than tribal Najdi culture, with its strict Wahhabi norms of sexual segregation. An increased emphasis on female honour has, however, developed among some of the Hijazi *'awa'il* in reaction to Najdi standards. The veiling of women and their protection forms part of a larger pattern of 'correct' behaviour that has emerged in response to fear of downward mobility, as a result either of changes in *wasta* or economic circumstances. As the Hijazi elite's honour, reputation and social precedence have come to depend on displays of formality and propriety, women's roles have grown more closely associated with and encumbered by ceremonial behaviour.

Likewise, the Hijazi *'awa'il* have become increasingly preoccupied with the definition and size of their families. The Hijazi family includes men, women and children who share a surname, as well as in-marrying wives. However, 'black sheep'—members who have 'blackened their face' (*yisawwidu bi wajhahum*) by indiscretions that have tarnished the reputation of the patronymic group—are excluded. For the *'awa'il*, the boundaries of acceptable behaviour for family members have grown in strictness and significance.

All recognised family members meet once a year during the month of Ramadan for the breaking of the fast, *iftar*, usually on a Thursday night at the house of the most prominent member (patron). Most patronymic groups among the *'awa'il* have a patron, although not necessarily an older son. Although members of the extended family meet weekly for *gayla* (the period on Fridays extending from before lunch until sunset), the annual reunion during Ramadan has a wider attendance and

27

meaning. It serves to confirm membership of the patronymic group, providing outsiders with an index of who is and who is not in the family. In other words, every family annually redefines its boundaries. The larger a family is and the more caring its members are towards each other, the higher its station and rank in Hijazi society. All of this has a peculiarly Hijiazi flavour in that the social ceremonies are invariably elaborate and are layered with an almost self-conscious awareness of being Hijazi.

Thus—despite official restrictions—the *'awa'il*, at the forefront of other Hijazis, use specific traditions not only to reaffirm their identity as Hijazis, but also to underscore their relative status vis-à-vis other Hijazis, and amongst themselves. As the *'awa'il* modify tradition in response to political, economic and cultural marginalisation, one aim is to legitimise their own newly acquired modes of life and conduct. These changes in traditional rules and practices are not considered innovations or additions to the culture, but rather an extension of values legitimised by the past. It follows that the concept of 'good taste' is constantly being redefined by the *'awa'il*, and that power within the Hijazi elite lies with those who innovate, define and legitimise new standards in fashion and propriety.

◆ THE CODE OF THE HIJAZI *'AWA'IL*

The Hijazi quest for an identity is at its most extreme among the *'awa'il*. Although small, consisting of around 25 families or patronymic groups, the Hijazi *'awa'il* is ethnically a heterogeneous group whose social cohesion is based on adherence to a rigorous code of public conduct relating to formal conversation, dress, food, gift-exchange, house type and decoration, and religious practice. This, combined with an acute sense of privacy, restricts and limits more casual social relations among all but one's immediate family.[13] At the same time, the social power exercised through formal ceremonies and strict enforcement of the code of public behaviour reinforces a sense of belonging among the members of the group as a whole.

The *'awa'il* are distinguished within the wider Hijazi community by criteria of status and respectability that serve to distinguish them as an elite and provide a basis for internal competition between the constituent patronymic groups. Although they change and develop, these criteria are widely understood at any particular point in time. As described by knowledgeable Hijazis, by the 1980s these criteria, in descending order of importance, included:

1) *Asl* (origin), *nasab* (lineage) and *hasab* (depth in lineage).
2) *Sum'a* (reputation) and *sira tayyiba* (good social standing).
3) *Mal* (wealth) and its appropriate display.
4) Adherence to *usul* (the correct rules of conduct) and *tagalid* (tradition).
5) *Tagwa* (religious observance) and its appropriate manifestation.
6) The size of the family and the 'love' and co-operation exhibited between its members.
7) Connections with the ruling elite.
8) Education.
9) Status of the *arham* (those linked by marriage).

Each of these criteria determines Hijazis' social status, but none is exclusive as a criterion for membership in *'awa'il*. As a result, all who are considered to have *asala* (good people of good origins), who practise *istigama* (right religious behaviour) and with knowledge of *usul*, are not necessarily considered to be or treated as *'awa'il*. Wealth as a criterion of status has gained in importance, although it remains insufficient for inclusion in the *'awa'il*. The *nouveaux riches* with shallow roots in the Hijaz are generally excluded. These include the families of Egyptian and Syrian advisers, medical doctors, lawyers and business consultants who settled in Saudi Arabia shortly after its unification, acquired nationality in the 1950s and gained vast wealth during the oil boom. Although some settled in Jeddah, their loyalty remained to the ruling elite.

Indeed, the criteria related to social rootedness—*asl*, *nasab* and *hasab*—are viewed by the *'awa'il* as the foundation for all other criteria of status. The *'awa'il* define origin or lineage as a minimum of three generations of respectable presence in the community. Because many people came to settle in the Hijaz from different Muslim countries, only when the reputation of the family is well established does good lineage, *nasab*, become relevant. Several prominent merchant families among the *'awa'il* came to settle in Mecca from Turkey, Iran, Central Asia, India, Malaysia and Indonesia. However, attempts are often made to disassociate from foreign, and especially non-Arab, origins. This reflects the historical obsession of the Arabian Peninsula's tribal rulers with the purity of Arab lineage.

Depth in lineage, *hasab*, is thus an important social resource. Patronymic groups who are known to have *hasab* have participated in elite activity and identity for four generations or more, and those who can lay claim to descent from the Quraysh have the greatest depth of lineage and hence high status. Examples of these patronymic groups are those descended from the Prophet Muhammed through the *Ashraf* or the *Sada*, the descendants of, respectively, Hasan and Hussain, the children of Muhammed's daughter, Fatima. Hijazis evidently do not acknowledge others in the Arabian Peninsula who claim descent from the Prophet.[14] Thus the criterion of lineage or origin serves to distinguish locals, and strengthens the basis of a regional identity that boasts its association with the cradle of Islam—the Prophet's birthplace, Mecca, and his home and place of death, Medina.

Sum'a (reputation) refers to the maintenance of basic values of honour and the moral conduct of all members of the patronymic group. This criterion of status combines most others: good origin, piety, family solidarity, education, wealth and propriety. Although in reality reputation is the sum of these standards, it is regarded as an independent criterion, perhaps because of the vulnerability of lineage in a heterogeneous society, especially in view of competition with the pure tribal culture of the peninsula's interior. Furthermore, reputation is instrumental to countering the effects of social mobility, with its threat to the *'awa'il* from newcomers and *arrivistes. Sum'a*, like *hasab*, can be built up only over time: to have enjoyed a good reputation over at least three generations means to attain *sira tayyiba* (good social standing).

Nevertheless, the achievement and preservation of status is not possible without *mal* (wealth). *Mal* enables the *'awa'il* to organise social occasions where they can display *usul, karam* (generosity), *tarhib,* (hospitality) and seemly behaviour, thereby 'honouring' or 'adding lustre' or 'adding credit' to a family or to an individual (*tajammul*). Conspicuous consumption becomes a virtue, which the *'awa'il* explain by the following Quranic verse: 'By the Bounty of thy Lord—rehearse and proclaim.'[15] Although this verse refers specifically to charitable donation, the Hijazis also apply it to all honourable and seemly spending. Wealth compensates for lack of political control while hinting at connections with the Al Saud family, the importance of which has changed the country's socio-economic stratification and significantly affected the long-term position of the *'awa'il.*

Indeed, the perception of money as a tool for the enhancement of social status and of Hijazi culture has grown with the increase in oil wealth. Money for the *'awa'il* can legitimise origins and is essential for attaining the education associated with cosmopolitanism. It is also necessary for the public display of religious ceremonies. For example, the celebration of the Prophet's birthday, the *mawlid*, disdained in the Najd and other parts of the Wahhabi-ruled kingdom, involves hiring professional reciters, inviting large numbers of guests, and providing a lavish dinner. The elegant and refined urban tradition—the most distinctive Hijazi attribute in a historically nomadic peninsula—is invoked by sumptuous decorated houses consisting of domes, marble courtyards and fountains.

There are no negative qualities associated with possession of large or even huge sums of money. Quranic support includes the verse: 'Verily, Allah rewards whom He will beyond all measure.'[16] The main cultural constraint on wealth is that it must be properly spent, or distributed—that is, if *sadagat* (alms) are given, and *zakat* (tax) is paid, [17] poorer families are supported and generosity properly demonstrated. Hence, men and women among the *'awa'il* partake in much philanthropic activity, such as the building of mosques and offering of *sadaga*, the scale of philanthropy being a measure of the patronymic group's 'piety'. Participation in charity organisations confers honour and respectability, and those run by wealthy Hijazis stand out in today's Saudi Arabia, their size and assets matched only by those run by the Al Saud. In short, a family's wealth and the way it is displayed internally and externally form a key determinant of social status. Hijazis quote the popular Arab saying *sit ghina wala sit fagr* ('a reputation of wealth is better than a reputation of poverty').

On the other hand, the tension between wealth and the other criteria of elite membership has grown since the 1980s. As social mobility has increased the threat to elite status, the importance of *usul* has grown to the point of exaggeration. Well-established but less affluent members of the *'awa'il* thus acquire a sense of security from their knowledge of the appropriate rules of urban Hijazi conduct, while those who were enriched by the oil boom are able to strengthen their social position by spending their wealth properly. This can include the modification and even the invention of traditions to keep at the forefront of society, making *usul* an increasingly complex system of duties and obligations symbolising Hijazi solidarity.

◆ PIETY'S PURPOSE

Religious knowledge and piety have always been important criteria of status in the Hijaz, especially in Mecca and Medina. Prior to the unification of the country, the *'ulema* represented the highest social group after the Hashemite rulers. Even members of other professions such as the *mutawwifin* (guides to the pilgrims) and merchants attained respect from a reputation for piety. The take-over of all prestigious *'ulema* positions by the Wahhabi establishment since 1932 has, however, led the *'awa'il* to label as 'piety' some of their communal spiritual behaviour. The *'awa'il* continue to respect traditional 'piety', manifested in the observance of the five pillars of Islam. But public observance of certain distinctive religious rituals, such as the *mawlid*, and some Sufi trends, provide opportunities to display and affirm Hijazi status.

The Hijazi conception of piety is nonetheless clearly subordinate to other dimensions of social hierarchy. At ceremonies such as the *mawlid* or the *'aza* (condolence), the *'ala gad al-hal* (less affluent) will sit around the edge of the gathering, not in the front with the *nas kubar* (big people) or the *nas afadil* (eminent or distinguished people). This does not comply with the strict Quranic teaching of equality: 'The most honoured of you in the sight of Allah is the most pious of you.'[18] Nevertheless, strict hierarchical stratification is the norm throughout the country. Despite the official Najdi credo of tribal desert independence and Bedouin conceptions of equality, customs and body language of social deference are widespread among the puritanical Wahhabis and in the court *majlis* when the king and princes receive their senior subjects. In the Great Mosque of Mecca the front spaces surrounding the Kaaba, the monument to which all Muslims turn to pray, is reserved for the Al Saud.

For the Hijazi elite, a reputation for piety is also acquired through the company one keeps at formal gatherings, such as that of a learned man with spiritual powers, or a *sayyid*, a descendant of the Prophet's lineage. This contact helps reinforce the reputation of established members of the *'awa'il*. For aspiring members, such as those who have recently acquired wealth but lack the necessary lineage, it is a means of proclaiming their pious intentions and hence acceptability. As the number of knowledgeable and gifted men or *sayyids* is limited and some are known for more personal piety than others, competition to acquire their spiritual advice and guidance is keen.

Not all *sayyids* are from the Hijaz; some are from Morocco, Egypt, or Hadramout. They are Sunni and their learning has been influenced by the Sufi traditions of other Muslim countries, especially Egypt. Although the Wahhabi establishment repudiates these practices as deviant and superstitious, they have wide appeal and have been adopted even by some members of the royal family. Nevertheless, the *'awa'il* tend to be more inclined towards spirituality than the Wahhabis, whose dogmatic doctrine demands Islam's purification from *shirk* (idolatry), and who define and combat *haram* (sin) through the religious functionaries of the Committee of the Ordering of the Good and the Forbidding of the Evil (*mutaw'a*).

Piety is also displayed through physical evidence of long hours spent in prayer and devotion. The most obvious is the *halat al-salat* (gleam of prayer), which is mentioned in the Quran. It is a skin pigmentation caused by pressure exerted on the forehead through contact with prayer carpets, occurring on only a certain skin texture over a period of time. The condition is normally rare, but since the 1980s, there has been a sudden proliferation in the 'gleam of prayer' for Hijazi men. Hijazi women appear to develop it less frequently, but with advancing age they do seem to suffer bruising on their knees. It is quite common to see older women at formal occasions lifting their dresses to display their bruises as a sign of their sacrifice for prayers to God.

The return in the 1980s of religious rituals such as the *mawlid* is partly a symbol of Hijazi identity and partly a reflection of the increase in religious practice common to Saudi Arabia and other Muslim countries. Radio, television and newspapers carried more religious instruction than they did during the previous two decades, and the national school curriculum placed greater emphasis on religious subjects controlled by the Wahhabi *'ulema*. As a result competition in 'piety' became as prevalent as in any of the other indicators of status. This was partly the result of a broader shift in the Arab political arena. Nasser's secular pan-Arabism, dominant in the 1960s, did not challenge Saudi Arabia's position as the religious leader of the Islamic world. Since the Islamic revolutionary movement's victory in Iran in 1979, however, Saudi Arabians—especially Najdi officialdom, but also the Hijazi *'awa'il*—believe that they must show themselves to be worthy of guardianship over the holy cities.

This religious consciousness increased after the Gulf War in 1991. When United States forces not only defended the country but then remained, the non-Muslim presence triggered an Islamic movement of a radical kind among different sections of society. And yet it is noteworthy that the rejection of 'infidels' defending the Holy Land came from the Najdis and Wahhabis. The *'awa'il*'s reaction was a further assertion of religious devotion and of their belonging to the cradle of Islam.[19] The increasing elaboration of religious ceremonies thus also serves the *'awa'il* as an important means of distinguishing themselves from the Najdi political and religious elites. Rituals among the *'awa'il* are generally more emotional, mystical and even flamboyant, in sharp contrast with the more stern and strict way of life elsewhere in the Arabian Peninsula. Hijazis explain that their approach to Islam, unlike Wahhabism, is tolerant and respects plurality, as it has always been influenced by other Muslim trends. In general, by following piety the *'awa'il* are like the Najdis, but with a somewhat different content.

◆ THE MEANING OF FAMILY

Members of the *'awa'il* place a high value not only on family size, but also on its solidarity. As ever, the exaggerated ceremonies of the Hijazis refines their attitude to family. A large and united patronymic group can more effectively ensure that its claims to high status are respected. Strong kinship ties are a religious duty, with *'ibada* (care for one's parents) coming second only to worship.[20] There are several *hadith* that provide that severing *silat ar-rihm* (kinship ties) is a sin.[21] Relationships between all members of a family—those who share a surname (and in-marrying wives)—are expected to be cordial. Relations between brothers, sisters and cousins must appear strong, especially in public. At formal occasions family must appear and stand together and display the 'love' and unity between them. Internal discord should not be shown to outsiders, in accordance with the Arab saying, 'My brother and I against my cousin, but my cousin and I against the outsider'. This, as well as the norm of *'a'ila kabira* (large family), is overwhelmingly displayed by the ruling family, the Al Saud. Hence the domestic units of the *'awa'il* are larger than those of other sections of society (with greater financial resources required to maintain them). Obviously, the smaller the patronymic group, the more criteria for status other than size need to be met. Although the size of an *'awa'il* family does not measure up to that of the Al Saud, some number up to 200 members and others are as small as 50 members. The smaller size is due to less practice of polygamy and to the late realisation that larger families mean power. For the first and second generation Hijazis following the creation of the kingdom of Saudi Arabia the model was that of the smaller Hashemite ruling family. King (Sharif) Hussain had only four sons.

Although each individual family displays small distinctive markers during formal events, major differences of style and outlook that reflect city of origin, professional background or education are concealed except when in private. Similarities among *'awa'il* families—based on adherence to the common code of behaviour—are emphasised publicly at all times, enabling them to present a unified image of themselves as the dominant Hijazi elite. Ceremonial occasions associated with birth, marriage and death (i.e. life-cycle rituals) are the most public manifestation of tradition and correct behaviour. Strict adherence to the required social rules and emphasis on minute details of etiquette serve to distinguish the participants' status and reinforce their sense of identity. These rules determine, for example, how to walk and behind whom, how to greet and in which priority, where to sit, when to speak, what to say, and even the facial expressions to cultivate. Furthermore, specific meaning with regard to social status and identity may attach to a decorative object, to a type of spice, to a colour, to a motif on a dress or to the timing of an event.

Seemingly ordinary and unremarkable aspects of behaviour thus become highly significant to the extent that outsiders do not exhibit them. But status criteria are not only recognised internally. Elite status and distinctiveness are defined in relation to others, and competition between the elites of Saudi Arabia, expressed through regular interaction, is indicative of the country's degree of cohesion. This competition, both conscious and unconscious, between elites, remains strong in the field of decorum and ceremonials.

Special gatherings can take on a similar significance. Holding regular weekly *majlis* (formal reception),[22] where others visit to pay respects and enjoy hospitality, is a sign of status for men that also serves to distinguish members of the *'awa'il* from others. The Hijazi *majlis* is a formal gathering, comparable to an 'open house'. In the Najd only the king's reception and that of royal princes is called a *majlis*, and among neighbouring countries it is most popular in Kuwait, where such gatherings are referred to as *diwaniyya*.[23] In the sometimes uneasy political relations between the Hijaz and Riyadh the Interior Ministry discourages these regular weekly *majlis* with warning letters or telephone calls to the individual heads of households. It is evidently not the gathering itself that is objectionable, but the regularity of the time and place, and the topics of conversation, which sometimes address social, religious and literary themes. This makes the Hijazi *majlis* appear to approach the form of an institution—and thus potentially subvert the state.

Women also receive visitors regularly, but their gatherings have no designation like the men's *'majlis'* and have no political significance for the authorities. The women's gatherings are more elaborate; food, dress, language and etiquette are more ceremonial. A Hijazi woman of the *'awa'il* should hold evenings for many guests, preferably with a traditional singer. *Tarab* (music) is an important factor determining status and regional distinctiveness, since the Hijaz had richer and more developed musical traditions than the Najd, where until the late 1950s music was considered a *mulhi* (distraction) from religious duties.[24] Although the continuity and richness of Hijazi music and dance are threatened by an Islamist trend among Hijazi women, charismatic older women guard the musical traditions, whose display is not restricted to women's gatherings, as the *'awa'il* are known for holding mixed-gender evenings.

Even those rituals and ceremonies that pose a less obviously overt political challenge to Najdi hegemony are, however, vulnerable to the Saudi programme of national homogeneity, which confronts the Hijazi *'awa'il* from two directions. The first is from above, in the form of direct pressure—both coercive and co-optive—by the Al Saud to assimilate them to Najdi cultural norms. The second is from below, as social mobility within the Hijaz threatens the *'awa'il* with the vulgarisation or contamination of their culture by Saudified *arrivistes*. The rituals and ceremonies described in the following chapters indicate how the *'awa'il* have sought to preserve and assert a Hijazi identity against both challenges, thereby offering a challenge of their own.

3 The Political Awakening of the Hijazi 'awa'il

◆ THE DISPLACEMENT OF OCCUPATIONAL TRADITION

T HE HIJAZ developed for nearly 1,000 years as an international cross-roads, a melting pot of races and nationalities. Hijazis developed close ties with Malaysia, Indonesia, India, Turkey, Egypt and Central Asia, whose religious rituals, food and aspects of dress they adopted, and some of whose languages they spoke.[1] During the beginning of the unification 1925–7, compared with their Najdi counterparts, the Hijazi businessmen were wealthier and more accustomed to corporate political activity, having acquired experience during the Hashemite regime.[2] But Hijazis' sense of identity was more clearly defined before the unification of Saudi Arabia in 1932 than it is today. The relative absence of social mobility guaranteed the Hijazi elite a more closed and secure position. Families pursued professional occupations in which most adult male members participated and in which the next generation would be initiated as a matter of course.

By contrast, the far-reaching economic, social and religious changes brought about since unification, particularly since the 1950s, have significantly altered the ways in which elite Hijazis experience and perceive their status and identity within the Saudi state. As some of the most honoured traditional Hijazi occupations have become redundant or been usurped since the establishment of the Najdi state, the once-firm foundations of Hijazi autonomy have weakened. At the same time, hitherto obscure families have risen to prominence through access to oil money, posing a challenge to the exclusive world of the traditional Hijazi elite, the urban *'awa'il*.[3]

The pre-unification Hijazi *'awa'il* were comprised of four main groups:

1) The *Ashraf* (family of the ruling political elite).
2) Families of *mutawwifin* (guides to the pilgrims).
3) Families of *'ulema* (religious teachers, or the *a'yan*).
4) *Buyut tijariyya* (merchant or commercial families).

Each of these patronymic groups carried a particular status in the Hijaz and among the *'awa'il*, and all were recognised by Abdul Aziz Al Saud upon the foundation of the new state, as evidenced in his speeches. However, all of these groups have since undergone substantial transformation, in ways that steadily estranged the *'awa'il*—and the Hijaz's distinctive urban culture more generally—from the Wahhabi Najdi elite that gradually consolidated its control over all major levers of power in Saudi Arabia.

◆ THE *ASHRAF*

Under the Ottomans the Hashemite *Ashraf* were the recognised authorities in the Hijaz, with the emir based in the Offices of the Ruler in the great eight-storey palace of Muhammed Ali in Mecca. The *Ashraf* were the Hijazi chiefdom, political and military leaders of the Hijazi population. They enjoyed numerous privileges under the Ottomans, including payments to the emir of '3000 Lira per month plus food from Bedouin levies and undisclosed monies direct from the Imperial purse towards the upkeep of the Holy places in Mecca and Medina.'[4] Special laws protected the rulers, including decrees mandating that four lives be taken if a Sharif was killed, and that anyone striking a Sharif would lose the offending hand.

The *Ashraf* also enjoyed special titles that set them apart. They were referred to as *sidi*, master, even when amongst brothers or spouses: a custom of respect that survives among the *Ashraf* residing in the Hijaz and among Jordan's ruling Hashemite family. Sharifian men stood out at formal occasions, wearing a special headdress, *'umama*, while they mostly used a headband, *'iqal*, for travel.[5] They wore distinctive sandals and a dagger around the waist, in conformity with their rank. Sharifian women wore white trousers, a long shirt and short jacket with very long sleeves. They never covered their faces, but used a shawl to cover their heads, leaving their long plaits showing. Women's silk clothes came from China, often fashionably patterned with dragons.

As well as granting privileges, the Ottomans sought to exploit divisions in order to divide and rule. The *Ashraf* were divided into different groups, with both links and tensions between these branches persisting for many years. There were regional groups—those at Mecca, Taif, and the Bedouin *Ashraf*—and two branches of descent, of Zaid and Awn.[6]

In contrast to the desert armies of their neighbours, the *ikhwan*, who were religious zealots, the Sharifian military defences had developed into a sophisticated, organised system. At its apex were the distinctively dressed *'aqilis*, of whom there were 200 at the beginning of the twentieth century. There were also professional guards and the *naqabat*, a guild of camel drivers. For military training members of the *Ashraf* would spend two years in the desert with the camel patrol in order to learn the ways of the Bedouins and also to 'de-Turkishise'.[7]

Nevertheless, on the whole the *Ashraf* were not drawn to military asceticism, preferring an urban, cosmopolitan lifestyle. They spoke several languages, including Turkish and English, sponsored a variety of Islamic traditions, including the Sufi *tarigahs*, enjoyed many musical styles and travelled regularly to the Ottoman court, other Islamic countries and Great Britain. They received higher education abroad, with King Hussain's youngest son, Zaid Bin Hussain, studying at Oxford.

◆ THE *MUTAWWIFIN*

The second main group comprising the Hijazi *'awa'il* were the *mutawwifin*, the guides for pilgrims to Mecca. The more precise translation of *mutawwif* is a guide for the circumambulation of the Kaaba *tawaf*. However, in common parlance it means a guide for strangers (Muslims from other lands), implying guidance both for the *hajj* (pilgrimage) and throughout the city where it is performed.[8]

Prior to the 1930s the social status of the *mutawwifin* families varied considerably. Although the profession did not often enjoy the prestige of the *'ulema* or of the big merchant families, a *mutawwif* who had cultivated long-term relations with rich pilgrims was viewed with a relatively high degree of respect. Indeed, of all the Meccan guilds that of the *mutawwif* was most important,[9] because the city relied economically, socially and politically on the *hajj* and the income derived from it. All Meccans were, in one way or another, involved in the *hajj*, but the patronymic groups of the *mutawwifin* controlled the trade. One of the prayers said by pilgrims is, 'God make this a blessed *hajj* and a successful business', underscoring the lack of any perceived clash between spirituality and material gain.

From the moment of the pilgrims' arrival in the Peninsula until their departure the *mutawwifin* took care of all of their needs. Each main *mutawwif* had a *wakil* (agent) in Jeddah who met the pilgrims at the port and brought them to Medina and Mecca, protecting them from bands of marauding Bedouins. Once in Mecca, the guides instructed the pilgrims in their religious duties, interpreted for them, arranged accommodation and made everyday purchases. Agents who received and guided the pilgrims in Medina were called *muzawwir*, the one who enables the visit to the Prophet's tomb.

The professional services of the *mutawwifin* involved the whole family. The women of the family cooked for the pilgrims and cleaned their lodgings. Women have described the demands and hard work involved in caring for the pilgrims, who 'were our guests in our homes and in our city'. A Hijazi man detailed the task he performed at the age of eight:

> There were large numbers of pilgrims in any one group and no microphones in those days, hence my father [the main *mutawwif*] stood at the front of the group, my elder brother in the middle, and I at the end, repeating the required prayers as my father said them, to those who stood behind me.

Although the *mutawwifin* were mostly men, some women also held licences for the profession, generally by inheriting them from their fathers. A woman could not, however, project her voice in the mosque, as this is considered *'awra* (distraction from devotion), so she would appoint a *wakil* for this purpose. Outside the mosque she taught women pilgrims the appropriate ways to wash, dress themselves and pray. Since the advent of Wahhabism under the Saudi state, however, there have been no women *mutawwifin*, with gender segregation in the Great Mosque becoming strict and subject to the control of the *mutaw'a* (religious police).

By the very nature of their occupation, *mutawwifin* had to be familiar with the language, way of life and customary religious rituals of the country from which they received pilgrims. For this purpose, and in order to make contacts and recruit more pilgrims for the following year, *mutawwifin* travelled to these countries. The social and religious standing of *mutawwifin* derived from being *halagat al-wasl*, the 'circular link' through time between the Muslims of a particular country and the Holy Places.[10]

Payment for the services of *mutawwifin* was referred to as *amana* (objects of trust). At the end of their stay, pilgrims generally paid the head of the *mutawwifin* family in gold or jewels, which was then shared between the rest of the guides, including the *muzawwir* in Medina and the *wakil* in Jeddah, and those who handed out *zamzam* water (holy water drawn from the well in Mecca). Pilgrims fulfilling the fifth and final duty of all Muslims regarded those who guided them through it with a mixture of awe and admiration. Hence they tended to be as generous in their payment as they could afford. For their part, *mutawwifin* promoted and profited from foreign Muslims' traditional view of Mecca as 'other-worldly' and Meccans as blessed.

Prior to 1926 foreign pilgrims also paid a sum of money to the local government and the Sharif of Mecca. After the conquest of the Hijaz by Abdul Aziz Al Saud, the pilgrims' payment to the local government was abolished. But in 1932 King Abdul Aziz Al Saud issued a statement in *Umm al-Qura*, the official Hijazi newspaper, assuring *mutawwifin* that their positions were secure. He promised that even if the role and position of the guides did not improve, their status would not diminish.

These guarantees meant little. The Saudi government's Ministry of Hajj and Awgaf (religious endowments) has established six companies that administer the pilgrimage, each specialising in pilgrims from a particular region or country: Arabs, Turks and Europeans, Africans, Indians and Pakistanis, South-East Asians and Iranians. Each of these 'national commercial enterprises' has its own board of directors, leaving little scope for intervention by heads of the traditional *mutawwifin* families. Nowadays the pilgrims land at King Abdul Aziz International Airport in Jeddah. They are met and conducted throughout the pilgrimage by the relevant *hajj* company and stay in one of the many impersonal chains of international hotels or in smaller, cheaper accommodation.

Rationalising the *hajj* became inevitable after the 1950s, when inflows of oil revenues and easier modes of access to the Holy Places caused the annual number of pilgrims to soar, to around two million by the early 1980s.[11] As the rapid growth of the *hajj* strained the old personalised relations between *mutawwifin* and pilgrims, the state bureaucracy naturally took over. The enlargement of the Great Mosques of Mecca and Medina,[12] together with the introduction of loudspeakers, also took their toll on the Hijazi *mutawwifin*, facilitating the unification of the pilgrims' various religious rituals, norms and behaviours under Wahhabi rules.

With the institutionalisation and strengthening of the six national commercial enterprises, a Saudi attempt was being made to break the monopoly of the few Hijazi *mutawwifin* families, who complain that opening the profession to outsiders has compromised it. In the past, a *mutawwif* would be trained from childhood, and this was his sole activity. Nowadays a ministry employee in Jeddah or Riyadh might act as a guide during the pilgrimage season. The role of agents and brokers has grown, and they receive larger shares of the payments than the *mutawwifin*. Indeed, each *hajj* company has approximately 3,000 government employees, all of whom share the total profits, although only around 150 actually do the work.

Nevertheless, since the 1980s, the *'awa'il* have aimed to revive the profession's reputation as a Hijazi bailiwick. Several sons of *mutawwifin* who made their fortunes in commerce and built a reputation independent of their lineage now go to Mecca during the pilgrimage and work for the Ministry of Hajj as *mutawwifin*. They do not need the financial rewards, but instead seek to revive and assert a key component of traditional pre-Saudi Meccan identity. They say that 'For them only a Meccan could be a *mutawwif;* a Najdi could never really know or understand our city' or indeed compete with the Hijazi cosmopolitan tradition, which bestows a certain *savoir-faire* in dealing with other cultures.[13]

◆ THE *'ULEMA*

The *'ulema*, religious teachers, were the most highly esteemed profession, enjoying a status and respectability second only to the ruling dynasty. Most *'ulema* possessed key attributes defining membership in the Hijazi *'awa'il*, such as *nasab* (lineage), and a degree of *hasab* (depth in lineage). The *'ulema's* functions involved regulating communal and religious life by serving as judges, administrators, teachers and religious advisers. They also advised on temporal matters, such as marriage, divorce, inheritance and even medicine. The *'ulema* had circles of knowledge, *halagat al'ilm,* comparable to a religious academic class, in the Great Mosque of Mecca, where they taught. Each *'alim* (singular of *'ulema*) had his own students, some of whom came from as far as Indonesia, India or Egypt.

The leading *'ulema* in the Hijaz were mostly graduates of Al-Azhar, others studied in Meccan or Medinese mosques. The Hijazi *'ulema* specialised in *fiqh* (jurisprudence), Quranic exegesis, Arabic grammar and syntax, prosody, logic and philosophy. Their religious tradition was generally heterogeneous, following one of the three Islamic schools of law: the Shafi'i, Hanafi or Maliki. A prominent Hijazi *'alim* was in most cases multilingual, with knowledge of the Indonesian, Malaysian, Indian and Central Asian languages, including their various dialects. This theological openness set the Hijazi *'ulema* apart from the Najdi *'ulema,* whose religious education was mostly handed down from father to son and included little contact with outside scholars.[14] Religious training in the Najd was restricted to the principles of Wahhabism and Hanbali jurisprudence, with little interest in grammar, syntax or other traditional Islamic sciences.

Becoming an *'alim* in the Hijaz was a complicated matter. Sons of *'ulema* who wished to join the profession spent several years attending lessons in the circle of knowledge of their father or another prominent *'alim* who adopted them. Usually, after three years, the student obtained an *ijaza* (licence) to teach and was appointed by the four *muftis,* representatives of the four *madhahib* (Sunni schools of law). This allowed him to open his own circle, *halaga,* in which he would teach and be taught.

The high status held by the *'ulema* reflected their spheres of influence; although not necessarily affluent, they affected people's thinking and prescribed proper behaviour. The Hijazi *'ulema* lived mainly on donations, pilgrims' gifts, and *awgaf* (religious endowments), while some were engaged in commerce. Exceptionally, prominent *'ulema* received salaries from the political authorities in the Hijaz. However, unlike their Najdi counterparts, whose survival was entirely dependent on state subsidies, Hijazi *'ulema* enjoyed relative autonomy in the conduct and content of their daily life and professional affairs.[15]

The Hijazi *'ulema* had a distinct code of dress. They tied their *'umama* (headdress) in a unique fashion, their garments were made from a particular white cotton, they wore a relatively thin belt and *sirwal* (short trousers) under the outer garment. The older generation of the women (those born prior to unification) also had their own terminology, manners and way of thinking. This difference was also apparent in women *'ulema* (mothers, daughters, sisters and wives), who usually were literate and knew more of the Quran and *hadith* than other women. Some prominent female relatives of Hijazi *'ulema* debated in matters relating to *fiqh*, which would be literally unthinkable among women in Najdi *'ulema* families.

As dress was unified in accordance with the unification of the kingdom, so too were prayers and teachings in the mosque. Prior to the 1930s several *imams* led the prayers and taught different groups simultaneously, each according to one of the four *madhabib*. After the unification of the country there was only one *imam* representing only the Hanbali *madhhab*, as interpreted by the teachings of Muhammed Bin Abdul Wahhab. This homogeneity of religious leadership was facilitated and reinforced by the advent of the microphone. The *imam* could now lead thousands of worshippers at the same time. Earlier, the different *imams* had led their congregations independently of each other—and in more open debate, owing to Hijazi heterogeneity.

The long-term prospects of the Hijazi *'ulema* changed drastically following the conquest of the region by Abdul Aziz Al Saud and the adoption of Wahhabism as the state religion. The first Saudi king consulted with regional leaders, including the *'ulema*, and appeared to accept the predominant consensus. In 1924 he had arranged a meeting of Meccan notables and told them that, 'You are more aware of your country than those farther away. You should therefore take responsibility for the ruling of your area.' The Hijazi *'ulema*, seeking coexistence with Wahhabism, officially recognised the doctrine as consistent with the Islamic *shari'a*.

However, this was not enough, and Meccans quickly accepted the imposition of Wahhabism in the wake of the slaughter at Taif in 1924 by the Wahhabi army.[16] The Wahhabis killed hundreds of inhabitants that they considered heretics including the Shafi'i mufti, and the family of the guardians of the Kaaba. In return for protection from the jihadism of Wahhabist fundamentalist *ikhwan*, the Meccans opted to support Abdul Aziz Al Saud, who used the Wahhabi religious decrees to keep the Hijaz under control. In 1925–7, the Najdi and Hijazi judicial systems were unified by a royal decree, in accordance with the Hanbali school that governed Najd. The fact that Wahhabi law was applied caused this creed to become a dominant norm associated with the supremacy of Abdul Aziz Al Saud.[17] Many Hijazi *'ulema* opted to continue their teaching practices away from their preferred base of Mecca, and so lived and worked in Malaysia, Indonesia and elsewhere.

Hijazi *'ulema* became caught up in the political disputes within the ruling family over the country's future. The second king, Saud Al Saud (1953–64), sought a more conservative course with the support of prominent Najdi tribal leaders, Najdi *'ulema*, and those demanding an end to modernisation. King Saud, however, did not have the authority of either his father or his younger brother Faisal. He was unable to respond to the political uncertainties generated by pan-Arabism in the wake of Nasser's nationalism and, forced to share power with Faisal, was eventually coerced by a coalition of senior princes to surrender his political responsibilities to Faisal, who was known to be more sympathetic towards Hijazis. Indeed, Faisal replaced several of Saud's Najdi ministers with moderate Hijazi technocrats.

King Faisal pursued a policy of inclusion of educated Hijazis for pragmatic reasons throughout the 1960s and 1970s. He had been posted to Mecca by Adbul Aziz and developed a working relationship with many Hijazi notables, believing that modernisation, which he advocated, required the inclusion of the expertise and relative liberalism of the Hijaz. As part of this project, Faisal sought to reduce the political influence of the *'ulema* generally, while strengthening the position of more secular political elites.[18] Hijazi *'ulema* were seen by Faisal as useful, and were promoted as part of the development of a more technocratic state. In 1970, for example, the newly established Ministry of Justice was placed in the hands of an *'alim* of Hijazi origin who was more sympathetic to Faisal's project than were Wahhabis.

In 1975 King Khalid and his powerful half-brother, then-Crown Prince Fahd, reversed Faisal's policy of favouring Hijazis. This was partly due to pressure from Najdi *'ulema*, who resented the advancement of the 'secular' urban Hijazis and the supposed 'Westernisation' and corruption that they represented. The stricter Al Sheikh *'ulema*, descendants of Muhammed Bin Abdul Wahhab, secured preference over those from the Hijaz and came to fill the top positions of the judicial and educational systems. Under King Fahd they won more rigorous enforcement of Wahhabi laws, aided by external political circumstances, namely the Iranian revolution at the end of 1979 and the Gulf War in 1991.

During this period, Hijazis were discouraged from practising as members of the *hai'at kibar al 'ulema* (assembly of senior *'ulema*) on the grounds that their *'aqida* (ideology) is different: hence they are virtually excluded from the highest ranks of the profession.[19] The *'ulema* today are predominantly Najdi, the most prominent being the Al Sheikh. The qualifications required of an *'alim* have also changed: it is now sufficient that a student spends four years at the *shari'a* college in one of the state universities, such as Imam Muhammed Ibn Saud University in Riyadh, or the Umm Al Qura University in Mecca. Today's *'ulema* include all recognised religious scholars, judges of different ranks, religious lawyers, religious teachers and *imams* in the mosques. During the 1980s the *'ulema* numbered around 10,000.

The 1991 Gulf War had a dramatic impact on the religious and political atmosphere, the rise of Islamism and the creation of neo-Wahhabi opposition groups. One such group, led by Sheikh Safar al-Hawali and Salman al-Awdah, initiated the Intifidah of Burraidah in 1995, when more than 10,000 people demonstrated against US policies and military presence and criticised the corruption of the Al Saud. The group's leaders, like other oppositionists, were jailed, but then released in 1998. Some tamed leaders have since been permitted to address political issues in order to co-opt support for the feared underground religious groups that have emerged since the Gulf War.

The need to co-opt religious opposition strengthened the position of the Al Sheikh, who were already a major component of the Saudi regime, enjoying high prestige, influence and financial privileges. Indeed, the very foundation of the Saudi state continues to be based on the pillar of legitimacy afforded by the symbiotic relationship between the Al Saud and the Wahhabis. This is seen as defending the values and interests of the *umma* (the worldwide community of Islam). But in the Saudi Wahhabi way of thinking it was useful to promote a localised conception of the *umma* concerned with the fight against corruption and the presence of the US infidel forces on holy soil. The religious establishments and their various organisations, such as the Ministry of Islamic Affairs, Committee of the Order of the Good and the Forbidding of the Evil, and its employees the *mutaw'a* (religious police), the Ministry of the Hajj and Awgaf have gained more influence, particularly in the educational system. The growing numbers of Najdi graduates from religious and Western universities has reduced dependence on the secular outlook and professional skills of the Hijazis. By the time of the rule of King Fahd, Faisal's pragmatic attitude towards Hijazis was seen as no longer necessary or desirable.

With the Saudi political elite increasingly dependent on the legitimising support of the Wahhabi *'ulema* and the religious establishment more broadly, they reinstated the position of Grand Mufti after the Gulf War and provided wider scope for *fatwas* (religious decrees). The increase in the Wahhabi establishment's stature has offered it an opportunity to realise its founder's grand ambition: to abolish all *bid'a* (innovation) that came after the third Islamic century. As Wahhabism's inner puritanical drive has been unleashed, it has become increasingly intolerant of other interpretations of Islam, such as Shia, or the Sufi traditions of the Hijaz, which Wahhabis consider *shirk* (idolatory).

The distinction between the current Najdi *'ulema* and their one-time Hijazi counterparts is clear. The former are often referred to as *mashayikh* (singular: *shaykh*) and are mentioned in contexts that make it clear that they are seen by the *'awa'il* as representing strict rules and rigidity, whereas the latter evoke nostalgia for the moderate pluralistic Islam that they are viewed as having represented. As the increasing challenges of globalisation fuel a traditionalist response that has further magnified the role and influence of the Wahhabi *'ulema*, the Hijazis, who on the whole tend to be inclined more towards Faisal's brand of modernisation, have come to feel even more isolated. Very few Hijazis approve of the strict religious control that the *mutaw'a* (religious police) have on the everyday lives of people.[20]

However, the *'awa'il* still maintain observance of Islamic norms. Although there are no more Hijazi *'ulema*, the prestige traditionally associated with the profession has remained with their descendants. Hijazis often quote the saying of Muhammed, 'The *'ulema* are the inheritors of the prophets, *anbiya'*. Shortcomings that would be criticised in others are often overlooked when manifested in descendants of the *'ulema*. Four families among the *'awa'il* today are of *'ulema* origin, while several others descended from the *'ulema* are not included, because they have not attained the requisite standard of wealth and style of living.

◆ *BUYUT TIJARIYYA*

The status of the *buyut tijariyya* (merchant families) depended on their specialisation, wealth, moral and religious reputation and their lineage, with some exercising considerable influence in the community. Most merchant families traded in commodities; only a few specialised in specific items such as fabrics, perfumes, spice or jewels. Contacts with commercial centres in the countries were established and developed over several generations, and several patronymic groups became known by the trade established at some time in their history. Professional traders were widespread in the Hijaz, but only a few patronymic groups traded on a large scale or in luxury items, thereby increasing their status and prestige.

At the beginning of the twentieth century commerce was almost entirely based on imports of rice, sugar, grain, tea and textiles from India, although some goods were imported from Singapore, Indonesia or Ethiopia (coffee) and from the ports of the Red Sea and the Gulf.[21] Trade was almost entirely with the East and with other Muslim countries. The importing process was simple but effective. An Indian exporter would telegraph importing merchants notifying them of the dispatch of ships and of the price of the merchandise, set in rupees. Each interested merchant would specify the share of the cargo he wanted to buy. By the time the ship arrived, several Hijazi importers owned a share in its cargo.

Every merchant family owned a sailing ship or a share in one.[22] The ships went to India from the Hijaz to collect merchandise at special times of the year in accordance with the weather in the Indian Ocean. The Hijaz only exported a small quantity of almonds from Taif and 'balm of Mecca', an ointment extracted from wild plants and used universally as a medicine.[23] Nevertheless, the Hijaz was an international marketplace with a tradition of international trade. Goods from India were often transported on to other countries, and European goods arrived at the port of Jeddah via Suez. Trade from the port of Suez in Egypt was loaded onto the Hijaz railway, which carried it across Syria and Palestine.[24]

Unsurprisingly the outlook of the merchant families was international; indeed, some were in fact foreign, predominantly from India. These ties of international trade, along with the *hajj*, provided links through the Hijaz to the rest of the Muslim world that were a useful channel for Abdul Aziz Al Saud, who relied heavily on the knowledge and expertise of Hijazi traders to maintain them. After 1925 members of the Jeddah Chamber of Commerce joined the new political administration to deal with foreign representatives and the kingdom's trade, serving Abdul Aziz Al Saud and, later, his son Faisal.

But the Hijaz, which was previously the richest region in the peninsula, suffered a serious material setback at the beginning of Saudi rule in the 1930s. One reason was 'the transfer of the [pilgrimage] tax out of local hands to the new regime'.[25] Moreover, onerous new rules and conditions were also imposed on commercial activities. The currencies used locally in the Hijaz were the English gold coin (guinea), the Ottoman gold coin, the *maskufi* gold coin, the *bantu* gold coin, the Egyptian gold coin and the Hashemite gold coin; in addition there were the silver currencies. Upon the unification of the country, however, the Saudi rial became the only currency. Gold, traditionally stored and used by the merchants as capital, was no longer allowed out of the kingdom.[26]

This posed great difficulties because the mode of payment for Indian merchandise was either gold upon its arrival at the port of Jeddah, or rupees in the country of export. Furthermore, many merchants maximised their profit by paying in gold in India, where it was worth more. As a result, some Hijazi merchants continued to smuggle gold to India. But a crackdown by King Abdul Aziz Al Saud led to the imprisonment of several well-known Hijazi merchants, bringing an end to the practice.[27] The new government also took loans from leading Hijazi merchants during the 1940s, some of which were never repaid.[28] And finally, the government issued trading permits to foreign brokers, thus ending the monopoly of the few Hijazi merchant families that had a registered trade bureau.[29] Several Hijazi merchants were financially crippled, either directly or by rising competition from newcomers and *arrivistes*. Since the 1930s, and especially since the Second World War, the source of imports has shifted almost entirely from the East to the West, particularly to Europe, America and Japan. Merchants turned to Western countries for electrical appliances and cars. As tastes and fashion changed and as the kingdom opened itself to Western products, even commodities previously bought from the East such as rice and fabrics were now imported from the West.

Together with the changes to the laws and regulations surrounding commerce and trade, a more significant transformation occurred in the very concept of trade and commerce, and in the role of money. Prior to the 1940s and 1950s, a certain mystique surrounded money, generated and preserved by a few select merchant families in the Hijaz, who benefited from heightened status and respectability. These merchants traded in goods that were important because they were in short supply and thus became a substitute for money. But in the 1950s and later, when oil revenues made many people suddenly very rich, storing or exchanging money was no longer considered to be a specialised profession. Everyone made their money (and a great deal of it) in the same way. The transition from a non-monetary to a monetary economy thus cost many of the Hijazi merchant families—even those who managed to preserve their wealth—their previously secure status and prestige. Indeed, with the rapid increase in social mobility brought about by oil money, some members of the *'awa'il* became very poor relative to the *nouveaux riches*.

◆ OIL AND POLITICAL DEPENDENCE

Until the conquest of the Hijaz by Abdul Aziz Al Saud, Mecca and Jeddah were the richest cities in Arabia, with annual incomes of £7 and £8 million, respectively.[30] In the period immediately following the defeat of the Hijaz, the most serious material disadvantage of Saudi rule was the redistribution of proceeds from the pilgrimage tax—which previously had remained entirely within the Hijaz—throughout the rest of the kingdom. But between the unification of Saudi Arabia and the first oil boom in the 1950s, the Hijaz remained the country's leading area, although by 1940 it was already on the way to becoming relatively impoverished in comparison with the other regions.[31]

Since then, however, the country's main source of income shifted dramatically from the *hajj*, which provided 60 per cent of the government's total revenue of 12 million rials in 1932, to oil production, which provided 90 per cent of revenues of 757 million rials in 1952.[32] With traditional sources of income and wealth effectively eliminated in the Hijaz, direct connections with members of the royal family and patronage became necessary for generating income, security and prestige. Agents made hundreds of millions of dollars in commissions on oil contracts. Government oil revenues soared again during the second oil boom in the 1970s, went up from $36.5 billion in 1977 to $102.2 billion in 1980 and $113.2 billion at their peak in 1981.[33] The prosperity of the *'awa'il* and the Hijaz in general came to rely on money filtering across from the oil wells of the Eastern Province.

Nevertheless, until the mid-1970s Hijazis were prominent in some areas of government service. The value that King Abdul Aziz had seen in the Hijazi merchant class was just as apparent to Faisal, first while he was crown prince and later when he became king (1964–75). Faisal needed the co-operation of the more moderate, better-educated elite to whom he offered the immediate incentives of a share in the administration of development as well as the more distant prospect of eventual participation in political decision-making.[34] He even drew political appointees from the membership of the Saudi Association of Chambers of Commerce, which grew up from the Jeddah Chamber, as he replaced Najdi ministers installed under Saud.

Hijazi modernisers were eager to assist Faisal in his effort to use the oil windfall of the 1970s to advance the development of the country. But oil revenues undermined the traditional socio-economic and occupational structure of the Hijaz itself. A Western-educated Najdi middle class began to control in both government and business, while the Wahhabi *'ulema* asserted control over religious affairs. In short, oil wealth increased social mobility in Saudi Arabia, producing a new elite whose emergence depended on its members' relations with the ruling family and on what was a far more common and hence more important determinant of success—regional Najdi tribal affiliations.

Indeed, changes in the ruling elite were made possible by economic and social change, but were brought about politically by Faisal's successors, Khalid and Fahd. Since the 1960s Fahd had been using his patronage powers as Minister of the Interior to 'implant members of the "Sudeiri seven" clan, the six full brothers of Fahd, their clients and their "tribal" relatives in the government'.[35] King Fahd's first cabinet in 1975 began the process of 'Sudeirisation'—the displacement of largely Hijazi technocrats with a new generation of Najdi ministers, governors and top administrators. Despite his continuing dependence on Hijazis, Fahd was succumbing to pressures from the more orthodox Wahhabi *'ulema* to reverse the 'Westernisation' pursued by Faisal.

King Fahd and his allies were also able to exploit lingering doubts about Hijazi loyalty. Despite the predominance of Hijazis within areas of the administration, the Hijaz also produced determined opponents of the Saudi Arabian state. Some, along with others from neighbouring regions of the country, have participated in the sporadic political revolts that have occurred since unification. A small minority supported Nasserite pan-Arabism in the 1950s, with Ba'athism finding favour in both the Hijaz and Asir. Several Hijazis were jailed in the 1960s for their involvement in political plots, and a series of abortive coups throughout the 1970s involved small numbers of senior administrative and military personnel. Notwithstanding the politically marginal character of most of this activity, it did nothing to endear the Hijazis to Faisal's brother princes.

As Hijazis were increasingly pushed from senior positions within the state under King Fahd, they lost access to oil contracts and suffered steady reduction in most other opportunities for political and economic advancement. By the 1980s, the unification of Saudi Arabia and the development of the oil economy had fully displaced the Hijazi *'awa'il* as the dominant social and economic elite in the Arabian Peninsula. They had become a peripheral and subservient elite within the Saudi state, whose economic strength now depended entirely on the political patronage of the non-Hijazi royal family.

◆ THE PRIVATISATION OF RESISTANCE

At the start of the twenty-first century, several Hijazis fall into the category of the mega-rich. Given the accretion of vast wealth to the Hijazis—and the cradle-to-grave welfare state that the government established with a portion of its windfall oil revenues—it is sometimes difficult for Najdis to understand the *'awa'il*'s feelings of relative deprivation in present Saudi society. It is argued that the oil boom of the 1970s benefited the urban Hijazis. As a Najdi merchant said:

> It was Hijazis who benefited most from the wealth in Saudi Arabia. They would have stayed on pilgrims' income if they remained Hijazi; instead they had a large share of the oil wealth situated in the Eastern Province. But they are still complaining.

Hijazis, on the other hand, believe that they would have benefited from the oil wealth of the Eastern Province even if the Hijaz had never been incorporated into Saudi Arabia. A Hijazi elder explained that:

> Its importance, since pre-Islamic times, as a trading nation, along with the relative backwardness of the rest of the Peninsula, would have established the Hijaz as the financial, industrial and commercial services centre for the rest of the Peninsula, much as Singapore is for South-East Asia.

Such aspirations, much like those of a previous generation for a renewed Hashemite Kingdom, have come to naught. In practice, unification has steadily drained away many of the institutional advantages that the Hijaz once possessed. Administration migrated to the new capital in Riyadh, as did the offices of the businesses and banks. But it was 'the departure of the [foreign embassies] that was received by the sophisticated and extrovert Hijazis as the supreme insult, particularly because the traditionally introvert and xenophobic Najdis had discouraged westerners until the 1960s even from visiting Riyadh'.[36]

The Hijaz has been eclipsed by the growing power and authority of the emergent generation of educated, technocratic Najdi who now dominate the heights of Saudi Arabian business, administrative, religious and military life. This, combined with the inhibiting effects of the rigorous Wahhabi *'ulema* on social debate has left many Hijazis with a sense of fear and hopelessness. It is within this atmosphere that there has been a return to rituals and symbols to assert a distinctive Hijazi identity. Excluded from the political and, indeed, public life of their own state, the Hijazi *'awa'il*, in particular, have set about creating a new milieu in which they can feel at home—a world whose contours describe the powerful latent challenge facing the Saudi authorities.

4 The Rites of Passage I: Ceremonies of Birth

◆ INTRODUCTION

E VERY SOCIETY has its own rituals that define key elements in the lives of its people, usually in the form of birth, marriage and death. The moment of birth provides Hijazis with an opportunity to display what they consider to be their importance. A community obsessed with its own sense of identity—however self-conscious at times—is bound to exploit the rituals surrounding birth. Hijazis are no exception. The birth of a child is the occasion for a manifold celebration of both individual and cultural life. It also provides a special opportunity to assert family lineage and reinforce continuity with past and future. Both on the symbolic and practical level it highlights the renewal of the patronymic group, just as the ceremonies associated with it express a renewal of Hijazi culture. The communal recognition of a child's birth serves to reinforce the structure of family relationships, bringing to prominence many of the criteria of social status. At this time lineage, patronymic group size, solidarity with the patronymic group, wealth and, as always, the observance of piety and propriety receive particular emphasis.[1]

The importance of this event must be judged in the context of Hijazi society, in which the patronymic group is the dominant social, economic and even political unit. As in most patrilineal societies, an established patronymic group gains potential and vitality with the birth of each new member.[2] This is especially important in Hijazi society, which is under the external domination of a very numerous and ever grow-ing ruling family. Consciously or unconsciously, the celebrations focus on expansion of the patronymic group in response to that of the Al Saud.

However, birth is distinguished from other Hijazi rites of passage in so far as it is the only event that, by honouring motherhood, focuses almost entirely on celebrating woman-hood. The ceremonies surrounding birth acknowledge the *hadith* (saying of Muhammed), *aj-janna tahta agdam al-ummahat* (paradise is under the feet of mother).[3] Despite female subservience, Hijazis pride themselves on elevating women to a special status after they give birth. More than in other parts of Arabia they are encouraged to play a more prominent role within the family. Upon giving birth, a new mother achieves her highest personal status and religious position. Her role around delivery as a perpetuator of the patrilineal family line is publicly acknowledged, as it will be again in the performance of marriage and death rituals. Women thus take active roles in the observance of 'tradition', although modification and invention of rituals are initiated mostly by male patrons of the extended families.

Birth ceremonies are smaller in scope and scale than those of marriage and death. They are particularly Hijazi in that as only Hijazis—relatives and close friends of the patronymic group—attend them. The rituals associated with birth are, indeed, a concrete expression of the acceptance of the rules of a distinctive Hijazi society, and an expression of the hope that the newborn will observe these rules. However, with every birth the patronymic group is also offered opportunities either to lay claim publicly to its status in the community or to negotiate new identities by demonstrating a complete understanding and acceptance of social values and norms.[4]

More importantly, the ritual and tradition that relate to pregnancy and birth are replete with a complex layering of social significance that extends beyond the patronymic group. The revival of tradition becomes a tool for the self-conscious assertion of Hijazi identity. Birth brings the hope of, and provides some assistance in, the creation of a romantic vision of the Hijaz—at the expense of the Najdi vision of a unified Saudi people.

◆ THE HOSPITAL SCENE AND MODERNITY: REDEFINING BIRTH CEREMONIES

With the advent of modern medical practices, the physical and social setting under which some traditions are reinvented has changed considerably. The location of the birth itself, along with many of its required rituals, has been transferred to the hospital, removing them from the traditional domestic setting. Reviving traditions in a modern setting imposes constraints on which practices re-emerge and which do not. Those practices and rituals that are selected as 'traditional' must be adaptable to a novel context, which lends them new qualities.

The first hospital opened in Jeddah in 1924 for pilgrims coming to Mecca via the sea.[5] The rest of what would become Saudi Arabia had no hospitals. During the late 1950s, public and private hospitals emerged as a direct result of oil wealth. Most medical staff came from other Arab countries, predominantly from Egypt; later some came from Europe and the United States. This period saw a de-traditionalising of many social and medical aspects of birth, such as the role of the Hijazi midwife, *daya*. Hijazi female doctors were pioneers in the male-dominated profession, becoming the first Saudi women to train in Egypt and later in the West and work in hospitals in Jeddah, Mecca and Medina. Hence, the medical profession escaped the traditional concepts of shame, i.e. dishonouring the family, and gained a prestigious status.

With the advent of technological advances the concept of hospitals and medical practice have been adjusted to local ideas and behaviour with regard to sickness and childbirth.[6] This process of transformation began to take place deliberately during the 1980s, in contrast to the 1960s and the 1970s, when changes in Hijazi society were less self-conscious and less resistant to Saudi Najdi influences. During the later period, since the 1980s, Hijazi society was largely developing into a profoundly ritualistic one, reflecting people's attempt to preserve elite status and cultural identity in an increasingly competitive and uncertain environment.

In the context of ritualisation, social conceptions of the hospital have become more formalised. The interior design of hospitals in Jeddah has been adapted to local ideas regarding presentation. In Jeddah, during the 1970s, several individuals among the *'awa'il*[7] responded to the appearance of grand government-built hospitals in Riyadh by founding Hijazi hospitals with the highest standards of medical care as well as with deluxe suites.[8] Hospital-building and design became part of the Hijazi–Najdi rivalry. In contrast to the more functional designs of the Najd, Jeddah hospitals have come to resemble the homes of the elite, providing a conducive environment in which to maintain Hijazi rituals. Suites and reception rooms now become places in which the mother and baby are at the focus of a series of events into which an expanding circle of family and friends are drawn. It is a peculiarly Hijazi characteristic to transform a hospital birth into an occasion for large-scale formalised social rituals.

The series of events and rituals that surround a birth serve numerous functions. They focus on the mother and/or the child, with some of the ceremonies being held separately for the mother and baby.[9] At different times family and friends all have a more or less formal place in the series of rituals. First, there is the birth itself, at which female members of the mother's immediate family are present. Afterwards, once the baby has arrived, the mother receives congratulations from her relatives and the wider network of friends. Later on there is the naming ceremony. Needless to say, outside the Hijaz the whole process of giving birth is much simpler and less charged with social meaning.

Hijazi cultural mysticism, regarded by conservative Najdis as superstition, is particularly evident in attitudes towards pregnancy and birth. An impending pregnancy is often fore-told by an older relative or an especially pious person such as a *sayyid* in a *ru'ya* (vision). This vision usually foretells not only the existence of the foetus but also its sex. These beliefs and practices are prohibited by Wahhabi principles. Wah-habis believe that visions interfere with the idea of the oneness and absolute power of God. Then, after the delivery and until the end of the 40-day confinement period, the ritu-als are designed to protect the couple, as mother and child are considered particularly susceptible to the evil eye during this time. The confinement period also brings with it a social support system that safeguards and shelters the mother so that she may regain her strength before recommencing nor-mal duties.

To help with her transition into motherhood, the woman receives a re-education in tradition. After each birth, her sta-tus changes, regardless of whether the newborn is a boy or a girl. Every time she gives birth the mother enters a new rela-tionship and has to find her way into a new role. She is expected by her extended family as well as her long-term friends—*wifyan* (literally 'faithful ones')—to transmit the prevalent social values to the newborn.[10] These expectations are expressed in popular sayings, such as, 'May God support mothers in their tasks'.

◆ RECEIVING THE NEWBORN INTO THE WORLD

Upon feeling her first labour pains, the mother-to-be leaves for hospital, taking her clothes and other 'necessary' objects. The 'necessary' objects include ornate paraphernalia, includ-ing plates on which to serve the dates, Hijazi sweets, traditional tea, coffee utensils and traditional incense. Veils and prayer mats are also necessary for prayer time.

At the moment of birth, a woman has several of her closest female relatives standing by her and reciting particular verses from the Quran to ease the delivery.[11] In addition they implore *ahl badr* (those who fought with the Prophet in the battle at Badr) to save her, or they make *nadhr* (vows to God) for the woman's safe delivery, for example, 'Oh! God save her, let her deliver with ease and I will hold a celebration for the birth of the Prophet, a *mawlid*'. Such overt references to the powerful Meccans of the past and in particular to the Prophet Muhammed's spirit are frowned upon by the Wahhabis as *bid'a* (dangerous innovations departing from the fundamentals of religion).

Within only a few hours of the delivery, the *wifyan* with whom one has *wisal* (social ties), come to celebrate the new life and define its status, establishing it within the social network. The *wifyan* are under an obligation to return each other's visits, known as *rad rijul* ('returning the legs'). Gifts are brought in order to reconfirm mutual belonging. The occasion of the birth offers a chance to repay a favour, *jamila*, and to perform both religious and social duties. This complex network of relationships and the terminology associated with it is unknown in other parts of Saudi Arabia.

The hospital room is transformed into the scene of a formalised gathering where the rules of conduct for visiting on the occasion of a birth are performed. Visiting rituals serve to unite the group in a shared recognition of an event of common importance and hence enhance the sense of group cohesion. At the same time, social status is dynamic and requires constant efforts and activity on behalf of those who are to be included within the desired group. As Kanafani puts it:

> Aesthetic display heightens group life during visits in which food and felicitations ... are offered. Visits are rites of passage in the sense that the guest and the host are in a marginal transitional state as they both undergo tests which will eventually either increase or decrease their prestige and esteem in the community or reinforce their original status.[12]

Visits are regulated by an elaborate code governing dress, gifts and ceremonial greetings. The dress that one wears on a hospital visit should comply with the 'traditional' rules of dress governing visits to the hospital. These colours are greens, white, blues, but not too bright, for the hospital is a solemn place commanding respect, which rules out red or yellow. Black is considered a bad omen, and is worn only to condolence ceremonies. Women of the Najd do not abide by these traditionally urban sartorial rules. Hence, colour codes serve to distinguish Hijazis at most rituals. Moreover, this minute attention to detail is particular to women of the *'awa'il*, who are acutely concerned to protect social status and identity.

On arrival guests perform the congratulation ceremony, *mubaraka*, with the appropriate set phrases. A visitor would never offer congratulations without an appropriate gift for both the mother and the baby. Gifts for the baby are preferably of gold, while for the mother they can be perfume or other feminine items. Gifts with the attached congratulatory cards are placed quietly on a table at the entrance to the room, for the rule is 'A gift is given in silence and received in silence'. The reason, in addition to discretion and elegance, is fear of the evil eye.

The specific set phrases, which are repeated by each guest at the hospital, include the subject of childbirth and the hardships that mothers go through. Women among the *'awa'il* regularly quote *hadith*, and every time a *hadith* is said the entire gathering acknowledges it by repeating 'peace be upon him'. Another topic of conversation derives from attempts to establish, feature by feature, who the baby looks like. This establishes the child's identity within the group, and thereby confirms lineage and maintains continuity. The interest is therefore more in confirming the status of the baby than in its features per se.

Relocating to the hospital, however, has not been accompanied by a wholesale re-appropriation of the past. Some traditional aspects of birth have not survived—at least intact—into the present. The practice of wet-nursing, establishing 'milk kin', along with the traditional midwives, has been relegated to the past. On the other hand, *tathir* (male circumcision) survives, but only as a medical practice. In the Hijaz prior to the twentieth century, male children were circumcised between the ages of three and seven, and *tathir* entailed lengthy and elaborate rituals involving music, chanting and special foods.[13] Nowadays circumcision's religious and cultural significance has been reduced to a minimum. This is most likely due to Najdi influence, as circumcision ceremonies are unknown in the Najd, where the practice is private. It has largely become a surgical procedure, usually performed by a doctor at the hospital when the newborn is only three days old, with close relatives merely congratulating the parents. Although circumcision denotes Muslim male identity, its celebration became less frequent in the 1950s and has since all but died out.

◆ NAMING THE CHILD: REASSERTING HIJAZI IDENTITY

There are two or three formal events related to the naming of the child. All of them have become contested territory in recent times. Both the name itself and the ceremonies by which the name is conferred on the child are subject to forms of official religious conflict. The child's name, in all Saudi Arabia, must be registered, giving the state the opportunity to limit admissible names. The Wahhabi authorities also restrict religious ceremonies through legislation. Hijazis have responded to these restrictions in various ways. They have adopted some Najdi practices, but have turned them in a distinctively Hijazi direction. They have also pursued 'traditional' practices, often in contradiction of the law and in the face of possible legal admonishment.

Officially, every name must be registered with four parts: first name, father's first name, grandfather's first name and family name. This establishes the newborn as a member of his patrilineal kin. The full name will always be used in public domains such as schools, military service, employment, etc. For the Hijazi *'awa'il*, using the father's and grandfather's name in a social gathering is a source of pride and an acknowledgement of regional belonging through more than three generations. When a man addresses a son of a friend of his, he will name him as 'son of so-and-so and grandson of so-and-so' in a reverential recognition of the family, specifically their depth of lineage.

Although names chosen by Hijazis are predominantly Muslim and Arab, they are easily distinguished from Najdi names and specifically from those normally chosen by the royal family. Arab names that are more easily pronounced in the West (e.g. Lana, Rana, Nada) became fashionable for girls during the 1950s and 1960s, but the 1980s signalled a return to traditional and Islamic names. Hijazis tend to choose names of members of the Prophet's family, including Ali, Hasan, Hussain, Hamza or Othman for boys, and Aisha, Khadija, Amina or Fatima for girls. In fact it might be said that these names, now so universal in the Muslim world, are actually all Hijazi in origin. Najdi names, by contrast, tend to be of Bedouin origin, such as Fahd, Mit'ib and Mesh'al, or names—universal to all Muslims—declaring obedience to God, such as Abdullah.

Many of these names are associated with the past and now help to emphasise Hijazi identity. However, in the 1980s the Wahhabi authorities officially forbade certain names and compound names, such as Muhammed Ali, permitting only one given name. Hijazis traditionally chose compound names because of their beliefs in the attributes of certain names. For example, the name Muhammed on its own is too great for a man; thus, it should be combined with another name. Likewise, a woman named Fatima will acquire an honourable and strong personality but will have to suffer hardships at a certain period of her life, as did the Prophet's daughter. The Wahhabis, for whom only God decides destiny and character, view such beliefs as superstitious.

Like the demise of circumcision ceremonies, Hijazis have emulated some Najdi naming practices, revealing that not all Hijazi 'innovations' are simply a rejection of Najdi dominance. In fact, one recently introduced practice has been adopted in the face of Hijazi superstition: naming a child after a living grandparent. In the past this was considered bad luck, for it could bring about the death of the person whose name the child had taken. It was the Al Saud royal family that set the precedent that reversed this traditional aversion. But adopting the new practice was clearly instrumental to the preservation of Hijazi identity: by naming the child after the grandfather, whether paternal or maternal, members of the family are reminded of their duties and responsibilities towards the patronymic group.[14]

This clearly has other implications. Naming a child after his grandfather indicates family solidarity and mutual love, and it means that there will be many first cousins with the same name. One's first name, therefore, is not intended solely, or even primarily, as an expression of individuality, but as a declaration of communal (Hijazi) belonging. As names will be repeated after every two generations, they are constant reminders of roots in the past, with all that this entails, namely romanticisation of the pre-Saudi Hijaz and Sharifian rule.

Once the name has been chosen but before the naming ceremony, the *khira* (divination) takes place. This is a special prayer, seeking a signal or answer from God, which may be performed before making any significant decision. It is said by the parents of the child or by a close relative or by a particularly pious man such as a *sayyid*. The *khira* is performed before going to sleep and the answer appears in the morning, either in a dream or just in a feeling. Although the name is chosen by the extended family, the divination prayer leaves it to God to give people a sign—favourable or discouraging—concerning its appropriateness to the particular individual.

◆ CONFERRING THE NAME

Until the naming ceremony, the child is but an extension of the mother and a member of the mother's patronymic group. It is at the naming ceremony itself that the men take possession of the infant and give it a new life as a member of its father's patronymic group. During the mother's 40-day confinement period there will be a major gathering at which this ceremony is held. This is either the *sabu'*, the ceremony of naming the newborn, which is held on the seventh day,[15] or sometimes the *rahmani*, the ceremony of the Merciful One, which can be celebrated in addition to the *sabu'*.

During the 1950s, 1960s and 1970s the naming was celebrated more privately and less lavishly, emphasising the basic formal religious ceremony, the *tasmiya*: the opening *surà* of the Quran was read, the call to prayer, *adhan*, was said in the child's ear and the name of the child was pronounced. Normally, unless a *sayyid* came especially for the purpose, it was the most senior member of the family present at the *sabu'* who named the child. This was followed by the *'aqiqa*, the sacrifice of two goats for a boy or one for a girl.[16] The *sabu'* was traditionally a male event, held after sunset at the child's paternal family home, with women having a separate celebration or holding a party for the Merciful One.

During the 1980s the rituals of the naming ceremony underwent a revival, resulting in the development of a number of variations on the ceremony, which is still undergoing modification. Among the more 'sophisticated' or open-minded Hijazis the naming ritual is performed in the presence of both men and women, so the mother is present. This mixing of the sexes befitted the Hijazis' historical cosmopolitan culture. However, conservative fundamentalist tendencies, which attach moral superiority to gender segregation, have strengthened among the Hijazis in the 1990s, as the power of the Wahhabi religious establishment and other Saudi Salafi groups increased. This is partly because of the US presence on Saudi territory since the first Gulf War, and the uncertainties of Western influence on Saudi values. Women's honour and gender segregation have become a focus of concerns about 'piety' and hence have become subject to increased religious control. This has established new terms of status competition, with the *'awa'il* believing that their identification with the cradle of Islam compels them to be at the forefront of piety by complying with a strict patriarchal system that excludes women from certain communal and public occasions.

The naming of a child on the seventh day, *sabu'* and the gathering for the Merciful One, *rahmani*, have become interchangeable. Both ceremonies serve the same basic purpose, uniting the *wifyan* of the particular extended family in order to share the celebration of the event and to establish and define the status of the newly born and its family. Both celebrations include the same necessary objects of ritual: congratulatory terms, gifts, food and dress. Furthermore, the form of these ceremonies is distinctly Hijazi, especially the *rahmani*, which is not celebrated at all by other Saudi groups. Some women's *sabu'* evenings are comprised of music, together with a large meal of several roast lambs and almond sweets in special containers designed specially for the event.[17]

The principal difference of the ceremony of the Merciful One is that it includes children. Bearing candles, the children sing for the newborn, 'Oh you, Merciful One, bless for us this child'. Although the *rahmani* takes place during daylight, the candles remain the central theme of the ritual. They symbolise light—specifically the light of the Prophet Muhammed. Sufi texts explain this as the light from which all angels, saints and ordinary humans were created. Not all participants in the ritual acknowledge the connection to Sufi beliefs; the event is seen as yet another gathering of Hijazis. But it is viewed as heresy by the Saudi religious establishment.

◆ THE RETURN OF THE *MAWLID*

In addition to the *sabu'* and the *rahmani* some among the *'awa'il* hold a celebration for the birth of the Prophet as a good omen for the event of birth. The *mawlid*—a segregated occasion that may be held either by men or women—remains an Islamic practice in most Muslims countries.[18] However, in Saudi Arabia the *mawlid* is not acceptable to Wahhabi establishment and is thus specific to the Hijaz. Here, the *mawlid* is not regarded as an anniversary celebration that must necessarily to be held on the twelfth of *Rabi' al-Awwal*, the date of the Prophet's birth, and only once a year; rather it may be performed whenever there is occasion to invoke good fortune.

The house of the Prophet's birthplace was treated with reverence since at least the ninth century.[19] By then the house was open on Mondays for *an naqqas* (prayers of special significance). It was around the *du'a* (an offering of a personal prayer of request) at the birthplace of the Prophet that the later public celebrations of the *mawlid* were constructed. After this prayer the life and good deeds of the Prophet were remembered. The earliest records of public ceremonies date from the thirteenth century (*Ibn Gubayr*), when the birthday itself was being commemorated on Mondays during *Rabi' al-Awwal*, the month of the Prophet's birth.

By the end of the sixteenth century the twelfth of the month had become established as *an nahrawali* (the day of celebration). It was widely observed as a public holiday and recognised within Mecca as one of the most significant occasions of the year, ending with a festival for which people generally were specially dressed. The important officials of the Great Mosque, four principal judges and many sheikhs would lead the assembled throng after the sunset *maghrib* prayer from the mosque to the Prophet's birthplace. Once at the house a sermon was delivered and prayers offered for the various authorities, including one for the Sultan (Ottoman authority). Following the procession there would be a distribution by the *Shafi'ite qadi* (judge representing the Shafi'i school of thought). After this the procession returned to the Great Mosque, where they again prayed for the sultanate.

By this time the *mawlid* had become a very public occasion serving both political and devotional needs. Questions concerning the propriety of the prayers were continually raised, however. In the thirteenth century the prayers at the house were described as *bid'a hasana* (a 'laudable innovation') by the commentator Al Azafi. But others record disputes into the sixteenth century, with some officials disapproving of the merry gatherings, with their musical instruments and mingling of men and women. The Wahhabis were not alone in considering the *mawlid* to be *bid'a*, an improper innovation.

Holding the *mawlid* today is not simply a matter of tradition. There are thirteen *fatwa*s (religious decrees) issued in 1993 by the late Binbaz, Grand Mufti of Saudi Arabia, forbidding the *mawlid* on the grounds that celebrating the birth or life of the Prophet places him over and above his ordained role.[20] Although chosen to be God's messenger, the Prophet was just an ordinary man, who lived and died like all others. Neither he nor the details of his life are to be invested with any special sacred significance. The ceremony held to celebrate his life is therefore considered *shirk* (idolatry), and under Wahhabi direction the house of the Prophet's birth has been demolished and replaced by a mosque. But it is noteworthy that these *fatwa*s followed the proliferation of *mawlid* celebrations by prominent Hijazis during the 1980s, a period of heightened regional consciousness.

For most Hijazis, however, the celebration of the Prophet's birth continues to be favoured as both religious and social event, forming part of their spiritual traditions and connecting them to their political past. Several prominent patrons of Hijazi patronymic groups are proud to hold regular *mawlids*. Since the 1980s they have even increased the frequency of attendance at these practices in defiance of the religious establishment, and as a manifestation of regional distinctiveness.[21] The ceremony is attended by a large number of guests—sometimes more than 200 people—beginning with Quranic recitations and continuing with songs enumerating and praising the Prophet's virtues and recounting his life. At the point in the story at which the Prophet enters Medina after the flight from Mecca, everyone present rises in a symbolic greeting gesture—re-enacting the welcome given to him by the people of Medina. At this moment, if the gathering has the required degree of piety and submission, the Prophet is believed to be present in spirit. The 'tears of the devout' are abundant at this climactic moment. Incense is passed around and rose-water is sprayed from Meccan containers. Most men's *mawlids* conclude with words spoken in justification of holding this auspicious event in the face of official opposition to it: if we do not celebrate the beloved of Islam and the

heroes who died for the sake of religion, who would we celebrate today?

Women generally gather in a separate area within the same
hall, enabling them to peer through windows at the men and
to see while remaining unseen. But it is the sound of the
chanting and prayers that really matters to them. The ceremony is sometimes held by and for women. On these
occasions even the leading reciters of the Quran are female.
This is the only event where women, usually of Malaysian or
Egyptian descent, can practise as professional Quran reciters.[22] Even though the reciter is not a Hijazi, this is a distinctly
Hijazi practice. The Quran is recited, then all the women
chant praises of the Prophet Muhammed together. In no
other part of the Arab Gulf do women recite the Quran, as
women's voices are considered *'awra* (faulty). Women's
mawlid gatherings are also more festive than men's, with jewellery and rich dress using colourful materials. The wearing
of the *tarha* (head cover) when the Quran is recited—a sign of
respect for the holy book—and for greeting the Prophet indicates the religious nature of the gathering.

The *mawlid* is an occasion when Hijazis who enjoy close
economic and social ties get together and express solidarity
while commemorating an event. The occasion also offers less
affluent Hijazis a chance to socialise with the prominent
members of their society, reinforcing ties of dependency and
affection. All of this is held in the privacy of the home and is
known only to the Hijazis; in other words, it is kept secret
from Najdis and others who do not appreciate the ceremony.
The food itself, consisting of several whole roasted lambs on
rice and traditional side dishes, is another vehicle for
reinforcing Hijazi social identity.[23]

There is some ambivalence towards the *mawlid* on the part
of Hijazis. On one hand the ceremony is another indicator of
the hosts' social identity and status; the quality and numbers
of the participants show the social standing of the person or
the patronymic group. Since the revival of this ceremony, by
a few especially financially and politically prominent members of the *'awa'il*, it has been held more frequently than

during the period before the rule of Al Saud. Some families hold *mawlids* once a week, just for *baraka* (blessedness). Others hold the ceremony only every two or three months, or for the occasion of a birth in the extended family. Still others stick to the traditional period, the third month of *Rabi' al-Awwal*, of the lunar year. On the other hand some Hijazis, concerned about Najdi disapproval and alienation from the political centre, refuse to attend a *mawlid*.

These Hijazis are also most likely to reject the growing revival of Sufism in the Hijaz that is reflected in the mystical aspects of the *mawlid* and with which it is associated. Sufism is part Orthodox Islam, sharing a belief in the *shari'a*, and part mysticism, believing that the Truth about God has not been revealed but continues to lie hidden. Sufi beliefs and practices vary widely, especially with regard to the *shari'a*. Mawlawis and Bektashis for instance, are heterodox and, while not rejecting the *shari'a*, they subordinate it to *tariqah* (method), considering it a superficial level of religious observance. Although there are different *tariqah* of moving through the *maqamat* (stages on the way to God), all Sufis hold that it is possible to attain a 'purity of vision' of God through various meditative or trance-inducing practices. Chanting, music and dance, contemplating the soul, meditation are all used.

The Wahhabis see Sufism in much the same way as they do the Hijazis: as the product of 'extraneous' and impure influences. For instance, while Sufis argue that the name is derived from the Arabic term for purity, *safa'*, some believe the name to have come from the Classical Greek word denoting wisdom, *sophia*. Sufi beliefs in the incarnation of God in man, in communing with spirits, visiting graves and regarding them as shrines, and many others, are condemned by the Wahhabis as belonging to non-Muslim traditions, such as Christianity, Platonism, Zoroastrianism and Buddhism. Although not specifically Sufi, the *mawlid* illustrates the affinities between Hijazi conceptions of Islam and Sufism, whose apparently heterogeneous origins appeal to the Hijazi sense of the cosmopolitan. Indeed, Sufism has had a prominent place in the Hijaz in the past, when the *Ashraf* not only accepted it, but actively endorsed it. The revival of the *mawlid*, then, has both heretical and treasonous connotations.

For these and other reasons some Hijazis try to be discreet about holding a *mawlid* by using the word *giraya* (Quran recitations) over the telephone. Some even believe that in every *mawlid* there is a member of the secret intelligence service. Given these fears, only individuals of high rank and connections dare hold the *mawlid* publicly, i.e. on a large scale in the courtyards of their capacious houses, using microphones etc. Those who are not in such secure positions run the risk of being raided by the *mutaw'a* (religious police) and even being jailed for up to two days. It is noteworthy that the revived *mawlid* does not include dancing and circus *darwish* performances. The celebration practised under Saudi rule is relatively austere, therefore not too heretical for the Wahhabis.

◆ CONCLUSIONS

This examination of the elite Hijazis' celebration of birth rituals indicates how the changes that have occurred need to be related to social processes occurring on many different levels. At a global level, cultural practices originating in the West are becoming increasingly widespread. Western cultural practices are clearly visible in the Hijaz in the form of the medicalisation of birth and the attendant professionalisation of medical skills. Similarly, the celebration of individual birthdays points towards tendencies to individualisation so prominent in the West. However, Hijazi rituals surrounding birth have a cultural character of their own. These activities involve family members and close friends in an affirmation of the patronymic group, rather than the individual, as the most significant cultural unit. The significance of naming a child, for example, is that it symbolises familial ties and belonging.

Neither are these rituals simply Saudi Arabian. On the one hand, although conditioned by the development of the Saudi state in many ways, as well as by the influence of

Wahhabism, Hijazi celebrations highlight the distinction between local and national cultures. They also underscore important contrasts between official Saudi culture and that of the wider Islamic world. Seen in context, then, the changing patterns of rituals surrounding birth in the Hijaz indicate a complex set of processes of cultural integration and differentiation that has global, regional, national and local dimensions. The following chapters investigate the process of 'Hijazification' from the perspectives of other celebrations and aspects of the life of Hijazis, with each one opening a different window on the wider horizons that shape their identity.

5 The Rites of Passage II: Marriage and Social Status

◆ INTRODUCTION: THE PULL OF THE TRIBE

T HE CONVENTIONS governing the making and breaking of marriage ties amongst the Hijazis, as well as the wedding ceremonies themselves, have undergone a series of changes during the twentieth century. Once again, the temporality of change conforms to a familiar pattern. Customs first passed through a kind of 'de-traditionalisation', with the patterns of social life prevalent at the start of the century giving ground to modernisation in a later period, a process associated with political change and economic growth. The past generation has been marked by the 're-traditionalisation' of Hijazi life, in which traditional rituals have been reasserted in modified form as a belated response to political exclusion.

Of key interest here is the introduction of what may be called the 'tribalisation' of marriage relations amongst the Hijazis. In contrast to past practices of marriage with non-Arab Muslims, marriages now take place within the Hijazi cultural group. The definition of what constitutes a Hijazi for marriage purposes has become more strict. This provides a greater degree of Hijazi autonomy over processes of cultural change.

One implication of 'tribalisation', however, is that it draws the cultural form of association that sets the standards for the

Hijazis from Najdi life. The emphasis placed on lineage, purity and related ideas confirms the superiority of a particular conception of what a social group should be: a tribe. On the other hand, emulation of the tribal form has not entailed wholesale mimicry of Najdi customs. On the contrary, like all forms of communal life, wedding rituals and celebrations allow for considerable variation of content, which the Hijazis exploit to the full. As with other areas of social life the conception of the distinctive nature of a Hijazi as a cultured, refined and wealthy person is asserted at every opportunity. The drama of marriage is replete with occasions for demonstrating the peculiarities of the Hijazi way of life and Hijazis' perception of their cultural superiority.

For members of the Hijazi *'awa'il*,[1] establishing and dissolving contemporary marriage relationships is now regulated by several sets of rules and considerations, most of which are relatively recent in origin. Some of these rules have been generated externally by the Saudi Arabian political and religious authorities, and carry legal status and sanctions. Other sets of rules represent another element in the internal development of a more tightly defined elite Hijazi culture, which hinges primarily on the elaboration of family status. The Najdis' de facto exclusion of Hijazis as potential marriage partners further restricts marriage options and reinforces the development of endogamous marriage. In all cases the rules are gender specific, providing more limited opportunities and placing greater restraints on women than on men. All of these changes are best understood in light of the contrast between the period prior to and that following the Hijaz's political unification under Saudi rule.

◆ TRADITIONAL GOVERNANCE OF MARRIAGE AND DIVORCE

In the period before Saudi political unification the rules governing marriage derived from largely religious sources, reflecting a very different relation between state and society to that which exists in the present. All contemporary marriage rules are closely related to these earlier ones, either as refinements or entailing new but subordinate principles.

At the most general level, the Quran is broadly permissive of potential marriage partners: 'Oh! Mankind! We have created you from a single [pair] of a male and a female, and made you into nations and tribes, that ye may know each other. Verily the most honoured of you in the sight of Allah is the most pious of you.'[2] There are, however, some qualifications to this open-ended approach. The first is that Islam permits marital ties between Muslim men and non-Muslim women, provided the latter are 'people of the book', *ahl al kitab*, i.e. Jews or Christians. The Quran tells male Muslims that, 'lawful for you are the chaste women from among those who have been given the book'.[3] Muslim women, on the other hand, are absolutely prohibited from marrying non-Muslims. A Muslim woman's marriage to a non-Muslim is considered to entail illegal intercourse and thus produces illegitimate offspring who are prohibited from inheriting the father's wealth.

The second qualification is to be found in the legal concept of *kafa'a* (compatibility), which is encapsulated in the *hadith* quoting the Prophet, 'If a man whose religion and character are acceptable comes to you [for your daughter's hand] give her to him in marriage.' The principle of *kafa'a* requires that prospective marriage partners possess appropriate status.[4] This imposes qualifying criteria on potential marriage partners, namely piety and good behaviour; it also appears to restrict the grounds on which requests to marry daughters may be refused.

In addition to religion, considerations of the nature of wider family life have been most influential in regulating marriage. Here the promotion and defence of patrilineal group status is of central significance. Family status is related to the *'ird* (honour) of its male members, which is defended by ensuring the chastity of female dependants.[5] The idea of *'ird* is a key reason why marriage based on overt love has traditionally been considered *'ayb* (shameful): admitting love implies a clandestine pre-marital relationship. Indeed, the idea that marriage should be based on an emotional bond between husband and wife conflicts with the primacy of maintaining well-integrated families; it implies putting one's personal interests and needs above the extended family's wellbeing. In this, Hijazis conform to general Arabian attitudes but, as ever, the Hijazi preoccupation with family creates a specific distrust of bonds based on emotion or sentiment.

Although the bride's consent is sought, it is only the leaders of extended families that negotiate the marriage.[6] As a rule a woman would be told of her prospective marriage, by the senior members of her own natal family, only once it has been negotiated. Then, once married, she would go to live in the house of her husband's extended family. Her family would tell her: 'His father is your father, his mother is your mother, his sisters and brothers are yours; seek their *rida* (contentment) like you seek our *rida*.'[7]

For divorce, too, religion has been the principal means of expressing ethical concerns, as well as the main source of rules that regulate the practice. For pre-unification Hijazis it was virtually unthinkable for a woman to get a divorce. Great weight was placed on the idea that divorce 'causes the Throne [of the Almighty] to shake' (*yahtaz lahu al-'arsh*). In Islam divorce is *makruh* (morally condemned) as the worst *halal* (permissible) act. There is a *hadith*: 'the most hated of the *halal* acts to God is divorce'. That divorce is nonetheless acceptable is supported by the rule: 'Keep them in good fellowship or release them in kindness'. According to the *shari'a* (Islamic law), there are several types of divorce, each involving different agreements.

Accounts of the late nineteenth and early twentieth centuries clearly show that these rules did indeed regulate Hijazi marriages. For instance, being Muslim, regardless of other origins, provided a sufficiently strong basis on which to build marriages. Mecca was a melting pot for the Islamic world, so mixed marriages were common.[8] Marriage made a significant contribution to the heterogeneous and cosmopolitan nature of Hijazi society.

By contrast, Najdi marriage was, and remains within the same lineage, with bonds among the tribal families usually reinforced by patrilineal parallel-cousin marriages. There is, however, an important distinction between *khadiri* (non-tribal, i.e. 'non-pure' Najdi), and *gabili* (tribal 'pure-blooded' Najdi). Strict patrilinearity allowed *gabili* men to marry outsiders, such as Egyptian, Moroccan or Lebanese women, but their female relatives have never married outside the tribe. In principle, then, men from the Hijaz would not have been able to marry into a pure-blooded Najdi family, while women would, although Hijazi women were not, as a rule, given in marriage to Najdi families, nor were they asked. In this intricate system of social boundaries expressed through marriage practices, Hijazis—both men and women—married from the Asir tribal region more easily than from tribal Najd.

Divorce has also been differently perceived in Najd, where it has been more socially accepted. Some Najdi women from the royal family and other politically or religiously prominent families have been married and remarried up to three times within the same section of the tribe. This is considered normal behaviour. Among elite Najdi men polygamy has also been more prominent.

◆ NATIONALISING MARRIAGE

For men, the Saudi state has not imposed any further restrictions; the range of potential spouses prescribed in Islamic tradition, including Christian and Jewish women,[9] has been sustained legally. However, the most significant secular elaboration to the earlier rules demonstrates the Saudi state's general willingness to introduce principles of social regulation which draw on Najdi tribal traditions. Saudi law now ordains that a woman may only marry another Saudi national; the rare exceptions require special permission. The Najdi tribal principle of excluding males has thus been extended outward, reinforcing the identification between tribe and nation. Non-Saudi males, even if Muslims, cannot achieve the status of a Saudi subject through marriage.

The extension of Najdi tribal and religious rules governing marriage has also changed patterns of divorce for Hijazis. Although divorce is a right available exclusively to the husband, the Saudi Hanbali school of law allows it to be granted to the wife where a marriage contract stipulates her *shurut* (conditions). In recent years there has been a remarkable increase in divorce, especially among the younger generation. Official Saudi statistics report that 24 per cent of marriages end in divorce. The Ministry of Justice calculates that in 1997, 15,697 marriages were recorded and in the same year 329 divorces were registered. The highest divorce rate was found in Mecca and the second highest in Riyadh.[10]

It is in terms of family and the newly adopted 'tribal' principles that the greatest changes to Hijazi marriage practices have been made. Particularly since the onset of re-traditionalisation in the 1980s, the *'awa'il* have elaborated considerably the legal principle of *kafa'a*, which requires appropriate status of marriage partners. In addition to the strictly religious interpretation of *kafa'a*, which relates to *din* (religion), two other criteria have gained great significance. One is 'material', i.e. *mal* (wealth), and the second is the essentially tribal notion of *asl* (family lineage). Patronymic groups also seek to establish *musahara* (marriage alliances) that will lend them honour in the eyes of society.

In terms of *kafa'a*, then, the criteria for selecting marriage partners concern the status of the patronymic group or the specific extended family more than the attributes of the individuals concerned. Marriage is a tie between two families; the bride and groom are first and foremost members of their respective families. A person's worth is evaluated on the basis of his or her patrilineal family of belonging. Hence, the first consideration when inquiring of a groom's suitability will be the compatibility of lineage, wealth and reputation of his extended family. Only then will other, more personal, qualities be considered, such as his education (especially if he has a post-graduate degree from a Western university) and his *istigama* (conformity to religious duties and moral values). A potential bride will be similarly judged primarily on the standing of her patronymic group. After this her own characteristics will be examined: 'Is the bride beautiful?' 'Is she *mitrabbaya* (well brought up)?' Although a woman retains her association with her own natal family and is known by its surname, the family she marries into also becomes important to her socio-economic status. It is viewed as proper and polite to inquire, 'From which family is your husband?' rather than 'Who is your husband?' or 'What is your husband's name?'

Prospective marriage partners will also be judged by the criterion of *tajammul* (appearing honourable and elegant). While the literal meaning of *tajammul* is limited to physical embellishment—its root being *jamal* (beauty)—the word has acquired a particular connotation in the Hijaz. *Tajammul* is 'seemliness': it indicates a condition of being 'presentable' and behaviour that is *comme il faut*—'adding lustre', 'honouring' and 'adding credit'.[11] A spouse who knows how to conduct herself in a becoming fashion or an elegant manner is said to be *tijammil*. For example, she will be correctly dressed according to the occasion, will know exactly how to present food, how to converse on specific topics and be an expert in the art of gift-giving. Her husband, on the other hand, will be described as *yijammil* if he properly displays his status and has a strong presence. Also, by offering a wife both the material means to perform her role and the social cachet of a good family name, he is viewed as honouring, adding credit to his spouse and her paternal family. The decision about a person's worth and suitability as a marriage partner is made by the patron of the family and not necessarily the father and is subject to change according to the times.

These regulating principles have different consequences for men and women because of the patrilineal nature of Islamic jurisprudence. A woman from one 'good family' should only be married into another extended family of similar socio-economic background, preferably a family with *sira tayyiba* (good standing). This implies having a long-established reputation. The rule is less strict in the case of a man, as his family's position would not be affected to the same degree were he to marry someone of lower status.

Once she is married a woman should seek the *rida* (contentment) of both her husband as well as her father, but ideally the husband's contentment should come first. Despite this cultural ideal, women tend to continue identifying with their own paternal family, from which they still take strength and support. A woman will develop ties of affection with her new family and her status will be affected by its fortunes. However, she generally feels more socially committed to her paternal kin and remains concerned for their prestige and reputation.[12] In the Hijaz one's *agarib* (kin) consist of both *ahl* ('blood' relatives) and *arham* (relatives by marriage). However, behaviour towards one's *arham* generally lacks the trust and intimacy displayed with one's *ahl* and is marked by a degree of social distance and ambivalence. Unless her husband is her patrilateral parallel cousin, his family is regarded like other people's parents.

Today couples tend to live as nuclear family units within the husband's patrilineal family compound. The couple and their offspring have one meal a day at the house of the head of the extended family. Despite the obligations and duties that she maintains with her husband's extended family, a woman's ties with her own natal family have generally led to a greater degree of marital independence. This is primarily a consequence of the wealth of the natal family and the absence of any concept of joint property in Islamic marriages. Such a degree of economic autonomy is in conformity with both *shari'a* law and that of Saudi Arabia. Women nowadays have control over their own money—many having been given private bank accounts by their father or guardian before marriage—and of the *mahr* (bride price). There is also an increase in women having their own businesses. Nevertheless, the husband continues to be obliged to spend on the household according to the legal concept of *iltizam* (obligation).[13]

Given that marriage can affect social standing, it has become a means of securing status within the context of increased social mobility. Some families who have acquired substantial amounts of wealth can heighten their status further by marrying into 'good families', just as 'good families' who have not acquired wealth can marry into families with wealth without losing any of their standing. There are limits to this; even today a woman will not marry a man whose status is very much lower than her own. For example, the offspring of a marriage between a slave and a non-slave would be unacceptable,[14] even if his patronymic group has acquired wealth, he is well educated and her patronymic group has good relations with his. The simple acquisition of wealth alone would not produce a sufficient change in status to allow for a marriage alliance between the families.

In some cases the marriage alliance provides a basis on which to develop other forms of social co-operation. Commercial ventures are developed or money is loaned between those related through marriage. Co-operation may also be political, such as when an influential person chooses to offer a post to his relative by marriage. These ties may be developed regardless of whether the patronymic groups are of the same social status.

Marriages between Hijazis and Najdis are very rare. The exceptions are one way, occurring between a *khadiri* (non-tribal, 'non-pure' Najdi) woman and a Hijazi man, especially if he is wealthy and offering a high *mahr*. Najdis do not marry Hijazis because their lineage is not considered pure enough. Therefore Hijazis are excluded from marriage with the Najdi elite. Conversely, Najdis' more lenient attitudes toward divorce and polygamy dissuade Hijazis, who say that 'Najdi men and women are constantly marrying and divorcing'. Hijazis use this argument to justify not giving their daughters in marriage to Najdis, and to console themselves for never having been asked to do so. The rarity of cases of inter-marriages between Hijazis and Najdis is the most significant expression of the social boundaries between the regions of Saudi Arabia and an obvious example of the cultural distinctiveness of the Hijazis. Despite the attempt at integration and national homogeneity, marriage practices and alliances demonstrate the fractured nature of the Saudi state.

◆ WEDDING PREPARATIONS AND CEREMONIES

Marriage ties, then, serve to create a more clearly defined social space in which the various elements of Hijazi identity may be elaborated. The series of events surrounding marriage, too, have undergone transformations that reveal re-traditionalisation. Typically, this has been conditioned by displays of wealth and conspicuous consumption, but homages to the values of piety, respectability, status and refinement are also prominent. As with rules governing marriage and divorce, changes in the ceremonial aspects of the wedding ritual are best illuminated by drawing out the contrast between the period preceding unification and the present.

Hijazi Traditional Rituals

Once the prospective bride and groom's extended families had arrived at an initial understanding, the *khira* (divination) was performed. If the *khira* was favourable, then the close kin of the future spouses read the opening *sura* of the Quran, the *fatiha*. The reading of the *fatiha* did not establish a tie, but only reserved the bride and held her by *mahabba* (good feelings). It was only in the light of the *milka*[15] that the couple were regarded as married in the eyes of God. At the *milka* the senior men established contractual ties between their respective families, ties sanctified by religious ceremony. Afterwards the bride and the groom were able to see one another in public without being chaperoned, and they would usually take walks together and visit close relatives. The bride would also receive gifts from the groom. The relationship was not sexual, however, until the *dukhla* (wedding party).[16] The *dukhla*, unlike the *milka,* is a social gathering of the women of the families, with no explicit religious purpose.[17]

One vital aspect of the marriage contract was settling the *mahr* (bride price). The *mahr* consisted of two tranches of money: *mugaddam,* given in advance (and often used for the bride's clothes, and *mu'akhkhar,* a sum to be given to provide security for the bride in case of divorce. These payments were called *mu'ajjal* and *mu'ajjal,* meaning immediate and later portions. Sometimes the *mahr* was set at such a high sum that it posed a problem for the groom, although Islam does not recognise it as an essential requirement for a man without money. According to the Prophet, 'A man can marry a woman for what he knows of the Quran [by heart] and without paying *mahr.*'[18]

The *milka* was just for men and was relatively short. The *'agd al-giran* (contract of association) ceremony, took place after the *'isha* (evening prayer). The ceremony began once the groom and his family, some of their close friends and the *munshid,* the man who sings in praise of the bride's and groom's families, had gathered at the groom's house. They would then go to the house of the bride's family, where members of the bride's paternal and maternal kin and some of their close friends met the men. For 20 to 30 minutes everyone stood to listen to the *munshid* sing the songs of praise. These songs were melodious—in contrast to the basically rhythmical character of the Najdi desert tradition—and recounted the lineage of the patronymic group of the groom, praised their merit, generosity and honour, and gave thanks to the guests. During the songs of praise, two men would carry in the *'ulab al-mahr* (boxes of the bride's dower).

An essential part of the *milka* in the Hijaz has always been the distribution of ten *halawa lawziyya* (sugar-coated almond sweets) of different colours to each guest, wrapped originally in a silver or white handkerchief.[19] More recently the *halawa lawziyya* have been presented to the guests in containers— either a plate, a vase, or a small bowl made of plated silver, glass or porcelain.

The period between the religious ceremony and the social events was comparable to the custom of betrothal in other societies, usually lasting between several months and a year. In other Arab countries the bride and groom may be allowed to see each other before the contractual obligations are established; in these cases the period between the two ceremonies is much shorter. This is because there is a separate betrothal period, the *khutba*, which takes place before the legal marriage contract and usually lasts for around a year. In the Hijaz this period allowed for either the bride or the groom to change their mind. Dissolving the relationship at this point would have been less grave since the bride was still a virgin. Hijazis did not regard a 'divorce' at this stage as the question of honour that their tribal Najdi neighbours would have.

The social events surrounding the wedding were numerous. An invitation to a wedding would be for several nights. There was a party upon receiving *al jihaz* (the trousseau);[20] the *ghumra* (henna ceremony), for the bride and women only,[21] which took place one night before the *dukhla*; and the *hilaga* (shaving ceremony) for the groom and men only, which took place at the same time as the *ghumra*. The *nassa* was the one party that mixed the sexes, briefly, and was also usually the moment at which the bride and the groom saw each other for the first time. The *dukhla* was also described as *mawlid* because of the chanting of the Prophet's biography by the guests.[22] The *subha*, the party on the morning following the *dukhla*, was also for women only, as was the *subu'*, a party in the form of a dinner with a singer in attendance that was held for the bride after she had spent seven days in her husband's home. The terms *khutba, henna, dukhla, zaffa* are common throughout Arab countries and the practices are variations on the theme and this includes Jews and Christians.[23]

A woman was hired to go from house to house to spread the news of the wedding on behalf of the bride's family and distribute invitations to these events. The *'azzima* (the inviting one) would return to the family after a day's work and tell them the number of persons she had invited, giving full descriptions of how the women had received her, what they had told her, and so on.[24]

At the beginning of the twentieth century, the *ghumra* was given by the extended family of the bride and did not concern the groom's family whatsoever. The *ghumra* ceremony revolved around the application of henna on the bride by a woman specialising in *hannaya* (henna decorations), while the bride's women relatives and friends sang and danced. The bride sat behind a decorated curtain, isolated from the guests. A part of the *ghumra* ceremony was the fastening of a *sakk al-khulkhal* (gold anklet) to the bride by a younger brother or a younger close male relative who only appeared to perform this ritual and left promptly.

A meal would be offered after the *milka* at the groom's house, consisting of traditional 'Meccan' sweets, namely *laddu, labaniyya, halawa tahiniyya, shurayk, ka'k* (special 'Meccan' bread), *harisa* (a puree of meat and barley served with honey) and *mahjamiyya*. Several of these 'Meccan' sweets (with a milk base, cardamoms and sugar) were originally from India, brought by pilgrims who settled in Mecca. A set of trays, the *ma'ashir*, would display gifts that the extended family of the groom sent for the bride. These included *'uda* (a chunk of aloe wood),[25] which could be decorated with silver, *cologna* (eau de toilette) in 'traditional' green glass containers, a tree of silver, an incense burner in silver, and the *'attara* (a font containing oil perfume). A gift of *'anbar* (ambergris) symbolised virility and was thought to be an aphrodisiac, while silver plates containing the spices betelnut, cardamom, cloves and mint, were said to symbolise fertility.

Although the *dukhla* was a women's affair, some men—the groom and the closest male relatives of both bride and groom—made a brief appearance. They would be present for only a few minutes to congratulate the bride and the groom, before promptly leaving the room. During the brief period of male presence at the party the women guests covered their hair and faces, uncovering them again only once the men had gone. In the absence of the men, no woman covered either her hair or face at the party; veils would instead have been left on *ash-shama 'at al-'amud* (traditional veil-hangers).

The *dukhla* was accorded a special honour by the attendance of a *Sharifa*, a daughter of the *Ashraf*, the ruling family of the Hijaz. It is said that a *Sharifa* would be 'hired' to attend a wedding in order to honour the family. When she entered the hall, it was announced, *'Sharifa ya sitat'* ('Oh ladies, a *Sharifa!'*), and everyone present would stand. The significance of this woman's status would be apparent throughout the celebrations. Some older women describe weddings in the first part of the century at which a *Sharifa* would only sit next to another *Sharifa*, her social equal. Social stratification would be acknowledged at this and any other social gathering; when an ordinary woman passed a *Sharifa* she did so barefoot, shoes being considered disrespectful. Needless to say, much of the *dukhla* as described here is particularly Hijazi in nature – especially the presence of a *Sharifa*, which by definition can only be a Hijazi aspect of a wedding event since the *Ashraf* are Hijazi families.

Such occasions in the Hijaz could only be held at certain times of the year. Marriages were effectively excluded from taking place in the period between *Sha 'ban* (the eighth month of the lunar year) and *Dhulhijjah* (the last month of the year). This period includes both Ramadan and the *hajj* (pilgrimage), and until the mid-twentieth century was thus unfavourable on economic, as well as religious, grounds, as Hijazis in general and Meccans in particular were occupied, acquiring their income from the pilgrimage.

'Modern' Traditionalism

Today, a wedding comprises one night for the men, the *milka*, and one night for the women, the *dukhla*. Some Hijazis explain this by saying that there is less time than previously, while nowadays the bridal couple travels for their honeymoon. Others maintain that guests have become more critical and more demanding—hence, 'One big night makes us appear elegant or adds credit to our name, *tijammilna*, and then we are finished with it.' This compression of matrimonial time exemplifies the ease with which the *'awa'il* have modified 'tradition' while claiming to be returning to it. The changed circumstances of their lives and the degree of consciousness surrounding 'traditions' and formality make it virtually impossible for them to be able to devote several days at a stretch to any one social event.

Some practices have been retained. For example, the *'awa'il* still prefer to have their weddings during the two months of *Rabi'*, that is, in *Rabi' al-Awwal* and *Rabi'ath-Thani* (the third and fourth months of the lunar year), and during *Rajab* (the seventh month). Despite changes in lifestyle and economic position as oil wealth replaced pilgrimage income, Hijazis regard these dates as a direct link with the past, to an identity as the true guardians of Mecca and Medina, as well as Jeddah, the route to the two holiest cities of Islam.

In other matters changes are quite significant. Among the *'awa'il*, the *mahr* has become largely symbolic (some 10–50 silver rials), and it remains only because it is *sunna* (the tradition of the Prophet). However, while the *mahr* itself is largely symbolic, there are various other financial responsibilities that the groom's family must fulfil. The groom, for instance, is expected to provide and furnish a house. For the rich *'awa'il*, then, the *mahr* has become a matter of inverted snobbishness. They do not need the bride price; they can afford to prepare a lavish wedding without 'burdening' their future *arham* (affines). It is considered *'ayb* (shameful) and in bad taste to discuss the *mahr*.

These modifications, and the concern with appearances that has accompanied them, appear to be specific to Hijazis, for other groups continue to regard the *mahr* a basic religious and practical requirement. It is also a matter of some contention, especially for the lower classes; inflation in Saudi Arabia has caused the bride price to rise sharply—a topic that is often discussed in newspapers. At Friday sermons in the mosques, worshippers have been routinely asked to be more reasonable in the demands they make.

Contemporary weddings may be completed more quickly nowadays, but preparations have become much more elaborate. There is the wedding dress to be ordered as well as the *jihaz* (trousseau), the dresses for *wasifat ash-sharaf* (maids of honour), who walk with the bride during the procession. There is the wedding hall to be booked, the flowers to be ordered, the singers to be engaged, especially those from abroad, for example from Egypt, Bahrain or Lebanon.[26] A professional group of six or twelve women, the *zafafat*, must be hired to chant the traditional Hijazi *zaffa* while the bridal couple walk down the aisle. The *zafafat* are generally of slave origin and are brought for the purpose from Mecca, where most of them live. The Hijazi *zaffa* differs from the Najdi in being more melodious and elaborate.[27]

The ceremony begins once the groom and his family, some of their close friends and the *munshid*, who sings the praise of the bride's and groom's families, have gathered at the groom's house. They then go to the hotel where the party is taking place, where they are greeted by members and close friends of the bride's family. These gatherings for Hijazi songs of praise were unknown during the period between the 1950s and 1970s. Like other ceremonials it made a comeback to celebrate the elite families of the Hijaz. Members of the *'awa'il* observe that the use of hotels is a particularly 'Meccan' custom, an attribution that, as with other Meccan 'traditions', confers high cultural value for all Hijazis.

During the songs of praise two men carry a large silver replica of a sailing ship, while the groom and some of his important paternal and maternal male kin wait to enter the wedding hall. The ship is about two and a half feet in width and contains objects ranging from gold bars, a box filled with money, an antique and ornate Quran, betelnut, cardamom, cloves and sandalwood. The ship's sails and masts are decorated with a multitude of perfumes, both traditional Hijazi scents and the latest French brands.

The ship is a gift from the groom's extended family to the bride and is regarded as an old tradition in the Hijaz celebrating trade as the source of wealth. There was, however, no sign of this supposedly venerable tradition for at least two or three decades, before it 'reappeared' in the 1980s. It has subsequently become a fixture at weddings of Hijazis who are able to afford such an object. It is bought either ready-made from local silversmiths or jewellers, or ordered from them. Hijazis report that the ships of the past were similar to those of today in size; the difference lies in the fact that the former were generally made of wood and were filled with fruits and one or two bottles of *cologna*. The reappearance of the ship can be regarded as part of the effort by the Hijazis not to 'forget' the glories of their trading past. For a people who conducted their trade by sea the ship was a powerful symbol of hope and prosperity. It also serves to highlight the difference between outward-looking Hijazis, who had access to prosperous trade routes via the Red Sea, and the nomadic tribesmen of the internal part of the Peninsula, the Najd.

After the parading of the ship, the groom and his male kin proceed to the wedding hall, where the *mumlik* (the person performing the marriage contract) is seated.[28] The groom sits to his right and the *waliyy-amr al-'arusa* (the guardian of the bride) to his left.[29] It is also important to seat a prince as a guest of honour next to the male members of the family, who invite him as a symbol of their connection to political power,[30] as well as an important Hijazi *sayyid* (a religious learned man) as a symbol of piety. Although Hijazi princes—members of the *Ashraf*—are present among the guests, it is only the Al Saud prince who is seated next to the male members of the family, perhaps so as not to offend or anger the authorities by reminding them of the presence of the rulers of the past. They are proud of the *Ashraf* but are afraid of flaunting it in the face of the Al Saud.

The ceremony itself is brief: a few words are devoted to the social necessity of marriage and its status as *sunna* (the tradition of the Prophet). Verses from the Quran are read and a few *hadith* are recited. Then the guardian of the bride says, *'ankahtuka wa-zawajtuka ibnati fulana'* ('I give you in wedlock and in marriage, my daughter so-and-so'). The groom replies, *'gabiltu nikahuha li-nafsi'* ('I accept her being wed to me'). All present then read the *fatiha*. Today, the number of guests at the *milka* ceremony of a member of the *'awa'il* is roughly 1,000–2,000. Following the contract, *'agd,* fruit juices are served and the *'ulab al-halawa* (containers of sweets) are brought in on large trays called *ma'ashir,* which are also used to display the traditional gifts to the bride from the family of the bride. These are covered by *bosh* (a coloured silk material embroidered with silver)—the same material that covered the *ma'ashir* at the beginning of the century.[31] The word *bosh* is Turkish (meaning 'empty'), Hijazis increasingly use such Ottoman terms to distinguish their dialect from that of the other regions in the Peninsula.

One aspect of the sweets distribution has evolved considerably during the last ten years. The *ma'ashir* must now be made of silver alloy and be engraved with the first names of the bride and groom, the date of the *milka* and the Quranic verse, 'And be placed between you mercy and compassion'.[32] Furthermore, they should be modelled on traditional objects such as a *mibkhara* (an incense burner), a *mashrabiyya* (a Meccan water container and cooler), a *marashsh* (a rose-water container) or just an 'Arabian' box. Although each extended family tries to be unique by introducing a new *ma'ashir* design, it must still conform to the traditional themes. The container should be a miniature of the original object. Its small size is considered *nazik* (refined), for the containers are not intended for practical use; they are miniature replicas, souvenirs of the wedding destined to be displayed later in living rooms.

The giving of sweets in containers is hotly contested. While considered a requirement of decorum by some, it is criticised from conservative religious positions. Many members of the *'awa'il* cite traditional Najdi Wahhabi interpretations of such practices as being *bid'a* (a dangerous innovation). The Wahhabi objections are partly related to the costs, which are very high—up to £300,000 for well-to-do families—for objects that have no practical use and are considered *bazkh* (lavish spending). But more importantly, the objections revolve around the symbolism of the objects. The *ma'ashir* serve to represent an imagined era of greater sophistication in the past in which great delicacies were served. These are displayed in the dining room (or dining area if food is served in the garden). However, the Indian origin of these sweets, like the possibility of Indian ancestry, is kept deliberately obscure. This is because the insecurity of the Hijazi *'awa'il* vis-à-vis the Najdi political elite is heightened by the Najdi boasts of the 'purity' of their lineage which they contrast to that of the 'remnants of pilgrims' as Najdis call Hijazis. Nevertheless, the display of this particular combination of objects, in this way, is yet another way of distinguishing the Hijazi elite from others.

The contemporary *ghumra* ceremony, which was 'revived' during the 1980s, is a novel affair that takes the traditional one as its frame of reference. The *ghumra* in its current form, as in the past, is a Hijazi ceremony that is not performed elsewhere in Saudi Arabia. But the new form of *ghumra* takes place only amongst the *'awa'il*, and henna is no longer used because it is now considered bad taste: only Bedouins actually apply the henna. Similarly, while the traditional dress, made in India and embroidered in silver thread as in the past, reappeared in the 1980s, following four decades of desuetude, the bride now changes into a Western-designed outfit. The *sakk al-khulkhal* has also been re-adopted, but it is now the groom who fastens the ankle bracelet.

The main change is that both men and women sometimes attend the ceremony. In these cases, the bride's male and female kin, those of her husband and some friends of both extended families now surround her. This new form of *ghumra* is practised only by a minority among the *'awa'il* who consider *ikhtilat* (mixing the sexes) a sign of sophistication that is particular to the Hijazi cosmopolitan elite. To justify *ikhtilat* within Saudi Arabia's conservative Wahhabi-dominated culture, however, the *ghumra* is still described as an 'intimate', 'family' gathering. Conservatives among the *'awa'il* continue to restrict the ceremony to women only.

♦ THE *DUKHLA* AND SOCIAL STRATIFICATION

The contemporary Hijazi wedding is the rite of passage that displays social stratification most obviously, as it is the largest ceremonial occasion gathering people from different classes in one place. During the latter part of the twentieth century, it became the custom among the *'awa'il* to seat guests during the *dukhla* at round tables, each holding about ten women. The *kusha*, where the bride sits, is still the central place, literally the 'bosom of the place', *sadr al-mahal*, while the stage for the singers is also important. Hence, tables closest to the *kusha* are, as Hijazi women describe, 'strategic places'. As tables get closer to the doors at the end of the room, they become less important in terms of hierarchical stratification. The tables closest to the *kusha* are reserved for the 'respectable guests', namely, princesses and those from the more established members of the Hijazi elite. The seating arrangements are partly determined by rules relating to age. As most gatherings of women are also meetings of social equals, age becomes important as a criterion of distinction in the absence of other social markers. Tables are therefore occupied by members of the same generation and of the same social status.

Guests are usually received by members of the bride's extended family and ushered to their seats. Seats are not reserved for particular individuals. If someone of a higher status arrives late and all the front seats are taken, immediate steps are made to accommodate her, such as shifting chairs or even people. If the standing of the latecomer is not so important, then she will have to sit in a less significant position. Even if there is no one free to perform this task, every guest is conscious of her ascribed social standing and accordingly knows where she ought to sit. Status, belonging to the group, depends principally on birth, but this is not as clear-cut as it used to be. Social mobility has generated a degree of uncertainty, especially in relations with those who have suddenly gained wealth. In most cases, people who fall into these categories sit next to the established members of the *'awa'il*, but they are not fully accepted since they do not fulfil other criteria for becoming members of the *'awa'il*.

While the positioning of the tables signifies differences in social rank, the appearance of every table is otherwise the same. On each there is a flower arrangement as a centrepiece, a silver or gold-plated container with dates, denoting tradition, and an identical one with Swiss chocolates, demonstrating access to Western goods. A third silver plate holds spices (whole betelnut, cardamom, cloves) and mint sweets (a combination considered distinctively Hijazi). A box of tissues is also placed in a special silver-plated container. Coffee in the 'traditional' coffee pot, fruit juices and water are passed around by women, usually of African origin, hired especially to do so.[33]

An ambiguous position to hold at a Hijazi wedding is that of a Najdi princess. Although every woman member of the *'awa'il* aspires to have a princess as a friend, and every successful businessman should have a prince as a patron, the *'awa'il* still seek to distinguish themselves from the latter, by their manners, dress, food and conversation, and relationships with the Najdi remain ambivalent. Such feelings, I was told, were not felt towards the *Ashraf* in the past for the latter were *minnana wa fina* ('from us and among us'), while the Najdi political elite today are perceived as a different people. The *Ashraf* are still present at weddings, but despite their special lineage and past dominance they cannot substitute for the powerful positions of an Al Saud prince or princess.

At the wedding princesses are, on the surface, accorded comparable respect to that previously offered to a *Sharifa*. A Hijazi woman feels proud to have a princess as a friend; it may sometimes be said of one who has a princess who visits her as a friend that she has become *nas kubar* ('big people').[34] A princess will be greeted with special formalities according her the honour her status demands; when the princess arrives, especially if she is an older woman, everyone in the room rises to greet her. Furthermore, the princess will be addressed with the words, *ya sumu al-amira* ('Your Royal Highness'), and *tal 'umrik* ('may your life become longer').

This exhibition of ceremonial behaviour is sometimes considered exaggerated even by the royal Najdis. But there is a widespread feeling among the Hijazi elite that Najdis, being of Bedouin (nomadic) origin, do not possess the same refinement or sense of propriety. Najdis are held not to know how to greet guests, serve food, or even eat or dress. They are regarded as continuing with practices, like eating with their hands in public and at formal gatherings, which members of the *'awa'il* now consider shameful, having adopted the use of the knife and fork since the 1950s.[35] Some among the Najdi elites, on the other hand, set themselves apart by wearing with their glossy *'abaya* (cloaks) and dresses with outsized flowers and other large motifs (they do not wear designs showing any representation of living creatures because of strict Wahhabi monotheistic beliefs). The Hijazi *'awa'il* on the other hand, consider small motifs and subdued colours more elegant.[36] Najdis consider these Hijazi refinements solipsistic and dull. These differing attitudes also translate into political and social relations; Hijazi motives and ways of thinking have been viewed as ambiguous, covert, aloof and difficult to understand by the Najdis.

◆ CONCLUSIONS

In this chapter the focus has been on changes to the community as a whole, as marriages, more than any other event, bring the emergent communal identity to the fore. Contemporary marriages establish ties between families and contribute to the formation of denser networks of social relations, which are vividly on display in the communal spaces in which marriages are celebrated. The norms regulating marriages and their celebration have changed considerably in recent years as part of the processes of communal formation, Hijazification. These changes have occurred partly as a result of the Hijazis having been forced by the pressures towards endogamy to become increasingly integrated into a more clearly bounded community. Within these constraining boundaries the internal structures of a common Hijazi identity have become much more clearly delineated. These attempts to clarify the character of the Hijazi culture are, however, subject to continual contestation and other pressures as attempts are made to define the terms on which relative status within the community is defined.

On the other hand, the increasing formality of the communal sphere has the consequence of minimising the impact of changes in economic and political fortune and of dampening its significance. The relatively high significance of status criteria other than wealth tend to retard social mobility by putting a premium on developing ties with prominent families. The emphases on lineage, seemliness and religious piety can all be seen to function to preserve this high status and cultural identity.

Nevertheless, there are signs that the changing demands of business life are making themselves felt on the relative significance of these criteria. Economic participation is increasingly dependent on the appropriate technical and administrative skills that individuals possess. As a result, educational and training qualifications are becoming relatively more important as criteria of status. All such changes, however, are contested as no single standard of judgement can be established. This is particularly so concerning religion, where a tendency towards greater emphasis on conformity to Islamic precepts clashes with intense pressures to accommodate political and economic change. A clearly emerging potential fault-line within the *'awa'il* is between what could be called 'conservative' and 'liberal' Islamic interpretations.

The various criteria used to judge status and identity specifically for determining suitability for marriage will continue to be combined and juxtaposed in new ways. The need to negotiate these changes carefully will continue to exercise the Hijazis in years to come. They will face persistent demands to accommodate globalisation, in such guises as professionalisation, as well as the internal Saudi order: pressures that are uneasily related to efforts at preservation of both Hijazi tradition and its specific expression of Islamic piety.

6

The Rites of Passage III: Death—The Final Vindication

◆ INTRODUCTION

D EATH IS A moment of crisis. Those nearest to the deceased are confronted by a host of difficulties. They suffer the grief of losing a family member, friend or associate, the uncertainty caused by the possible disruption of patronage networks, and the immediate demands of a speedy burial. As with other life-cycle rituals, such as birth and marriage, death brings the patterns of social relations to the surface. Like birth rather than marriage, however, there is a certain spontaneity with which the character of the network of family and friends reveals itself. This spontaneous moment is, however, underpinned by an increasingly well-established—more or less informal—code of conduct, as contemporary death, too, has become surrounded by reinvented and modified past practices.

The processes of tribalisation have shaped the rules governing the ritual aspects of acknowledging death, as with the other Hijazi ceremonial occasions. At stake in these cultural processes are the limits of the capacity of ruling Najdi Wahhabis to enforce their brand of religious conformity on the rest of the nation. Death, because of its peculiarly public nature, throws an unusual light on this question, affecting the moment of passing in particular ways.

The ceremonials already examined have been largely confined to what may be regarded as private places. The home of course, as an unambiguous familial space, epitomises this kind of privacy. The status of other places, such as the hotel and the hospital, are ambiguous from the perspective of the public–private distinction. From one perspective they may be regarded as home-like or quasi-private spaces in which people gather together under the auspices of a family. From another perspective they are public spaces in which people come together and are subject to critical external scrutiny. Such communal spaces, however, are relatively free of either direct state or Wahhabi influence. There is, nonetheless, an ever-present concern about spies from either the *mutaw'a* (religious police) or *mukhabrat* (intelligence service), or just individuals who will report Hijazi nonconformity. Indeed, the general fear of the Saudi state's security apparatus has become heightened to the point of paranoia, although direct interference in what are essentially domestic gatherings is not acceptable, especially when those involved are, like the *'awa'il*,[1] of high status.

Funerals, however, are different. These are events that take place in the open, in public. The procession moves away from the home, through the streets to the mosque, and on to the burial grounds. The terrain on which these events occur are public and religious spaces, which are inevitably more accessible to state officials and clerics. The proximity of official and officially endorsed authority is likely to make the effects of public power felt more strongly. At the same time, the contested nature of emerging Hijazi identities is more likely to come to the fore.

Funerals reveal the Hijazi revival at its most orthodox. Rituals associated with death are more restricted to a core set of practices determined by basic Islamic requirements. The extent to which the agenda of cultural change is set by external forces is relatively clear, as the space allowed for specifically Hijazi elaboration is much more restricted. Away from the privacy of the home and communal places, renewed traditions are less powerful in shaping behaviour and identity. However, public power too has its limits, for, as we shall see, at the moment of burial the secrets of the family are shared with the dead even as the corpse is finally laid to rest in public ground. In the reinvention of death rituals the stock of tradition has been called on to provide essential resources. The shift between the distinctive patterns of events associated with Hashemite rule in the early twentieth century and contemporary rituals surrounding one of life's pivotal moments can best be illustrated by providing an account of each pattern.

◆ THE HIJAZI WAYS OF DEATH

In the pre-Saudi Hijaz the moment of death brought on the initial period of *faz'a* (shock), which demanded that all relatives and very close friends—including *wifyan* (long-term formal friends) and *sudgan* (informal friends)—should have been present to lend support to the deceased's immediate family. Relatives of the deceased, in the sure knowledge that they could rely on the co-operation of friends, would take charge of the necessary practicalities: washing and preparing the corpse for burial, as well as making arrangements for the *'aza* (formal condolence gatherings).

Disposing of the corpse in the Hijaz followed the general rules set for all Muslims. Events proceeded cautiously in spite of this, with the principal actors first ascertaining from members of the deceased's close family whether any *wasaya* (particular wishes) had been left, either with wife, daughters, sons or even grandchildren. The rules of observance permitted some scope for variation in detail: how much of the Quran was read while washing the body; how much may be spoken to the deceased while he is being washed; what quantity of *'itr* (perfume) may be used on the corpse. The deceased's desires may have affected how these procedures were carried out, which people participated in washing and readying the corpse, or determining the place of burial. Some patronymic groups among the *'awa'il* have their own burial grounds where men and women of the same group are buried together. Women are generally buried with their natal family.

In the Hijazi tradition, members of the extended family would stand in attendance during the washing, carried out by a chosen *mughassil* (washer of the dead)—a man for a man and a woman for a woman. Then the *'aza* took place on three consecutive days, from the sunset prayer to the evening prayer for men and from the afternoon prayer to the evening prayer for the women. This gathering was also referred to as a *giraya* (recitation).

Assistance from supporters was very much a practical necessity, given the Islamic requirement that the corpse's disposal should be attended to as a matter of urgency. In the words of the Prophet, 'Burial is the best salute to the deceased' and 'Hurry up with the dead body, for if it was righteous you are forwarding it to welfare; if it was otherwise, then you are putting off an evil thing from around your necks.'[2] If the person died in the morning, the burial would have been in the afternoon or the evening. If the death was in the evening then the body was taken out at dawn. Burial was permitted at all times, but discouraged at the moment of sunrise, at sunset, and at the sun's height in the middle of the day. The timing of the escort of the deceased to the final resting place should have been according to the time of prayer.

As soon as the corpse was ready, and when the men of the extended family were all gathered together, the body was taken out of the house and sent on its way to the mosque for special funeral prayers before it could pass on finally to its burial. Men carried the body on a *na'sh* (bier), covered only by a green cloth, all the way to the mosque, the cities of Mecca, Medina and Jeddah being relatively small and distances not great. Green is the favoured Islamic colour, for it is the colour of dress in Paradise.[3] The *na'sh* of a woman was distinguished by being placed on a *gafas* (cage-like structure), with the green cloth placed from her chest to her upper leg, so that the contours of her body were covered—a show of respect that protected her honour. Gathered at a main window of the 'house of death', the female relatives of the deceased would let out *siyah* (screams) as the coffin was carried out by the men.[4]

Before the 1930s, in Mecca and Medina, the custom during a funeral procession was to put down the body every now and then and for one man to say, 'What do you have to say (or witness) about him?' The reply would be, 'He belongs with those people who are good'. The opening *sura* of the Quran, the *fatiha*, would then be recited by all. This aspect of ritual is distinctive of the urban Hijazis and is considered *bid'a* (dangerous innovation) by the Wahhabis.

Once the funeral procession reached the mosque—immediately after the prescribed prayer for the time of day—the *imam* (prayer leader) announced, 'The prayer for the dead man (woman), may Allah have mercy on you'. People lined up as for a usual prayer—standing closely together—with women behind the men in a separate section. With the body of a man the *imam* stood at its head and shoulders. If it was a woman's he stood at the middle of the body. The prayer started with the *takbir*, then the saying of 'Allah is greatest', *Allahu akbar*, followed by the reading of the *fatiha*, then a second *takbir* and a prayer for the Prophet Muhammed and his people. A prescribed prayer followed this. The *takbir* was repeated for the third time and a special prayer was said,[5] followed by the *takbir* and the *taslim*, the saying of *'a-salam alaykum wa rahmatu Allahu wa barakatu'* ('peace be upon you'). This was the form of the funeral prayer said for every deceased, at every mosque for all Muslims to attend.

After the prayer the funeral procession continued on to the burial. Before the 1940s, there were *hawta* (burial areas) especially for the *Ashraf*, the descendants of the Prophet, who ruled the Hijaz until 1925, as well as for several other influential patronymic groups. The *gabr* (grave) resembled a room (about two to three metres in length) lined with stone and had a dome. In contrast to the very basic and austere graves of the Wahhabis, the cemeteries of the *'awa'il* and others in Taif, Mecca, Jeddah and Medina, were distinguished by the greenery growing on the graves. Green plants were considered to be cooling and helpful in reducing part of the 'torture of the grave'.

As the corpse was placed into the grave the *talgin* (instruction of the dead) was performed. A son or a close relative, or any other person considered knowledgeable, took on the task of these final words. He began by speaking the *adhan* (call for prayer) into the deceased's right ear, and then recited the *talgin* in the left ear.[6] The *talgin* was for both men and women. If the deceased was a woman, then it was preferable that one of her close male relatives *mihrim* (one whom it was taboo for her to marry) tell it to her.

Hijazi condolence ceremonies took place over a considerable period. There were the three days of formal condolence, *'aza*, which started only after the burial, before which were visits to the family of the deceased, *faz'a*, which literally means immediate help, rescue and also fear and anxiety. On the third day after the burial a distinctive meal was offered to mark the *gat"aza* (the closure of the formal condolence).[7] Then there was the ceremony held on *yawm al-'ishrin* (the twentieth day), followed by the ceremony of *yawm al-arba'in* (the fortieth day) and finally an anniversary ceremony, the *hawl*. During the first 40 days, on three days of each week, Sunday, Tuesday and Thursday, the close extended family and relatives of the deceased would sit lined up to receive visitors who came to give *akhd khatir* (offering comfort). It is believed that these days were chosen because Saturday was the Jews' day, 'not ours', Monday, *ithnayn* (from the number two) was a bad omen and could even the cause the death of another person, while Wednesday, *arba'a* (from the number four) could cause the death of three! All these ceremonies included a large number of attendants, Quran recitations, and a large meal at the end. People accepted condolences at the *'id* (first feast) after a death. It was felt that, since the *'id* is an occasion of celebration and joy, the deceased's extended family must be missing them.

The majority of people in the Hijaz at the beginning of the century practised the ceremony held for the *hawl*. Snouck Hurgronje describes the yearly anniversary of death during the last part of the nineteenth century: 'On the *hawl* there are regular *mawlids* and Quran recitings, *qirayahs*, concluded like other *mawlids* with a meal. And this goes on until a new generation has forgotten the *hawl* of the dead ...'[8]

◆ CONTEMPORARY RITUALS OF DEATH

It has been observed that 'In all societies, regardless of whether their customs call for festive or restrained behaviour, the issue of death throws into relief the most important cultural values by which people live their lives and evaluate their experiences.'[9] However, in a society in which there are conflicting sets of cultural values their expression becomes more complicated. Occasions such as death are subject to forms of conflict and cultural competition whose outcome determines which values predominate at which times and places. Islam is the platform from which this power game is played in Saudi Arabia; so divergent religious practices are likely to be most sharply on display at the time of death.

Religious rules provide the essential core around which the ceremonials of death are organised. Knowledge of these religious rules is shared by everyone, but the *'awa'il* aim to surpass all others, as the display of piety has become such an important element of status and respectability amongst them. Today the *'awa'il* select aspects of the region's religious traditions in order to enhance their piety and their standing, but in doing so they challenge the Wahhabi orthodoxy. In the pre-Saudi Hijaz piety was directly connected to status, with the *'ulema* in Mecca and Medina traditionally constituting the highest social group next to the *Ashraf*. Since then Hijazis' alienation and marginalisation from Saudi political life have had profound social consequences, particularly in the Islamic revival that began in the 1980s. For the *'awa'il* securing status in the face of external domination and internal uncertainties has been achieved through the re-emphasis of a distinct code with clear rules regarding social relations.

The display of religious practice by both Hijazis and Najdi Wahhabis is one manifestation of competition for social and political status. Most Saudi Arabians observe the basic Islamic rules: the Islamic way of disposing of the corpse; the *salat aj-janaza* (prayer for the deceased), the presence of the corpse at the mosque, the burial of the corpse; and the *giraya* (Quran recitation) performed later. The *'awa'il*, however, in addition to adhering to the core rituals acceptable to the Najdi, have elaborated the way in which these should be carried out and have readopted other rituals with which to mark death. The *'awa'il* aim at surpassing others in their 'piety' by developing their own notions of what constitutes it. The most significant aspect of this is the stress they lay on their belonging to the cradle of Islam: the association with the Prophet informs a powerful alternative legitimising idiom with which to reassert social status and identity.

Spectacular displays confirm or deny standing amongst the *'awa'il*. Public gatherings announce to the world one's place in the social universe. The finality and inevitability of death, an event beyond the extended family's control, reduce the *'awa'il* to the same level as everybody else by subjecting all of the most important criteria of their status to an impromptu test: piety, solidarity of the patronymic group, the correct observance of tradition, wealth and propriety.[10] The spectacle surrounding death for the *'awa'il* offers a clearly visible final proof of their respectability; it is the final vindication that the life has been lived according to the rules. While birth offers an easy test for the status of a patronymic group, and marriage presents a more complex and dynamic test, death offers the most problematic test of status. Unlike birth and marriage, death can only be used as a vehicle to reinforce status in the most indirect ways.

From an abstract religious view all deaths would be marked in much the same way. It is a Muslim's duty to go to a condolence gathering and walk in the funeral procession, to stand by the extended family of the deceased during the critical moment.[11] But the Hijazis elaborate on this duty when, for example, several men carry the coffin. They alternate: one takes it for one minute, then another takes it, in order to receive *ajr* (a reward from God). Ideally, moreover, all criteria of status of the deceased except for his piety should be irrelevant. Practice, however, is often quite different. The *'awa'il* offer their condolences upon hearing of someone's death, but the mourning ceremony of an important figure is much larger than that of the less important. This is especially so when the deceased was well liked in addition to having held high status in the Hijazi community.

The social standing and number of persons who attend the condolence ceremonies give an immediate indication of how well the deceased's patronymic group are viewed in the community. The presence of those of high status, including Najdi royalty, at any occasion is highly valued. Such a visitor reveals the regard in which the deceased was held and indicates the nature of their social contacts. On the occasion of condolence such a presence is rare and is considered an even greater honour since it has taken place at the royal person's own volition.

The personal status of the deceased, or that of the family to which he or she belonged, determines the nature of the ceremony that surrounds it. Among the patrons of the *'awa'il* death is always a grand event with large audiences and much religious fervour. However, the emotion aroused by the death of a man, especially a well-regarded one, is more intense than that for a woman, even if she belonged by birth or marriage to a family of equal status.[12] These differences indicate gender inequalities justified by the Quranic verse, 'Men are the protectors and maintainers of women because God has given the one more strength than the other, and because they support them from their means.'[13] Nevertheless in comparison with others in the Peninsula, the Hijazis stand out for holding very grand ceremonies for their female deceased. Mothers, sisters and wives are mourned through poems in newspapers and mentioned by name publicly.

In order to understand the rituals surrounding death it is necessary to recognise the centrality of notions relating to the role of the deceased in reproducing the family and enhancing its prospects, such as 'protection' and 'maintenance'. Mourning ceremonies for men regarded as powerful, pious, wealthy or charismatic are very grand indeed. They have a strong public element, largely conducted in the open and subject to the gaze and scrutiny of others. The *'aza*, attended by men, takes place outside between *maghrib* (sunset) and *'isha* (evening prayer). The street—with the agreement of the mayor—is closed to cars,[14] and chairs for male visitors are lined up in the open space of the courtyard of the *bayt al-mawt* (house of death)[15] or *bayt al-'aza* (house of condolence), until they spill outside onto the street. Men and women are separated during most formal gatherings but, at death, the gender segregation is stricter than at any other event. The interior of the house is reserved for the women. The exterior of the *bayt al-mawt* is lit up by white lights set in straight rows, to enable the reading of the Quran, to identify the house, display prosperity and mark the importance of the event.[16]

At times of death, the family as a whole has a duty to stand together and to receive formal condolences as a single unit throughout the three-day mourning period. It is generally the patron of the family who leads the condolence acceptance group, whether the death has been that of a male or a female. The status of those attending the *'aza* may be more a reflection of the importance of those to whom the *'aza* is offered than the importance of the deceased person. The *'aza* is *mujamalat al-ahya* (a courtesy to those alive). Even if those offering their condolences did not personally know the deceased, their actions are directed towards those they do know.[17]

The Hijazi practice of giving and receiving condolences corresponds with those followed in the rest of Arabia but, as ever, the more sophisticated and polished city-dwelling Hijazis have managed to turn the rituals associated with grieving into something more refined than is found in the Najd or other parts of the Arabian Peninsula.

Women and children, however, are deemed to play a less significant role in securing the family's position. A woman's official status in contemporary Saudi Arabia does not generally lie beyond the domestic sphere, but, in contrast to a child, a woman has lived an adult life and has a whole lifetime of conduct, conformity to religious rules, values and duties, all of which must be recognised. Most importantly, her role as a mother is further commemorated in the offspring left behind. A child who dies before puberty, on the other hand, is not judged by people for his actions, since God does not judge a child for either the good or the bad deeds he has committed. The child has not lived a life that either shows achievements or proves anything. Upon his or her death, nothing moves or changes in the social standing of the patronymic group. Hence, for a child there is no condolence ceremony, but only *akhd khatir* (giving comfort), with the exception of the death of an only child for a family that has no hope of having another. All hope is not lost, however, that the child may yet contribute to the family's fortunes. On the death of a child people say that children become birds in Paradise.[18] Immediate family are reminded that 'on the day of thirst', which is the 'day of judgement', the child will come to his parents with a cup of water. On that day he will be their *shafi'nafi'* (mediator and benefactor). A child can usually be replaced but the head of the extended family cannot, and some Hijazis consider that a child's death wards off harm *daf' bala* from his father.

Meanwhile, the social standing of the whole household is so dependent on the 'head of the extended family' that his death often results in important changes, such as a restructuring of roles, rights, duties, loyalties and inheritance.[19] If he was prominent or had a high post in the government and none of his brothers or cousins were similarly placed, the status of the patronymic group could be significantly impaired.

◆ RELIGIOUS SPECTACLE AND THE CEREMONIAL REVIVAL

A distinctive characteristic of the Hijazi revival is to be found in its extravagant celebration of religion and in its idiosyncratic attitudes towards fortune and fate. Hijazis are encouraged in seeking to influence the standing of their families and themselves in the eyes of both other Hijazis and God. Indeed, the ritualisation of religious beliefs serves to blur the exact nature of the intended audience. Patronymic groups gather and, on the basis of what all Hijazis regard as their special relationship with the Prophet, seek to intercede with Him in order to secure the heavenly fortune of the deceased. Since the patronymic group is viewed to a great extent as a seamless entity, a person's conduct and achievements have a bearing on its name and reputation, even after death. There is a tendency, therefore, to create and use every opportunity for displays of duty and proclamations of family honour.

As with much Hijazi ceremony it is Orthodox Islam that enables such practices. When a person dies it is generally recognised that three aspects of their lasting influence in the world continue to earn them *ajr* (reward or recompense) with God, but the *hadith* to this effect is especially well known to the *'awa'il* and taken very seriously. First, in addition to the good deeds performed during one's lifetime, there is recognition of the knowledge that the deceased acquired and which continues to benefit others. Second, there is the provision of *sadaga jariya* ('perpetual' charity)—investments held in the name of the deceased. Some members of the *'awa'il* keep a house, rent it out, and distribute the income to the poor in the name of and for the soul of the deceased. Some also construct mosques in the memory of their deceased.

Third, prayers are said by a 'good son', and the *'awa'il* believe that a daughter's prayers—indeed, prayers by male and female generally—are spiritually equal in the eyes of God. For every situation of death there are appeasing and consoling remarks by relatives and close friends, designed to show that the deceased *intagala ila rahmat Allah* ('has gone to the mercy of Allah'). If the deceased died as a victim it will be said, 'How lucky he has died a *shahid*' (martyr). The prayers for the deceased, the family's as well as those performed by hired *mugri*, are often said and also frequently spoken about. The *'awa'il* believe that the Prophet has encouraged the praise of the dead, and regard it as the extended family's duty to do so.[20] Family members will say, 'The corpse was so light! The coffin was running, nearly flying', implying that angels were helping to carry the corpse or that a good soul was in a hurry to meet its creator and receive its reward. Another favourite story is: 'When they opened the grave of my grandfather so-and-so, six months after his death, they found his body intact'.[21] This refers to the belief that two angels, Munkar and Nakir, interrogate the deceased, and that the more advanced the decomposition of the body, the greater has been the 'torture in the grave'.[22] Most of these elaborations of belief have special significance for the Hijazi *'awa'il*, whereas Najdis regard their importance as exaggerated and even *bid'a*.

Any social meeting will provide the opportunity for putting the pious duty and honour of the family on display by making such statements, but the *'awa'il* do not leave gatherings to chance. Reviving the long series of ceremonies from the past provides the *'awa'il* with more formal settings in which to seek to enhance perceptions of their standing. However, the only ceremony that is common to all Hijazis is the closure of the formal condolence, *gat''aza*, on the third day after the burial.

Since the birth of the Saudi state and its alliance with the official Wahhabi establishment, some of these elaborate ceremonies have been discouraged, but not formally suppressed, as deviant from Islamic dogma. Some among the *'awa'il* believe that disparaging these ceremonies is an attempt to suppress Hijazi identity. But others among the Hijazis regard some of these practices as overly elaborate and have been willing to subject them to critical re-evaluation. Several among the *'awa'il* believe that extending the grief up to one year could be *mifawala* (a bad omen).[23]

Extended families which are very 'traditional' will observe the 40-day mourning period. They will sit every Sunday, Tuesday and Thursday in their home to receive those who could not come to give comfort immediately after the death.[24] Despite the differing opinions on the practice, Hijazis regard the 40-day mourning period as a way to reassert both the social status of the patronymic group and Hijazi identity. In addition to the 40 days there are some among the *'awa'il* who still hold a *hawl* (annual commemoration).[25] It is significant that in this respect the pattern of ceremonies is not dictated by a strict interpretation of the Quran. The Prophet said: 'The mourning of a Muslim for another Muslim is three days.'[26]

The *hawl*, which commences with Quranic recitations and ends with a large meal, is another occasion on which a *mawlid* may be performed. The display of the patronymic group's solidarity, their oneness, especially for the purpose of prayer, serves to enhance their good image in the community by employing the key criteria used to prove status: piety, wealth and the correct observance of tradition. It also denotes, as the *mawlid* does, Hijazi identity versus that of the Najdi Wahhabis. A great deal of what differentiates the Hijazi from the Najdi is contained in their oral traditions, and the *hawl* is just one occasion on which these traditions are kept alive. It is significant that *mawlid* poems are not published and sold in Saudi Arabia as they are Egypt, Jordan or Malaysia. In fact, the *'awa'il* do not circulate any written material except for the Quran. Hijazis feel that 'it is safer this way, that there is no written record' to provoke government censorship and bans.

The gathering held to commemorate the *hawl* takes place after the sunset prayer. Attendants read the Quran quietly. Then, professional Hijazi Quran reciters read several *suras* from the Quran for about one hour,[27] after which the *mawlid* begins: the life story of the Prophet and his struggle in spreading his message are recounted and his qualities are praised. All *mawlids* have the same themes and messages, yet they vary in the manner in which the poems are recited, in the words used and the melody, according to whether they are performed by an Egyptian, Jordanian or a Hadrami (from Hadramout). However, the aim is the same: to express love for and devotion to the Prophet. The *sira* (good conduct) of the Prophet is recited as it is known in Orthodox sources, and not embroidered with wonders and miracles as in the Turkish narrations.[28] The ideas of Sufism are given expression, with those who participate aiming to achieve a spiritual bond with God through discovering the 'light of Muhammed' or the 'truth of Muhammed'. By exhibiting Sufism they are display-ing this knowledge of what they consider the truth, thereby gaining religious power. At the same time, they are radically distinguishing themselves from Wahhabi dogma.

Prayers are then said for the dead, for all pious Muslims who have passed away, the Prophet's companions and the particular individual for whom the ceremony is held. At the end of the prayers a *sayyid* of acknowledged piety talks of the importance of prayers in general and about the blessed-ness of the evening, finally asking God for mercy on those who have died. The entire ceremony—except for the silent reading of the Quran in the beginning—is performed from memory, in accordance with Hijazi oral tradition and the importance attached to memorisation by the *kuttab* school (schools for the memorisation of the Quran). The entire pro-ceedings are conducted with a microphone—a modification of the ceremony required by the large size of gatherings and which also helps to emphasise the emotions felt. Moreover, loudspeakers in every corner of the house enable women— who remain invisible to the men—to hear the recitals.[29]

◆ TRANSFORMING THE JOURNEY TO THE BURIAL GROUND

Not every element of the traditional spectacle surrounding death has proved useful or viable in the present revival. The crying out in grief and offering of witness that once com-menced the funeral procession and accompanied the bier to the mosque and burial ground is no longer heard. The Ortho-dox interpretation of Islam holds that devout Muslims should ideally distinguish between two attitudes to the world: one emphasising the importance to be attached to *ad-dunya* (temporal things), and the other viewing *al-akhira* (the hereafter) as better, for it implies meeting God. The critical event of death represents a trial of a Muslim's religious belief and practice. Since death is the will of God, a believer—how-ever great his grief—should meet the calamity with faith and patience. Mortality should be discussed with little show of anxiety, since death is in the hands of God. According to the Quran:

> To the righteous soul it will be said: 'Oh (thou) soul in complete rest and satisfaction! Come back thou to thy Lord, well pleased thyself and well pleasing unto Him! Enter thou, then, among my Devotees! Yea, enter thou My Heaven!'[30]

On this matter the sayings of the Prophet are now effective guides to behaviour. There is a *hadith* quoting the Prophet: 'The deceased is tortured in his grave for the wailing done over him'.[31] Another *hadith* warns: 'He who slaps his cheek, tears his clothes and follows the ways and traditions of the Days of Ignorance is not of us.'[32] Hence, believers should control the urge to cry aloud or scream. A *hadith*, quoting the Prophet, says, 'Allah curses the wailer, *an-na'ya*, and who so encourages her, *al-mustami'a.'* Similarly another *hadith*, 'If the wailer dies without repenting Allah will cut for her clothes made of tar and clothes of flames.'

A sober, controlled and 'dignified' atmosphere thus now prevails throughout the deceased's last earthly journey. Seldom are there loud expressions of grief at a condolence ceremony of the *'awa'il*. Other formal events are similarly controlled, but the funeral procession stands out. Silence predominates, interrupted only by occasional whispering or by the recitation of the Quran by a *mugri*.[33] The practice of giving witness died out with the Wahhabist attempt to simplify and purify religion upon the inception of the Saudi Kingdom. Several Hijazi men have said that during funerals nowadays, 'men in short garments and long beards have interfered in the way we bury our dead'.[34] This is a reference to the presence at Hijazi funerals of representatives of the Committee for the Order of the Good and the Forbidding of the Evil, to ensure that conduct is in conformity with official Wahhabi religious doctrine.

The implications of the activities of the Committee for the Order of the Good and the Forbidding of the Evil for the pattern of re-traditionalisation are clear: in public the terms under which the Islamic revival occurs are more strictly determined by Wahhabism. This is not simply a matter of giving public credence to the Wahhabist interpretation; there is an active disowning of the past. Nowadays many Hijazis view the wailing of women as un-Islamic. Men and women criticise the practice, saying that it was an influence from Egypt, where there are *naddabat* (professional wailers).[35] Wailing is now considered to contradict the belief that there will be a good *al-akhira* for the deceased. Today the rule is that when the corpse is brought out there should be total silence. The belief in silent prayer is also explained or justified by some Hijazis by reference to the Prophet's companions, who walked in silence in a funeral procession with birds circling their heads.

During the journey to the mosque the body is transported most of the way in a car, followed by a large procession of others. The procession stops at a short distance from the mosque, and the final leg is completed on foot. The prayer for the deceased may be performed at any mosque but people prefer it to be at the Great Mosque in Mecca or the Mosque of the Prophet in Medina. These are not only the two most important mosques for all Muslims but they remain the heart of the Hijaz. The size of the mosques also means that there will be more people to pray for the deceased, thus bringing greater mercy and blessings from God. The funeral prayer is said immediately after a prescribed prayer at the mosque. At any mosque, whenever a body is brought in for the funeral prayer, everyone present, men and women,[36] participates. People say, 'Lucky the one who dies during Ramadan', or 'Lucky the one who dies during the pilgrimage season', or 'on a Friday', because so many people are gathered in the mosques at those times.

◆ THE BURIAL GROUND

Once prayers for the dead have been said the funeral procession continues to the *hawta* (burial ground). Several patronymic groups among the *'awa'il* possess their own *hawta*. The royal family also have their own *hawta* in the capital, Riyadh. But these are the old patronymic groups who bought land in the graveyard (or adjacent to it). There was also land bought in the form of *waqf* (religious endowment). Hence any other Muslim can be buried here. The *Ashraf*, the descendants of the Prophet, as well as other influential patronymic groups of the Hijaz, can no longer buy burial land in this way.

As new money cannot purchase the prestige attached to a family grave, these are now reserved for the 'old', 'good' families among the *'awa'il*. Patronymic groups that have a space in the *hawta*, especially if it is in Mecca or Medina, continue to use it, but they do so with circumspection. The burial grounds are given symbolic names not related to those of the patronymic group, for example, 'the Section of Light' or 'the Flower'. These names, known only to the patronymic group and those close to them, are not written down near the graves for fear of offending the authorities.

Burial groupings are generally based on the patrilineal system: a man, his sons and daughters and all those who hold the paternal grandfather's *hawta*. Wives are not buried with their husbands and his paternal family, unless they express a wish for this. However, the rules on gender separation continue to be observed even after death, with men and women of the same extended family buried in separate graves, *gubur* (singular: *gabr*), in the same *hawta*. For a Hijazi *hawta* the land is divided into separate cement-lined plots, in each of which several bodies can be buried. There are still no burial grounds in Mecca and Medina where Najdis are buried with Hijazis. Older Hijazis explain: 'Najdis do not inter-marry with us, and do not wish to be buried with us.'

Abdul Aziz Al Saud, upon conquering the Hijaz, aimed at purifying the House of God (Mecca with the Great Mosque at its centre) of idolatry. Stones identifying graves were forbidden. Likewise thousands of graves and shrines of the *Sahaba* (the Prophet's companions) were destroyed in the early days of the Wahhabi-Saudi rule—mainly in Al Baqi' cemetery in Medina and Al Ma'la cemetery in Mecca—along with other historic monuments, such as the reputed house of the Prophet.[37] Hijazis especially lament the destruction of the tomb of Khadija (the first wife of the Prophet), the tomb of Ali Bin Abi Talib, the Prophet's son-in-law, and the tomb of Amina bint Wahb, the Prophet's mother. Domes that identified the graves of the *Sahaba* were destroyed according to a *fatwa* (religious decree) issued by Abdullah Bin Balhid, who claimed that Muslims would worship these domes rather than God. Wahhabis condemn these adornments, especially those erected under the rule of Sharif al-Hussain Bin Ali, as representing myth and heresy. There must be no indication of the deceased's identity, putting a somewhat odd twist on the Prophet's saying: 'May Allah have mercy on a tomb whose occupant is not known'. Indeed, domes are no longer permitted to top any graves, for, according to the Wahhabis, a tomb must not be higher than the human forearm.

The same fate has greeted another distinguishing mark of the graveyards of the *'awa'il* and others from Taif, Mecca, Jeddah and Medina. As mentioned before, people in these areas have considered greenery around the graves as cooling and helpful in reducing part of the torture of the grave. Wahhabism has seen to it that the greenery was removed because it too was considered un-Islamic. The inherent asceticism of desert life, combined with state-sponsored Wahhabism, has imposed desert-like conditions on these burial grounds, stirring silent resentment.

Najdi Wahhabi followers also believe that since the Prophet was buried in the ground in a *lahd* (in direct contact with earth), Muslims should do likewise. Hijazis, on the other hand, hold that both types of burial conform to Islamic criteria: the Prophet was buried in a *lahd*, but many of his companions were buried in *gubur*, which contain a barrier of stones or cement. Of course, these distinct practices have sources other than the teachings of Islam. Hijazi urban prosperity and the availability of materials enabled the building of stone graves, and the practice was allowed to develop in the absence of literalist religious fundamentalism. Before the twentieth century brought vast oil wealth to the Najd, its tribes, living in tents and mud houses in the desert, had few resources with which to build stone graves.

The considerable impact of Wahhabism on the conduct and site of Hijazi burial is clear enough, but despite the pressures for a particular brand of religious conformity the *'awa'il* continue to find some space for a certain measure of defiance. For example, *talgin* (instruction of the dead) is still performed, despite its being carried out in public and hence under possible surveillance. This custom is practised by most other Sunnis, in Egypt, Malaysia, India and Pakistan. In Saudi Arabia *talgin* is a controversial practice because the Wahhabis view it as unacceptable, excessive and unnecessary. Official Saudi doctrine holds that the Prophet never recommended nor practised the instruction of the dead. Members of the Committees for the Order of the Good and the Forbidding of the Evil will therefore reprimand any group practising it at the graveside.

Nevertheless, Hijazis continue the practice, whose correct performance is of the utmost importance to particular patronymic groups in order to confirm their position in relation to the other members of the *'awa'il*: it symbolises their group solidarity and the specific character of their Hijazi identity. Justifications for the practice are varied. Some observe that, 'Since the call for prayer is the first thing to be heard by an individual at birth, it should be the last thing heard by him at death'. They add: 'The authorities cannot follow and supervise each one of our dead'. This instruction is not taught in the national school curriculum but it continues to thrive, like other Hijazi religious rituals, via oral transmission from father to son. At the grave a relative of the deceased who has been 'schooled' in this way usually performs it.

◆ CONCLUSIONS

The instruction of the dead offers a poignant demonstration of the limits of the power of Wahhabism to shape the cultural and spiritual life of Saudi Arabia. In particular, the Hijazis continue to use indigenous traditions—especially those associated with the Prophet—selectively, which serve to lend a sacred justification to one set of cultural practices while providing a religious rationalisation for attacking another. The Al Saud can dominate but not assimilate. Under the auspices of Islam the funeral party occupies the burial ground, briefly imprinting its own version of social relations onto the public space.

Such practices demonstrate the resilience of a collective social life with its roots in the structure of family life. Orality is a vital aspect of this resilience, matched by a cautious attitude towards written records. The highly personalised network of social relations among the *'awa'il* provides a framework within which the spoken word is an effective means of transmitting information. This framework, reinforced by trust, also protects those who pass on information. It is not open to public scrutiny, and is therefore largely immune to state intervention. At the graveside, in the face of official disapproval and in a gentle mockery of the limits of official power, these oral traditions are passed on for the last time to the deceased.

However, the social structures being built up around the *'awa'il* are by no means completely autonomous. Beliefs and attitudes have developed and changed, in part according to the practical possibilities open to urban Hijazis, and the process of tribalisation seems to be regulated by a certain pragmatic realism. Re-traditionalising attitudes on specifically Hijazi terms is much less likely to occur where the practices they inform have been effectively repressed. The pressures to abandon wailing and giving witness have not only succeeded in marginalising these practices but have also produced a clear shift in attitudes amongst some Hijazis. The more discreet instruction to the dead, despite similar

121

pressures, has been sustained, injecting life into the family traditions on which it depends.

Indeed, while the previous chapter examined how the process of tribalisation was built up around the restrictions placed on marriage, it is clear from the rituals surrounding death that the Hijazis' assertion of tradition requires specific communal spaces. From the perspective of individual families, these spaces are public and subject to communal rules, but from the perspective of state or religious authorities they are still familial spaces, which are protected, to varying degrees, from the imposition of national rules. Organised under the auspices of family heads, communal gatherings are key to the development of the ceremonies and rituals through which a distinctive sense of the Hijaz has been developed. The contrast between the character of these spaces and that of public spaces that do not benefit from the protection afforded by the institution and status of the family could not be greater.

7
Cultivating the Social Arts I: The Art of Formal Conversation among the Hijazi 'awa'il

◆ INTRODUCTION: COMMUNICATION AND CONCEALMENT

T HE BIG 'OLD' families of the Hijaz like to think that they alone have been cultivated in the ways of mannered society. They look down upon those who have suddenly acquired wealth as not having had time, in a single generation, to learn how to conduct themselves. It is said that 'they may have money or power, but they do not know how to behave'. Familiarity with the codes of formal performance provides a sense of unity and identity. To the 'older' but less wealthy members of the 'awa'il,[1] knowledge of the rules of formal conversation provides a sense of security in a context of fierce internal rivalry with the *nouveaux riches* and competition with the Najdis and other Gulf Arab elites.

Throughout the 1980s and 1990s — a period of religious and economic insecurity — the importance of concealing the secrets of the family and communicating approval of the status quo was enhanced, even exaggerated. Mastering verbal formalities became a means of protecting and strengthening social status and Hijazi identity. Moreover, by emphasising the rules of formal, polite conversation, the 'awa'il were laying greater stress on what they perceive to be their strength and distinguishing feature in Arabia: a sophisticated, urban

123

background that allowed them to assert their own sense of social precedence over the Najdis, who are perceived to lack such refined cultural roots.

In the everyday world of the *'awa'il* one should not underestimate the significance of facades: a person's appearance, the frontage of a house or a family's public face. All the families collude in fostering rules of social intercourse that minimise the chances of being dishonoured in the eyes of others. The elaboration of rules of good conduct at formal occasions is crucially important in this respect. These codes eliminate all scope for even a note of criticism to slip in, whilst encouraging the speaker to declaim with an elegant air. Concealment within communication typifies the art of conversation amongst the *'awa'il* of the Hijaz.

◆ ORGANISING SPACE AND TIME

There is a fundamental distinction to be made between the world of domestic family relations and that of formal gatherings. Virtually every aspect of life is marked by its belonging to one or the other of these domains. The manner and content of speech, styles of dress, the nature of food and eating, gifts given to friends—all of these are subject to discrete sets of rules. The barriers that separate these spheres even give physical shape to the homes of the *'awa'il* and to the pattern of activities during the week.

These boundaries, and developments within them, give a rich texture to the world of the *'awa'il*, whose complex internal structure depends on the way in which time and space are organised. It is a commonplace that religious performances lend to the secular calendar divisions between sacred and profane times, and separate designated places in a similar fashion. More surprisingly, this is also true of family life in the Hijaz, which, at each of its different levels (the patronymic group, the extended family and the nuclear family) is treated as sacred territory into which outsiders cannot enter.

Outsiders' first impressions of an *'awa'il* house are made by its symbolic defences—particularly very high, encompassing walls, intended to protect the family from the scrutiny of others, ensure privacy and mark the boundaries between the 'inside' and 'outside' worlds. There are two gates in this formidable barrier. One small and simple entryway is for the *ahl* (family) and their *sudgan* (close friends). Another entrance, larger and more ornate, is reserved for more ceremonial welcoming of 'outsiders'—*ajanib* (non-family), including *wifyan* (formal friends), and non-Hijazis, specifically the Najdis. When receiving these categories of guests, who come only by previous appointment, the house is more brightly lit, incense is burnt and behaviour follows all the rules of formality and propriety.

Insider/outsider distinctions do not dissolve once visitors are within the confines of the house. There are two reception rooms, one referred to as *al-ma'iyysha* (the living room), where male and female members of the family and close friends gather in an informal, more relaxed atmosphere. The formal reception room, called *al-salon*, is usually closed to family members, as it is seen as a communal space which is opened only for special occasions. The *salon* usually hosts each gender separately.

Formal visitors will normally be invited into the home at certain times of the week, which is divided into two parts. Saturday to Wednesday, the working days of the week, are for the non-family: men go to work and women perform their 'duties' towards their formal friends—visiting them in hospitals if they are sick, and receiving and returning their hospitality. The weekend, Thursday and Friday, are reserved for the family. The extended family comes together on Thursday evening for dinner, and on Friday (after the men come back from the noon prayer at the mosque) for the *gayla* reunion that lasts from lunch until sunset. The only formal event that is routinely given priority over 'the family part of the week' is a wedding, which takes place on Thursday night, though of course an unexpected illness or a death would also take priority. As one woman put it: 'From Saturday to

Wednesday we finish with our duties towards "people", then, from that time onwards, we are free to be with our family. We all get together, old and young'.

The Hijazi emphasis on family as a source of rituals—even in its extended form—is greater than in the rest of Arabia. The explanation lies in the urban–tribal divide between the Hijaz and the Najd. Najdi attitudes to their kin are very much governed by the fact that the linkages are tribal and therefore extensive. In this context relations with siblings and cousins count for less than among the city-dwelling Hijazis who form part of smaller more intimate family networks.

◆ RESTRAINTS ON SCANDAL AND GOSSIP

The *'awa'il* have long cherished privacy and formality, and practised their concealing arts. Greater geographical and social mobility, coupled with the growing dominance of the Najdi political elite, have made the demand for privacy more acute, especially for those in more vulnerable positions. The increased danger that the protective, regularised pattern of time and space might be disrupted has called forth supplementary defences: codes of honour and the art of concealment. If the hostess is not properly dressed, or if she sees a guest come upon something else that is not up to the appropriate standard, she will appeal to the visitor, *'asturi ma wajahti'* ('put a veil on our shortcomings'). The hostess relies on the reciprocity implied in the popular saying, *'illi ma fi kheir fi ahlu ma fi kheir fil-nas'* ('He who has no goodwill for his family will have no goodwill for others'). She trusts that her guest appreciates the obligation to others not to 'touch' their honour or slander their good name. Hijazi guests who appreciate these matters will be perceived in the community as akin to loyal, considerate family members and will be honoured accordingly.

There is more than a sense of mutual interest to protect a family's reputation. Religion provides a powerful reinforcement. Every day one hears repeated aloud prayers to God to *'ya rabi sitrak'* ('protect us or veil our embarrassment from others'), and *'ya rabi la tifdahna'* ('preserve us from scandal'). Similarly, people often refer to the Quranic verse comparing scandal-mongering to the sin of cannibalism: 'Spy not on each other, nor speak ill of each other behind their back. Would any of you like to eat the flesh of his dead brother? Nay, ye would abhor it'.[2] For the *'awa'il* the *hadith* 'leave the created for their Creator' underpins the symbolic wall around the family.

These shared feelings and values mean that people feel the need to keep their *dimma* (conscience) clear of gossip. People do satisfy their curiosity about rumours of others' private lives while talking to *wifyan* (formal friends) over the telephone and privately with relatives. But nobody admits to 'talking about people'. In addition to weighing on the conscience it would offend dignity. There are, though, known gossips, or 'news carriers', who have acquired a reputation as 'reporters'. Although sought after, they are not respected.

◆ BEHAVIOUR IN THE COMMUNAL SPHERE

Within the communal sphere, where families are precariously exposed to outsiders, there is a rising premium on maintaining the formal barriers that guard the family from scrutiny, which guarantee its secrecy and protect its honour and reputation. In this competitive milieu all families come together with the aim of showing only the best of Hijazi culture. These deep-seated concerns about honour and gossip cast a fascinating light on the formal sphere, the organisation of which revolves almost entirely around the status competition between extended families. From the moment of entry into a formal gathering a family will deploy its repertoire of offensive and defensive strategies: conspicuously exhibiting every available piece of evidence to reinforce the family's claim to high status and resolutely fending off critical scrutiny by restricting the range of permissible topics of conversation.

127

At all life-cycle rituals women enter as one family to be received by another. They strictly follow the rule of age precedence, with even slight gradations being acknowledged. Seating is then arranged on the basis of perceived social status, such that two to four members of each extended family are together amongst their respective age and peer groups. Mutual status is commonly known, so at every formal gathering the same people sit next to each other. Women can therefore regularly sit next to their favourite *wifyan*, and will reserve places for them.

Formal behaviour of members of the extended family towards one another is ritualistically marked by an emphatic propriety. For example, a daughter behaves more courteously towards her mother, getting up more often and more ceremoniously for her, stroking her hair and kissing her hand, and remaining largely quiet while she speaks except for the set responses of approval and phrases such as, 'May God not deprive me of you!' Although such set compliments are heard between family members at home, they are more usually encountered in formal public gatherings.

Hijazis express the good feelings or 'love' they have for each other during formal conversations. One often hears a woman asking another, *'billahi awhashtik ya fulana?'* ('by God, did you miss me?'); *'keif'* ('and how!') comes the reply, *'Allah wada' mahabatik fi galbi'* ('God has placed your love in my heart'), *'Allah yi' lam 'an al-mahaba al-akhawiyya illia fi galbi laki'* ('Only God knows the sisterly love that I have for you'). Hijazis consider such declarations to be a desirable Islamic practice that enhances feelings of solidarity, quoting the *hadith*, 'If a person feels love for his brother let him tell him so'. This stylised approach to language and behaviour distinguishes the urban Hijazis from the more rough and less demonstrative Najdis, while the theme of 'love'—so consistent with Hijazi Sufism—stands in sharp contrast to Wahhabi puritanism.

The aim of seating arrangements at a formal gathering is not to exchange controversial 'ideas' or learning something 'new': the aim is not to separate people from those they meet during their everyday life nor to place those who sat together before with other compatible guests. Rather, the purpose is to affirm and consolidate old familiar values. Formal conversation avoids 'taboo' subjects, such as politics or social problems. This is especially true in women's gatherings. Broaching such topics evokes no response, instead making the female listener feel uncomfortable, even bored. Such topics are not traditional, and hence fail to fulfil the primary aim of formal conversation: emphasising the authority of tradition and custom. Such conversation is guarded and neutral, and does not deviate from a script that specifies both the lines and the speakers with whom one repeats them. Both the form, i.e. the manner of speech, and the content of formal conversation are carefully regulated by the concept of *tajammu* ('seemliness' or adding lustre). How one speaks and what one speaks about should reveal only that which helps one's own extended family, and that of others, to *yirfa' al-ras* (hold their head up high) and *yibayyid bil-wajh* (whiten their face).

Valorising the family and concealing its defects in the communal sphere is by no means considered hypocritical. On the contrary, it is regarded as a Muslim's duty towards both family and community. Hence men and women among the *'awa'il* of all generations take pride in this religious observance. All information should substantiate the hidden themes of conversation, accentuating the family's 'piety', verifying how 'traditionally' Hijazi, refined and wealthy it is. The Hijazi *'awa'il* relish giving full accounts of family members' regular and frequent visits to the Mosque of the Prophet in Medina, of the dreams they have of the Prophet and his companions and of the messages revealed to them. The Prophet Muhammed was a Hijazi and the more they assert their closeness to him, the more they strengthen their Hijaziness. They recount the many *sura*s of the Quran they read each week, specifying the days specially reserved for *wird* (additional private worship). Topics of conversation denoting financial capacity and Hijazi good taste are favoured. Trips abroad are elaborated upon. Concealment, on the other hand, means that anything that would present a family in a bad light in front of others, such as inter-familial disputes or financial problems, is defined as private and therefore off-limits. This concealment applies even to discussions of rivalry or tensions within or outside the boundaries of the Hijazi *'awa'il*.

◆ SHELTER FROM SCRUTINY

Conversational proscriptions extend far beyond discussions of 'private' matters to include direct commentary of any kind, be it criticism or compliment. Open remarks about material matters, dress, or designs could be considered as lacking poise and elegance. Such subjects are discussed discreetly, in private.

A wide range of ritualised exchanges has supplemented these restrictive conversational options. These include elaborated forms of everyday comments, florid means of bestowing praise, and entertaining resources for filling the inevitable silences. Children are among those aspects of life never commented upon directly. Women asking about each other's families always speak of children as *al mahafiz* (the protected ones), or *ism Allah aleihum* (those upon whom be God's name). One another's husbands are politely referred to as 'the father of the protected ones'.

Women of good Hijazi families pride themselves on mastering the art of passing elaborate indirect compliments. For example, upon seeing one of the guests walking into the room she repeats, *'khatwa 'aziza'* ('dear foot-step'), or *'khatawat fi haram al-nabi'* ('foot-steps in the Mosque of the Prophet'). The reference to the Prophet expresses blessedness and also serves as a reminder of Hijazis' connection to Muhammed. Even these remarks might be prefaced by saying, 'May my eye fall cold on you', to ward off the evil eye, which is considered to be hot. A polite woman's concern for others extends to those dear to her but absent. For example, when eating the food that her hostess has prepared, she might say with a sigh, 'I am *mitnaghghisa* (desiring the presence) of so-and-so, she particularly enjoys this dish'.

Formal conversation between the *'awa'il* is marked by frequent pauses, which partly reflects its lack of spontaneity, its controlled and ritualised patterns. Nevertheless, since some social conversation is necessary, *'awa'il* women pride themselves on being able to keep it flowing by citing proverbs and poetry, *hadiths* and verses from the Quran. If there is a silence that is too prolonged, an elderly lady will say, 'Why is there silence? Is there one among you who is pregnant with a girl?' This will lead to either the same woman or another known for her *labaga* (eloquence) reciting a line of poetry or recounting a Meccan story with a good moral. Silent periods at such gatherings are also punctuated by sudden cries of supplication to God.

All the enforced politeness needed to promote family honour understandably puts individuals under a certain degree of strain, from which they need some release. Fortunately, belonging to a family also provides some respite from the controlled and impersonal atmosphere, for one is allowed to whisper to close family members and express true feelings. This is partly facilitated by the large numbers gathered together, enough to allow individuals to have a more private talk without attracting too much attention to themselves. Talking about bodily functions is also suitable for the formal sphere, and can be a source of more relaxed conversation. People will discuss anything from haemorrhoid operations, to kinds of contraception. When women among the *'awa'il* are told that such topics are considered embarrassing, not 'delicate', or shameful in other societies, they reply, *'la haya'a fil-din'* ('There is no embarrassment in religion'). Illness, birth, death: all come from God. To discuss them is non-controversial.

Nevertheless, a woman who is accomplished in the use of polite language and performs to good effect is viewed as having a 'tongue like honey'. She will replace even basic, neutral phrases such as, 'Thank you', or, 'We will come', with the pious and ritualistic expressions that now constitute a major part of any verbal discourse. The cultured hostess will appeal to her departing guests, 'Do not desert us, do not desert us, by God do not desert us'. She will be reciprocated with the reply, 'We will come to see you even if on our eyelashes'. This ornate language, decorated with extensive details and elaborations, stands out as peculiar to Hijazis.

The requirement that relationships appear good at all times helps to protect the stability of the underlying relationships, such as those between *wifyan*, from any temporary strain. A space is created by shielding tensions from the scrutiny of others, thereby allowing relationships to be re-established with a minimum of repercussions. Although people in formal surroundings may know that *x* does not get along with *y* they act as if they have not noticed, thereby maintaining the facade of normality, Hijazi good manners and solidarity.

Indeed, women among the *'awa'il* pride themselves on their ability to suppress feelings of animosity; they consider it *'agl* (wisdom). It is highly complimentary for a woman to be described as *mitabtaba* (very tactful). There are, however, subtle indicators of hostility that are not easily detected by outsiders. Refusing to greet another in a formal gathering or failing to repeat to her the appropriate set phrases and set compliments or not accepting the seat that a long-term friend has reserved for one, and thus changing one's place, will not only affect their relations but will also have a bearing on the relationship between their respective families. Such acts of hostility may lead to a cooling or even to a temporary severing of relations until some compensatory gesture is made.

Even so, conventions such as the *'itab* (friendly reproach), which do not immediately express the speakers' underlying feelings, help maintain long-term 'faithful' relations between the formal friends, and contribute to the cohesion of the group. *'Itab* only occurs between those who genuinely want to resume good relations, as it provides the other person with the chance to apologise. However, only a woman of comparable, or higher, social status to another can offer *'itab*. A younger woman who reproaches an older woman, for instance, would be considered too presumptuous: she waits for the older to reproach her, for she can only apologise. The reproach is offered directly, 'I have *'itab* for you', and is followed by a brief account of the cause of the offence and an assurance that, 'If I didn't love you I wouldn't have reproached you!' The other woman then answers, *'a'zurini ana migasira ma 'aki'* ('Forgive me, I have fallen short with you (in my obligations, duties towards you'). *'Itab* is also a form of sorting out relations between men but to a lesser extent, for in their more complex public world there are various functional means to balance and control relations.

◆ CONCLUSION: THE SUBTLETIES OF REGULATED COMPETITION

The previous chapters brought out the importance of communal spaces to the emergence of a distinctive Hijazi identity. In this chapter there has been a closer examination of interactions in these spaces. This has revealed ways in which social standing is a precarious good, and how entering communal spaces requires that a special kind of attention be given to nurturing it.

The structure of formal gatherings bears comparison to a subtle, competitive game such as chess. There are well-defined sets of rules, within which one must advance one's cause whilst simultaneously defending oneself from the possible attacks of others. One's defence entails closing off avenues of attack, in this instance, by concealing anything which might lead to being diminished in the estimation of others. The offensive strategy entails putting on the best possible show of familial solidarity, wealth, poise etc., in order to augment one's social standing. As with the best chess the most skilful moves are those that combine the achievement of strategic advantage with the greatest economy. Knowing the rules and understanding how best to take advantage of the opportunities they afford is therefore crucial.

The rules of formality and propriety, however, have not been developed for the sake of competition but in order to regulate it. Their function is to give the social milieu a certain thickness, or viscosity. The aim is to inhibit mobility, to restrict the downward movement of those less able to function in the new environment, and to retard the upward motion of the aspiring *nouveaux riches*. The rules may generate many occasions for potential disruption to existing relations, but they also provide vital opportunities for reconciliation.

The painstaking acquisition of a working knowledge of these rules has become a condition of social ascendancy. Adherence to these common conventions also demonstrates approval of the system and ensures the continuity of the family world of the Hijazi social elite. Accepting the rules entails an acknowledgement of the social positions they confer, and therefore strengthens the positions of those who gain most from them. To be ambitious, therefore, is at one and the same time to reinforce the social superiority of those one is seeking to challenge.

8
Cultivating the Social Arts II: Reasserting Culinary Tradition

◆ INTRODUCTION: THE DOMESTIC SPHERE IN
THE RECREATION OF A COMMUNAL IDENTITY

T HE PREVIOUS chapter, on the rules of formal conversation, stressed the structured resistance towards
innovation within the communal sphere. There the
Hijazi *'awa'il*[1]—not being part of a larger tribal network as
the elites of other regions—seem to be interested only in
maintaining and strengthening the familiar contours of their
self-enclosed world. The *'awa'il* do sometimes like to hear
'new' things in public, but not when these will threaten their
'tradition' or identity. They are cautious with the idea of open
changes, partly because of the Wahhabi definitions of *bid'a*
(heresy), which encompasses any innovation that departs
from what is deemed authentic in the Islamic tradition. The
'awa'il like to 'progress' and 'modernise', but to do so while at
the same time remaining true to Islamic values and a specifically Hijazi way of life. 'New' is not necessarily 'better'.
Whatever they collectively adopt as new must be made to
appear as a continuation of tradition, to resemble the 'things
of the past', to supplement the reconstruction of the romantic
Hijaz. The *'awa'il* are well aware that life is altering, that modernisation and globalisation mean change and sometimes
improvement, but they stress that change is not synonymous
with 'Westernisation'. They like to think that what they have

now grows out of the same soil as that from which sprang the things of their great-grandparents in Mecca, Medina or Jeddah.

The *'awa'il*, descendants of cosmopolitan Hijazis, have persistently assimilated novelties, and continue to do so. Now, however, they only accept into the communal sphere what seems to them to be traditionally Hijazi. In order for a novelty to become established as a part of today's living traditions it must pass through the rigours of a transition phase. Failure to pass the challenges of transition results in its becoming an unacceptable innovation. During this period people are suspicious, subjecting the novelty to certain tests: what is its relation to traditional values? Can it be said to be seemly? Who introduced it? What was their status in Hijazi society? Is it acceptable to the important opinion-makers? This process offers some security, a sense of stability. By affirming the rules for legitimising new social actions it also regenerates group cohesion.

Any novelty might be perceived as a departure from tradition, or in 'bad taste'. Maintaining custom and tradition reinforces social status and Hijazi identity, while innovating can threaten it, especially the status of those in vulnerable positions. Only the very secure have the confidence and thus can afford to take the risks involved. Individuals of unassailable social standing can experiment and introduce innovation in dress, food or manners. A consensus usually emerges on the acceptability of the change to 'good taste', which both reflects admiration for the person who introduces the innovation and illustrates the extent to which tradition remains open for reinterpretation.

There are thus various stages in the contemporary adoption of a 'new' element. It must be carefully chosen, and important opinion leaders will usually select it. It might then be accepted by the wider community, perhaps in a modified form, and become a feature of tradition. The following discussion of food examines this process further. Some aspects are of special significance. First, there is the essentially 'private' or 'indoor' character of assessing acceptability. As the discussion of conversation showed, formal occasions do not permit open comments and therefore shield an experiment from immediate critical scrutiny. Debates on the merits or otherwise of novelties take place amongst friends and families in an informal manner. Second, and relatedly, the home is the site of assessment and also, most importantly, of the resources for innovation itself. This is especially true in the case of food, where culinary knowledge from earlier times continues to thrive as a marker of Hijazi identity, despite the displacement of some older eating habits from formal life.

◆ A TRADITION OF COSMOPOLITAN CUISINE

It is hardly surprising that Hijazi attitudes towards food have emphasised novelty. The social background, education and outlook of Meccans, in particular, has long been characterised by their belonging to urban centres and association with travel, from extensive foreign trade and the *hajj* (pilgrimage). For centuries the *hajj* has brought Muslims to Mecca from many different cultures, and since the last century Meccans have sent their offspring to study in other Islamic countries. Their way of life, including eating habits, has been continually subject to the modifying influence of other cultures.[2] A meeting point for the movements of people across the Islamic world, the Hijaz became a site of rich cultural, and particularly culinary, transactions. This open, urban character sets Hijazi cuisine decisively apart from its basic Najdi Bedouin counterpart.

Many of the pilgrims to the holy city of Mecca ended their journey by settling there or in neighbouring cities, in the process introducing a variety of customs and traditions, including those concerning food. With time these were adapted to the local sensibilities and so were gradually added to the collection of what may be termed 'Hijazi' food. This richly diverse cuisine is proudly referred to as 'Meccan', 'Medini' or 'Jiddawi' food. Some of the dishes still retain names that betray their origins in Indonesia, India, Iran,

Egypt or Turkey— the originally Indian sweet, *laddu*, for example. Others have acquired new names precisely to indicate the country of origin, e.g. *ruz Bukhari* (rice from Bukhara). Yet other names were modified to sound Hijazi Arabic, such as the Indian rice dish *buryani*, which became known as *zurbiyan*.

Becoming Hijazi meant changing more than names. Meccan food was presented in 'refined' and 'elegant' ways. Meat and vegetables, for example, were cut into very small pieces. The only thing to be presented in large chunks was the whole lamb, which was reserved for special occasions. This contrasts with Najdi Bedouin cuisine, which has been customarily presented in larger pieces and viewed as rough and less 'refined'. There were also specific rules for the serving of *al mubashara* (guests) with an appropriate formal language of designated expressions and compliments to be exchanged. There was also an elaborate vocabulary of words and phrases to describe the presentation of food known only to members of the *'awa'il*, who prided themselves on their mastery of this knowledge.

◆ RITUAL MEALS

Many different events are traditionally marked with either a single dish or a combination of dishes specific to the occasion. There are special meals for the several days of the religious calendar, to mark the significant life-cycle events of birth, death and marriage, as well as for special occasions, such as the arrival of clouds promising rain.

The *hijri* (Muslim new year), is celebrated with special food—milk, fruit and a special local goat's cheese, all representing purity. The traditional meal served during the *mawlid* (the celebration of the Prophet's birth) consists of lamb and rice or *'ashuriya*, a special sweet dish made from ten different kinds of grain, which is prepared to commemorate *'ashura*. *'Ashura* is a Shia commemoration but also has significance throughout the Muslim world. Many Sufis in Turkey and other Sunni lands observe the mourning for Hussain, grand-son of the Prophet, martyr and iconic figure for the Shia. There is also a legend in Turkey and elsewhere that it is the day of the landing of Noah's Ark after the flood, and that Noah was the first to make *'ashuriya* with the ten grains that remained in the Ark from initial provisions. Within Saudi Arabia, these traditional meals are distinctive to Hijazis and indeed are central symbols of rituals—such as the *mawlid*—but are frowned upon or even forbidden by the Wahhabi Najdi establishment.

Ramadan has dishes reserved for it: barley soup, cooked fava beans, *sambusak* (cheese and meat pastries) and *fatta* (meat on a bed of bread immersed in stock and covered with yogurt). There are also sweet dishes particular to Ramadan, such as *kunafa* (filo pastries filled with almonds and immersed in honey). The *'id al fitr* (end of Ramadan) is a feast for which *al minazzala* (roast lamb) is cooked after being cut into pieces. It is served with *dubyaza*, a sweet dish made from cooked dates, apricots, figs and almonds.[3] On the fifteenth of *Sha'ban*, the month proceeding Ramadan, Meccans prepare another pastry dish, *mishabbak*.

When at Mina, the final place to visit during the perform-ance of the pilgrimage, *zallabiyya* (a very fine layer of pastry covered with powdered sugar) is prepared. The other feast following the pilgrimage, *'id al-hajj*, was distinguished by a local variety of *ma'mul* (pastries filled with dates or with almonds, flavoured with cardamom). Although the majority in Saudi Arabia performs these religious rituals, each event is marked as particularly Hijazi by a distinctive dish or a combi-nation of dishes that only Hijazis know, prepare and share.

There is a unique meal for the event of death, cooked and served to mark *gat'aza* (the end of formal condolence) on the third day, as discussed in Chapter 6. The central dish for this occasion is rice with chickpeas and meat, and a dish of finely chopped tripe, liver and sometimes squash, a vegetable con-sidered to have been the favourite of the Prophet Muhammed. Another meal consisting of a whole lamb on rice with accompanying dishes such as sesame and cucumber salad is served at the *hawl* (ceremony commemorating a death anniversary).

There are other meals that are cooked and shared on special occasions. For example, the meal given on a cloudy day to welcome *al ghaym al sukkari* ('the sugary clouds') consists of *ruz bi 'adas* (rice with lentils), *salata/humar* (salad of tamarind) and fried fish. All of these dishes represent a Hijazi culinary tradition distinguished by location: a physical environment bordering the Red Sea, which offered varieties of fish not available inland, and the mountainous areas of Taif, south of Mecca, which provided traditional vegetables and fruits. Other varieties of staples and greens came through trade and pilgrimage.

Extending hospitality and showing generosity to *al mubashara* is a crucial part of Hijazi good manners and therefore one way of establishing or maintaining status and respectability. Hospitality requires that the hosts show their guests every *mujamala* (courtesy) and *tagdir* (recognition). This means that from the beginning of a party until the last guest leaves, the host or hostess should remain attentive. Also, Meccans consider serving *al mubashara* to be chivalrous, revealing a sense of honour and *muruwa* (chivalry). Until the beginning of the twentieth century, the food would be served from dishes placed upon the floor, on *misaffa* (a circular mat of palm leaves about one metre in diameter). It was usual to use the hand for eating, but subsequently urban Hijazis adopted the spoon to eat most of their food, whereas in the other regions of the Arabian Peninsula the hand remained in use.

Food is also traditionally offered as a gift to others. Nearly every day, one's table would be graced at mealtime by at least one *tu 'ma* (plate) sent by a relative or friend. This plate would never be returned empty but always laden in return, if not with food then just with sugar. Such gifts of food are always brought to the house by messenger, never personally. A *dakhla* is another gift of food sometimes sent to the home. It is usually given in the form of a feast in honour of a homecoming. Food might also be offered to an extended family afflicted with a death. Distant relatives and close friends send cooked food, especially during the first three days of formal condolence.

◆ THE GASTRONOMIC REVIVAL

Meccan food all but disappeared from formal gatherings during the 1960s and 1970s, but saw a revival in the 1980s. The importance of food as a signifier of both relative family status and collective cultural distinctiveness has greatly increased during the phase of competitive tribalisation, especially for those Hijazis claiming origins in Mecca or Medina. The ways food is cooked, presented and consumed all serve to augment a common sense of identity amongst a people who are increasingly conscious of those cultural factors that separate them from others. Furthermore, food serves as a status indicator that distinguishes the elite from other sections of society, bolstering their standing as *wujaha* ('the face of the people') or *a 'yan an nas* ('the eyes or the example of the people'). Socially defined status, as we have seen before, is closely connected to conceptions of *tajammul* (seemliness) and to 'whitening the face' of the family. One way of exhibiting *tajammul* is through mastery of the minute details of consumption, quality, quantity, and presentation of food at formal events.

It is during the more religious traditional ceremonies, such as the *mawlid* or the *hawl*, that the meal is taken in a manner most closely resembling the ways of the 'romantic Hijaz'. On these occasions the meal is served on the floor, although white plastic tablecloths have been used in place of palm leaves. For everyday meals, as well as at other less traditional events such as a wedding party at a hotel, food is served at Western-style dining tables. Also, a wider variety of dishes are prepared for these latter occasions, drawing on the traditions of many different countries, Arab, Western and Oriental. At the more traditional religious events, forks are not used; instead the right hand or a spoon is used in order to emphasise tradition.

In addition to all the regular formal events, Meccan families hold 'Meccan nights' wherever they happen to be living. These events are replete with Meccan themes, objects and food, some of which are recreated from the past. There are, for example, special combinations of typically Meccan dishes, *mabshur* (small grilled meat balls), *mantu* (steamed pastry filled with mince meat) and *mittabbag* (a fine layer of pastry filled with eggs and chives) and sweet *mittabbag* (made with honey and bananas or with cheese and honey). Water flavoured with rose and other plants, like the *kadi*, is drunk from special Meccan water containers and bowls. These are all are served by men dressed in old Meccan dress and consumed by guests seated on high-backed Meccan benches, for which a brisk trade in reproductions has developed.

Other regions in the Arabian Peninsula have their own emphasis on honouring the guest, albeit in less detailed ceremonial ways, but this behaviour is particular to the Hijazi and especially to women. According to the rules for serving *al mubashara*, the more honoured guests, seated at 'the head of the table', are served by the more senior members of the family while the younger or less important guests, seated at the opposite end, are served by the younger members of the family. The *'awa'il* refer to the fact that, in Islam, the hosts should always be on hand to serve the guests, only eating later, regardless of differences in their status. They repeat the hadith: 'He who loves Allah and his messenger should be generous to his guest'. Even with an ostentatiously large number of domestic staff it is the 'people of the house' who actually serve the guests. The servants bring the food from the kitchen while the host or hostess and their immediate family offer it in the appropriate manner to the guests.

The guest is not left for a moment without being offered food: juice, nuts, dates, coffees (Nadji Arabic, Turkish) mint tea and Lipton tea, then dinner and again teas, coffees and a mixture of 'digestive' spices, betelnut, cardamom, cloves and peppermints; this combination is particularly Meccan. Before and especially after food is served *'uda* (incense) is burned and passed around as another sign of hospitality. Throughout the party the host or hostess and their extended family implore the guest, by God, to eat. Set compliments are exchanged in acknowledgement of the generosity, such as, 'May Allah make your house always prosperous', to which the host replies, 'with your presence only'.

◆ CONSPICUOUS CONSUMPTION AND PROTECTION FROM THE EVIL EYE

At first sight there appears to be a curious paradox related to conspicuous displays of status, including those related to food. On the one hand, it is imperative to make a show of it, to present it both quantitatively and qualitatively to guests, and to have a sufficient surplus from any party to be able to make widespread gifts to members of the extended family. On the other hand, there are almost absolute restrictions on what can be said about it. Food must be seen and noticed, but not witnessed or commented upon. The embargoes on the public criticism of food are deeply rooted, being closely tied to anxieties about *hassad* (the evil eye). Although the hostess and her family have gone to the trouble of preparing more than 30 dishes to cover their table for a 'tea invitation', when she asks the guests to proceed to the table she will say only, 'Please oblige us, come and drink some tea'. Traditional food has been safely reintroduced into the ceremonial meals of the *'awa'il*, and Hijazi 'superstitions' have played their part in the revival.

Re-emphasised tradition is closely linked to conspicuous consumption. A well-presented meal is very large and costly. Wealth allows people to organise social occasions at which they display grand meals, demonstrating their generosity and propriety. However, as widely abundant wealth becomes something of a social leveller, people are returning to traditional themes in order to set themselves apart. In the 1980s people placed less stress on quantity than on quality. If it is

143

suitably 'Meccan' even a very inexpensive dish will stand out in a grand meal of many Eastern and Western dishes. For example, what was once a poor man's meal, *ful midammas* (a dish of fava beans prepared with a sauce of clarified butter, cumin and lemon juice) now assumes pride of place in the eyes of the *'awa'il.*

Nevertheless, at a communal event there is nearly always considerably more food on the table than can possibly be consumed by members of the household and their guests. This gives the host family the chance to demonstrate their wealth and generosity to an audience far beyond the confines of the house or banquet hall, for every respectable, wealthy family has several other families to whom they regularly offer charity, in food, clothes, money etc. The leftovers from lavish banquets are usually distributed to relatives and poorer families by way of *sadaqa* (alms). On the evening of a big dinner or religious event, or the morning after, the chauffeurs go around from house to house distributing the food, with most relatives receiving their share. The food is such that it keeps well, even improving in flavour overnight.

The danger of *hassad* is greater in respect of certain categories of person and types of food, i.e. those who are either vulnerable or in a position to be envied. For example, *masluga*, the special chicken broth that the new mother consumes, is especially prone to the evil eye, as is the milk for an infant. These are always covered by a cloth or opaque paper for protection. Fruit is another vulnerable type of food, so baskets of fruit always stay covered until the moment their contents are about to be consumed. Any food that used to be a rarity or considered a delicacy is also held to be more susceptible.

There are various preventative measures against the evil eye, other than covering the food. One is not to mention the names of particular dishes such as *laham* (meat), but instead to refer to it obliquely by another word, such as *cucu* or *haila*. The latter is taught to children, for they are most vulnerable. Displaying strong feelings towards food, such as eating heartily in front of a large group, or passing comment upon the dishes, not only is considered inelegant and similar to Bedouins' manners, but also risks exposure to the evil eye. For this reason it is customary for women to eat a light meal called *talbiba* or *tasbira* (appeasement of hunger) at home prior to attending a formal dinner party. This is also partly to convey elegance and refinement, for appearing to be hungry in front of others is not considered dignified. Upon seeing a banquet polite guests will always say only *masha'llah*, ('whatever Allah wishes'), in a stage whisper, to express their goodwill and admiration without remarking directly on the fare.

Opportunities for passing judgement on the meal are limited, for although people do exchange a few words at meal times, there is no tradition of formal table conversation. It is considered bad manners for those who have finished eating to sit 'counting the morsels', which could cause the evil eye. According to Quranic verse, 'If you have eaten, disperse even if you are enjoying conversation'.[4] All guests are seated at the same time, and the rule is that guests should get up on finishing without waiting for those who are still eating. The time spent sitting at a meal thus depends solely on how much and how fast an individual eats.

When a person is suspected of having received the evil eye while eating, a condition people describe as *jatu lugma* ('receiving a morsel'), a *sayyid* is sought to remove the 'morsel'. The stomach is rid of the evil eye by the application of a piece of wet cotton wool to the afflicted part and by the power of the *sayyid*'s prayers. Not many people engage in this type of remedy today, but other beliefs and healing procedures frowned upon by the puritanical Wahhabis are still secretly practised. The only measure publicly acknowledged as being sound is the repetition of a particular *sura* from the Quran.[5]

◆ THE HOME AS THE SITE OF INNOVATION AND TRADITION

The home makes an unequivocally vital contribution to guarding and developing Hijazi cuisine. Traditionally, the only places for eating outside the home have been the *gahawi* (popular eating places) or cafes where men eat outdoors seated on high benches, rounding out their meals with tea and *shisha* (waterpipe). No woman would ever eat in a public place. Even for men of the *'awa'il* it is considered *'ayb* (shameful) to eat in the public environment of the *souk* (market). Western-style restaurants have now opened. Most are part of the international chains of hotels offering Chinese, Japanese, European and Middle Eastern food. These cater to expatriates living in Saudi Arabia, although some Saudi Arabians, including Hijazi *'awa'il* have started to patronise them. Nevertheless, the segregation of genders continues to be enforced by patrolling *mutaw'a* (religious police) .

Food in the home has always been the responsibility of women (although some Hijazi men take pride in gourmet cooking). Visual and oral transmission has passed the recipes down from mother to daughter. In the past, female slaves who lived as part of the family helped in cooking the family recipes. Today most women of the *'awa'il* do not cook, leaving it instead to male foreign cooks, usually Filipino, Lebanese, Sudanese, Egyptian or Moroccan. These professional cooks, however, are taught the Hijazi recipes by the lady of the house or by a knowledgeable female member of the maternal or paternal family. Although she may pride herself on not having to cook (since having a cook is an indicator of high status), a woman of the *'awa'il* will still pride herself on possessing the knowledge of traditional Hijazi cuisine.[6]

It is common amongst men to explain the difference between men's and women's food, dress, elaborate manner of formal greeting, speech and so on, in terms of women being more concerned about 'appearances' than men. They like variety, which is not in the nature of men. Of course, this understates the significance of women's concerns. Bringing customs and ceremonies back into formal life has depended a great deal on the capacity of the domestic, female sphere. Without this repository of historical knowledge, and without the interest in 'appearances' needed for innovation and the detailed elaboration of formality, there may have been little to show for the Hijazi revival.

◆ CONCLUSION: CYCLES OF INNOVATION AND JUDGEMENT

Given the dense web of formalities among the *'awa'il* that regulate their communal spaces, these cannot be places in which innovations occur and are developed. Communal spaces, rather, are testing grounds for innovations made in the relative safety of the private sphere. The focus here has therefore shifted back to the family. This sheds new light on the significance of the metaphorical walls built around the family. Within these walls, shielded from critical communal and public gazes, innovations can be developed before being subjected to wider and potentially damaging scrutiny.

Similarly, communal spaces are not public spheres in which critical judgements are formulated in more or less formalised debates. Judgement, like innovation, belongs to the private sphere. It is in the private sphere that people decide whether or not to accede to innovations encountered at communal gatherings. It is here that people seek to determine whether or not innovations meet the criteria of acceptability. The privacy of the family sphere provides a place in which judgements are exercised and where the criteria of judgement are elaborated. Such judgements, however, are not made once and for all, for both innovations and judgements are advanced only tenuously, as moments of a continuous process of development.

9

Cultivating the Social Arts III: The Adaptation of Hijazi Dress to the New Social Order

◆ INTRODUCTION: CHANGING THE HABITS OF A LIFETIME

C LOTHING AND OTHER bodily ornamentation generally express an individual's or a group's sense of identity, belonging and cultural distinctiveness. Dress links people to specific times and places, to a community, a particular socio-economic position, an age group, a gender role and so on. Identities, however, are historically fluid, as social, economic and political arrangements in any given society change, and such changes may be marked by and influence the way people dress. As a result, dress is a persistently shifting cultural phenomenon that indicates a person's social, geographical and historical location.

The character of the Hijazi *'awa'il*[1] has been shaped by their responses to key historical moments and processes in contemporary Saudi Arabia. This has left profound traces on the nature of dress, which has become an increasingly important means of expressing and perceiving social status and identity. Changes in the pattern of dress broadly correspond to three phases of recent history. The first years after unification were marked by efforts to promote national cohesion and homogeneity, resulting in the standardisation of

149

Najdi dress as the Saudi norm in public or outdoors. From the 1950s until the 1980s, Western fashions exerted a growing influence on women's indoor dress, worn under the black Saudi *'abaya* (veil), while men maintained the uniformity of dress. This period reached its height during the oil boom of the 1970s. Enthusiasm for unadulterated Western tastes then began to dim, and Saudi Arabia has since been characterised by various attempts to assert local, regional, Arab and Islamic 'models' onto cosmopolitan fashion for women, along with subtle re-adoption of Hijazi Islamic dress for men, constituting the *jubba* jacket and the *'umama* turban, which distinguishes them from Najdis and their looser fitting robes.

Focusing on changing patterns of dress allows a number of themes to be explored in greater detail. In particular, distinctive dress reflects the gendering of Hijazi social life, such that men and women register social and political influences somewhat differently. Women's dress, especially that adopted for the more formal *'awa'il* gatherings, provides a very clear illustration of the relations between the two phases of 'openness' and subsequent 'Hijazification'. Throughout these two periods there was, for example, a continuous emphasis on subtle indicators of status and *savoir faire* that was expressed in the transformation of the demands made by the *'awa'il* on Western fashion houses. The shifts in women's dress also accentuated the distinctions between the private, communal and public spheres, with distinct patterns of change occurring in each.

◆ PATTERNS IN MOTION

Prior to 1932 dress was but one aspect of widely differing ways of life, so it varied from one cultural zone to another. Equally, within each zone dress served to mark out a variety of social distinctions. Political unification under the Al Saud rulers entailed an effort by the ruling elite to control the vast country through the elimination of potentially separatist tendencies. Abdul Aziz Al Saud, anxious to harmonise cultural variations, decreed that all men serving in government positions must wear the Najdi Bedouin dress (the one seen in Saudi Arabia today).

Regional differences still persist, however. Asir, for example, has kept its local colourful dress for both men and women because this largely peasant community maintained a greater degree of independence from the government until the 1990s.[2] The use of colour marks regional differences. Desert people from the heart of the Peninsula, for example, traditionally favour brighter, stronger colours: reds, orange, yellow, blues and greens. This is both for house decoration and women's clothing. Urban Hijazis prefer pastels or muted greys, blues, greens or beige. Older Hijazi women explain that it is more 'elegant' to wear quiet, subdued colours with smaller motifs. They also add that it is only the Bedouins who wear 'loud' colours with big motifs.

Urban Hijazi men in the early twentieth century wore a long white outer garment, with trousers underneath, and a belt. The head was always covered by the *'umama* (head-dress). Minor distinctions were apparent, signifying differences in occupation and status.[3] These distinctions were mainly based on the manner in which the *'umama* was tied and the type and colour of the material, as well as the width of the belt and the length of the *sirwal* (trousers) worn under the outer garment. For example, *tujjar* (merchants) dressed differently from *'ulema* (religious teachers) and *mutawwifin* (guides to the pilgrims), while the dress of the *za'im al-hara* (head of the district) differed from that of the *'amat an-nas* (common people) and the *shabab* (young men).[4]

Prior to unification, the distinction between inside and outside the home, and that between domestic and formal occasions, regulated urban Hijazi women's dress. Formal wear for women of Mecca, Medina and Jeddah commonly consisted of a *zabun* (long fitted dress).[5] Under this was a *sideriya* (blouse or bodice), which showed through an opening in the *zabun*. The blouse was fastened by six buttons of silver, gold or diamonds, depending on the wealth of the women. For facial make-up, traditional oils were used, as was *kohl* to line the eyes. The hair was centre-parted and partly covered by a *midawwara* (white head cover). Older Hijazi women explained that women prided themselves on the art of wearing the *midawwara*: The way it was wrapped revealed a woman's elegance and social status. There was also a vocabulary elaborated specifically to describe such elegance in upper-class urban female dress. When going out, Hijazi women wore pale coloured veils, which left the face and some of the hair uncovered.[6] The women of the *Ashraf* Hashemite ruling family were particularly famous for their long plaits, kept on both sides of their shoulders.

Formal occasions traditionally placed an accent on exhibiting a family's wealth. It was common practice, for instance, to borrow or rent expensive jewellery to display on the occasion of a wedding. All those involved, the bride and her family, as well as the guests, would adorn themselves in this way. The more jewellery the bride had on, the more the spectacle was appreciated and admired. There are stories about how young brides swooned under the weight of the jewels in the intense heat. This was a matter of pride as it reflected the wealth of the family (even if most of the jewels were rented), as well as showing the youth and delicacy of the bride. Her jewellery and everyone else's in those days were Eastern in origin, made in India and Indonesia.

◆ SQUEEZING OUT REGIONALISM

While the distinctions between private, communal and public spheres have persisted, the various forms of pre-unification Hijazi dress have now become, in effect, 'museum pieces'. Early twentieth-century dress has succumbed to transformations comparable to social changes imposed during the colonial era. Current Hijazi feeling regards this as the denial of their particular identity, holding that such radical change simply emphasises the political dominance of the Najdi ruling elite. Behind this general disappearance of traditional

Hijazi dress, though, there are different explanations for the ways in which dress has changed.

The nature and pace of change to Hijazi dress codes have been gendered. For male dress the influence, not to say pressure, for change has had a clear political character. For female dress the influences have been, initially, those of the Wahhabi religious establishment in public spaces, the international market in private spaces and, since the 1980s, Hijazification in specifically communal spaces. Without being required to cover themselves in the same way as women when they move between home and the outside world, men experience less of a distinction between dress requirements for the two spheres. Male dress, due in part to the proximity of the Hijazi elite to the Saudi government, is therefore far more dependent on developments regulating appearances beyond the home. Between the 1930s and the 1970s many Hijazi *'awa'il* men occupied significant positions, benefiting from the area's economic and cultural position in the centre of the Arabian Peninsula.[7] Since the 1980s, however, they have been subject to relative political marginalisation from government. The proximity to government in the earlier period dictated that outdoor wear conformed rigorously to the Najdi requirements for national dress. All men of high status, such as ministers and senior government officials, wear the *mishlah* (cloak). Among the Hijazis, young men only wear a *mishlah* on formal occasions such as the *milka* (men's wedding party) or the *'aza* (condolence ceremony). For these occasions the more formal black cloak is worn in preference to the beige. During the wedding the groom stands out in a white *mishlah*. Older men wear it at all formal occasions, such as dinner parties, as well as when going to the mosque. The *mishlah* can be seen as a status indicator of those Hijazis included in the official political order.

Women, of course, faced pressures to conform to national outdoor dress codes after unification. Officially sanctioned moves against regional identity required the wearing of a severe black veil by all women. The principal justification for its prevalence, however, has been provided by Wahhabist

153

strictures on women's modesty. Equally, the enforcement of this measure has been left to the members of the Committee for the Order of the Good and the Forbidding of the Evil, who make sure that women are veiled properly in all public places.[8] Failure to be veiled results in serious reprimand, even punishment. Attitudes toward the veil, as between strictly religious and more liberal Saudis, remain subject to intense debate. Since the 1990s there has been an increase in dogmatic trends, symbolised by an even more severe form of veiling apparent across all regions and sections of Saudi society.[9] Nevertheless, regional differences remain. The stricter version of the national veil is more likely to be seen in Riyadh than in Jeddah or Mecca. The veil-enforcing Wahhabis are all non-Hijazis. Most Hijazi women resent being bossed around and they increasingly recognise the political significance of this. A Hijazi woman in her thirties recounted to me with enthusiasm her recent encounter with a member of this committee in a Jeddah shopping mall. She said that as he ordered her to cover her face she replied 'No, by Allah! I shall not cover my face, my grandmother did not cover hers, nor did my mother, why should I do so?'

◆ A TASTE FOR THE WEST

Hijazi women have enjoyed relative freedom of choice in matters of clothing for both indoor and formal life, these spheres being insulated from the political pressures on women to follow in men's footsteps and transform their dress. In the formal sphere there has been tremendous change in women's dress, initially from traditional Hijazi forms to Western and then to an admixture of the two, which was both more gradual than that experienced by men and driven by other forces. Indoor wear has been the least open to external pressures of any kind, so here we find the greatest degree of continuity with tradition.

Three broad phases of change in female Hijazi formal dress may be discerned. The first two belong to the periods of 'openness' and indicate the growing proximity of Saudi Arabia to the Western core of international markets, while the third reflects the impact of Hijazification on those same markets. The first major steps towards forms of Western clothing were taken during the 1950s. Fashions were inspired by the West, but via Egypt, generally through Egyptian films popular during that period, reflecting Egyptians' closer relations to the West. By the 1970s Hijazi *'awa'il* women not only had immediate access to Western fashion, but with the advent of oil wealth they had their pick of the very finest clothes on offer. However, as time passed the direction of influence changed, and Hijazi women experienced these changes in common with many others in the Islamic world. As Nicholas Coleridge has commented, 'Between 1976 and 1986 Islamic taste first embraced Western high fashion and then, in a most striking way, modified and in some respects even undermined it'.[10] By the end of the period Western designers were responding to these changing demands from the Arabian Peninsula, and in particular to those of the *'awa'il*.

All Saudi Arabian women, as well Hijazis, enjoyed the fruits of oil wealth, but the latter also faced certain problems. Rapid changes in fortunes, both economic and political, meant that Hijazi women found themselves in a situation of increased social and geographic mobility in which they needed to maintain status and respectability, especially vis-à-vis the Najdis. The women of the *'awa'il* drew on their sense of superior refinement in a competition that was particularly fierce among themselves. As a result, a highly nuanced appreciation of Western dress became a significant status indicator among the *'awa'il*. All women must always dress 'suitably' for the social occasion, acknowledging the status of the hostess and her guests and, most importantly, expressing their own social status and Hijazi identity. There are, however, generational differences as the pattern of change partly reflects the changing economic contexts within which new generations have grown up. The *zabun* is still seen at the start of the twenty-first century but is only worn by older women, on whom it is considered dignified.[11] Younger women happily wear the *zabun* to express their 'Saudi Arabian herit-age' at charity parties and so on, but would not otherwise appear 'ridiculous', dressing inappropriately. As these public charities only express Saudi national identity, the Hijazi dress is referred to as Saudi while all attending know that it is spe-cific to the Hijaz.

◆ ASSUMING A GREATER MODESTY

There was no diminution of the significance of designer dress or of the requirement to make a show of one's wealth during the 1980s and 1990s. However, with a general return to 'tradi-tion' and to more narrowly and rigorously defined Islamic practices, Hijazi women became more conscious of the requirement for modesty in dress. Knowledge of and adher-ence to religious consideration is, alongside Hijazi identity, as much a source of pride as being fashion conscious. As a result, the direction of influence between producers and con-sumers has been reversed, to some extent. The women of the Hijazi *'awa'il* do not want to fall behind in the competition in 'piety' and have the purchasing power to make demands on fashion designers. Women only consider *muhtasham* (mod-est), and not *'uryan* (naked), dresses by named designers suitable for formal occasions. Similarly, Hijazi women find attractive and appropriate to their status jewellery that looks Eastern but is made in Europe by famous designers. This both keeps and reinforces their cosmopolitan status and iden-tity, and serves to conform to emerging domestic standards.

Since the 1980s *'awa'il* women observed well-defined codes of formal dress. A modest dress is one that is long, covering the ankles, with long sleeves and preferably a high collar. The collar also keeps the chin high and thus looks 'dignified'. The dress preserves modesty by minimising exposure but must be well tailored and close fitting, following the lines of the body and especially the *mikassam* (waist). The dress is some-how reminiscent of the Hijazi *zabun*.[12]

Colours generally are a vital expression of Hijazi women's status and reputation. There are, for instance, social sanctions against cross-generational dressing. At weddings black is considered elegant for all, with the exception of the unmarried, for whom it is considered too 'heavy'. Equally, Hijazi older women would not wear red or the various shades of pink, as such colours are thought to indicate vivacity and sexuality. An older woman wearing red or pink would be criticised as being 'light', without poise. Generally older Hijazi women wear pale colours, light grey, mauve, pale green or blue. It is the younger women who wear darker and more vivacious tones. This colour consciousness among the Hijazis stems from their urban background, which brought together women from diverse origins who wore all colours irrespective of age. These colour-conscious rules for dress are much more relaxed for women of the Najd.

On the whole, Hijazi women's colours are worn regardless of season, while masculine colours are only white or pale cream during the hot weather and beige, brown, grey, black or navy blue during the winter.[13] Men are also restricted in terms of the material they may wear: for them silk is considered a *haram* (sin). There is a known *hadith*: 'It has been forbidden, *haram*, for the males of my nation, *umma*, to wear silk and gold but it has been permitted for the females.'[14]

◆ AT HOME IN THE *SOUK*

During the 1950s and 1960s Western influence spread, borne by markets, to large parts of Saudi Arabian society. Markets did not only penetrate the formal spaces of the *'awa'il* but breached barriers surrounding the more private spaces of the home. Most people, both the rich and other urban strata, began to wear Western-style clothes indoors and informally with friends and family. The patterns affecting everyone were very similar. Clothes 'hanging in the *souks*' were imported from nearby countries, such as Morocco and Egypt that had established clothes manufacturing industries.

In the privacy of their own homes, the *'awa'il* are simply not under the same pressures as they are in the communal sphere to make every effort to accentuate distinctions in status. Changes to elite indoor dress are not driven by the same persistent attempts to create distances from others. Indeed, if anything, the pressures run in the opposite direction, as elites have been forced to demonstrate greater identification with popular sentiment across the Islamic world. Indoor dress therefore conforms more closely to that of the rest of the society, with the women of the *'awa'il* wearing clothes and jewellery similar to that which may be found 'hanging in the *souks*'. For instance, whereas the women of the *'awa'il* would never wear Indian or Bahraini Eastern-style jewellery at a formal gathering, they do wear it in the privacy of their own homes and among their relatives. Consisting of bangles, chains or multi-layered necklaces, this jewellery is what is used by most other people. It is also bought and worn by foreigners, mostly Americans and Europeans, who view it as traditional 'ethnic' jewellery.

Similarly, women from all regions and different sections of society now wear a dress known as a *thob*, a long, relatively loose garment that usually has some embroidery on it. It resembles the originally male garment but is more 'feminine' in appearance: its cut is more close fitting and it can be different colours.[15] It is worn frequently since it is comfortable and easy to care for, straightforwardly cut and without difficult pleats. Although there are more expensive versions of the *thob*, it is not considered suitable for formal gatherings, except for Ramadan evenings. As a result of its ubiquity, women of the elite would not ask a famous European designer to make a *thob* for them for fear that it would be mistaken for a common one 'from the *souk*'. Most elite women now wear it at home, when amongst the extended family and close friends, and they would also wear it under the veil when going shopping to the *souk*, and while visiting relatives and close friends.

Curiously, the *thob*, a tradition invented during the early 1970s, has today become a kind of national dress for women, and is widely believed to be 'traditional'. However, the custom appears to have originated with some Western women who wore the men's Saudi *thob* as 'ethnic-chic'. It then appeared amongst some women of the cosmopolitan *'awa'il*. After this it spread throughout urban areas, where it carried 'intellectual' connotations in the view of its relatively better educated and more travelled domestic initiators.

There have, then, been notable changes to indoor dress. Women of the *'awa'il* had given up, for a few decades, dress that indicated their specifically local identity. They had put aside dress which indicated their regional background and city of origin for the cultural anonymity of Western styles. The new dress, the *thob*, combines aspects of Arab dress in general, whether it is Palestinian, Jordanian, Syrian, Lebanese, Egyptian or North African. It indicates a wider Arabian identity. The *thob* can therefore be seen as something of a return to traditional indoor dress, its use part of the general assertion of self-consciously indigenous codes and the 'return' to Arabic, non-Western values. The garment being worn in their everyday lives is seen as especially comfortable and reassuring at a time of increased globalisation and homogenisation. By wearing it, women of all ages are identifying themselves as Arabs and as Muslims in what is perceived to be a Western-dominated world.

◆ CONCLUSIONS: PATTERNS IN TIME AND SPACE

Changes in modes of dress over time can be a register of shifting social relations such that history might be said to expresses itself in dress. *'Awa'il* dress has indeed registered changes of this kind in recent history, as it has been imprinted by Najdi nationalism, Western-oriented markets and the two cultural strands of contemporary tribalisation: Islamisation and Hijazification.

The pattern of change reveals the many forces pulling the *'awa'il* in various directions, as well as demonstrating their own attempts to exercise some degree of control. Outdoor dress both for men and women has seen little change since the 1930s and remains under the virtually total control of the Committee and its employees, the *mutaw'a* (religious police). Dress codes in this sphere conform to the political-religious strictures of Najdi nationalism, highlighting the scope of the state's imposition on personal life. Western influence on women's indoor and formal dress remains strong, but it has passed its zenith. Nevertheless, dress codes express the extent to which these spheres have become increasingly com-modified. They also illustrate how trade has become, more or less directly, occidental rather than oriental, even though ties with the East have by no means been broken. The manner of the 'return' of the *thob* reveals a very peculiar pattern of change. The *thob* comes out of indigenous traditions, but its present character depended on as Western tastes for exotica, Hijazi and cosmopolitan tradition and indigenous re-adoption.

The *'awa'il*, then, have been both trendsetters and have responded to trends emanating from elsewhere, such as mar-kets and popular processes of Islamisation. One result of the coincidence of these two processes is that indigenously gen-erated Hijazi values have, to some extent, been woven into existing market relations, regionalising and Islamising mass produced commodities and *haute couture* alike. In this con-text, the *'awa'il* have played a significant role in creating new choices for others to follow. Their status is such that they can establish new rules and codes, which may then filter out into the rest of society.

Shifting dress codes express a complex interplay between the historical phases of political and economic change and the differentiations between the private, communal and pub-lic spheres. Each sphere is subject to different pressures and possibilities, and changes within each have a rhythm of their own. These differentiations are significant for the processes of Hijazification. Indeed, as the evolution of dress has revealed, the processes through which the identity of the *'awa'il* have been transformed in recent times cannot be understood without taking into consideration both the place of the Hijaz in the wider world and the internal relations between the different spheres in which Hijazi life is lived out.

10 Conclusion

◆ THE GLOBAL HIJAZ

T HE CENTRAL AIM of this study of the Hijazi *'awa'il*[1] has been to provide a close analysis of Hijazification and to demonstrate that the most important of the processes to which it is a response is the Saudification of Saudi Arabia. The twentieth century saw the institutions of the national state spread throughout the world. This transformation of political geography has necessarily entailed attempts by state builders to integrate diverse communities and group identities into relatively homogeneous national cultures. But, just as political elites the world over have sought to establish themselves as leaders of unified nation-states, their efforts at cultural integration have been contested, not least in Saudi Arabia. Hijazification attests to the huge variations in these forms of contestation, and their outcomes.

There have been three broad phases in the relationship between the Hijaz and Saudi Arabia. The first began 1932 with the unification of the country, when Saudi and Arabian identities came to the fore. The second period, characterised by openness to change from the West, began soon after, with the discovery of oil in the late 1930s. The *Zeitgeist* became clearer in the 1950s, when large oil revenues began pouring in, and reached its peak in the oil booms of 1973 and 1979. The start of the most recent period, characterised by internal and external religious revivals,[2] can be dated to the collapse in oil prices in 1983 and the subsequent recession in Saudi

Arabia, with the Gulf War in 1990–1, which re-entrenched American presence in Saudi Arabia, representing the era's greatest watershed. It is during this final period that the criteria of social competition and status definition have shifted towards 'traditional' or qualitative themes, as opposed to 'material' or economic ones.

Trade and communications have of course been of central importance to the political and cultural processes of contested national integration. They have also been profoundly significant in relation to cross-national, regional and international integration, which has also been contested. Overall, the forces of economic, political and cultural integration, and their opposites—those of differentiation and contestation—occurring in the Hijaz could be said to be common features of globalisation.

In general terms, then, Hijazification is no different from ethnic identity formation elsewhere in the world. This study, though, has been concerned with the specific nature of Hijazi ethnic transformation. It has used a careful and detailed ethnographic approach to investigate the ways in which the Hijaz has acquired its peculiar qualities through a series of historical phases, each of which combined distinct international, regional and national processes, and contained its own mix of economic, political and cultural characteristics.

◆ CULTURE AS POLITICS

The modification and invention of tradition in the Hijaz has served several fundamental purposes. First and foremost, it is primarily the *'awa'il*'s attempt to compensate for a relative decline in political and economic influence by emphasising cultural distinctiveness. In the Saudi Arabian context this turn towards the cultural sphere is largely due to the constraints imposed by the Saudi state on explicitly political controversy. The limits are such that, for example, it is forbidden even to make public reference to locally specific identities: Najdi dominance has come to be reflected in the narrow definitions of cultural life prevailing within the public sphere.

This dominance has meant that the political elite in Saudi Arabia centres around the Najdi royal family, who have exclusive title to political office. The Wahhabi religious elite are closely connected to them, with each reinforcing the legitimacy of the other. In practice, though, the relative position of the religious elite has fluctuated according to the personal stance and determination of the ruler and the prevalent internal and external political, economic and religious circumstances. The broad pattern of the stratification of the political elite is determined by the Najdi tribal system of alliances. Those closest to the royal family (besides the religious elite) are their affines, largely the Al Sudeiri family. Next in rank are *gabili* (members of families of 'pure' Najdi blood); third in line are *khadiri* (Najdis of less pure blood). Hijazis rank below these and are thus effectively considered to be fourth-class citizens.

The Hijazis' low political status is based on wholly different criteria than those used to determine the position of *gabili* and *khadiri*. It is not predicated on kinship ties of any kind, but on the utility and necessity of relationships arising out of the accidents of history. The families of the Hijaz owe their position within the elite of Saudi Arabia to their having been the political and economic elite of the Hijaz prior to unification, and to the fact that their skills and experience proved invaluable during the first 50 or so years of the Saudi state. While there is recognition amongst Najdis that the historical background of the *'awa'il* deserves some respect, it is not of the same significance as that given to members of family and tribe. Although the *'awa'il* have been inside the state elite, they have remained outside tribal boundaries. The Hijazis have therefore been vulnerable to the perception that they are no longer necessary. Their status, and the potential vulnerability it confers, has not changed in recent times. Rather, since the 1980s, political power has been concentrated under the authority of seven Al Sudeiri brothers. It is as a part of this process that the *'awa'il* have been relatively marginalised, both politically and economically.

Prior to this period, Hijazi cultural distinctiveness was not of great significance, except insofar as it ultimately ensured low status within the national elite. There was little to be gained in emphasising such distinctions as long as Hijazis could look forward to playing an important role within the state. However, once the Sudeiris embarked on the business of displacing Hijazis and monopolising the top political, administrative and economic positions, Hijazi cultural distinction and status came to be seen in a quite different light. Saudification marked an intensifying of the process of homogenising public culture, but it also reinforced the significance of regional differentiation. That differentiation had already been fostered by the effective encouragement of endogamy amongst Hijazis. Within the relatively clear boundaries created by intermarriages, the *'awa'il* responded to their displacement with the process of Hijazification. They adopted the language and practices of tribalisation, and they set about clearly defining what it meant to belong to a rival tribe in the Hijaz.

◆ THE COMPENSATING COMFORTS OF DISTINCTION

The ethnographic accounts provided here describe the specific stances that the Hijazi elite patronymic groups have been adopting in order to reassert their cultural heritage and their sense of social importance, in response to their displacement from above. Hijazi culture has come to be perceived as not only distinctive, but as superior in relation to those of the Najd and other groups in the Arabian Peninsula. Members of the *'awa'il* appear to think that 'If we do not have political precedence then at least we have social precedence', or 'If Najdis, *gabili* or *khadiri* are nearer to the King, we have something that these people do not have. Their social world is not ours'.

Hijazification should thus be seen as a response to tremendous changes in the way national integration took place. Relative marginalisation partially explains why the process occurred at all, but from one of the first of the ethnographic investigations, on marriage, it became clear that the *'awa'il* were quite selective in drawing on the past. By locating the emergence of this new tribe within a broader context, the varying levels of emphasis given to different aspects of the past can be better understood.

Amongst the most salient features of the wider context of Hijazification is widespread popular Islamisation. Hijazification is a challenge to Najdi cultural dominance and a rejection of the pretensions to national cultural leadership of the Najdi elite. It is a rival form of social integration that, like the Najdi-dominated project, has both embraced and sought to regulate the growth of popular Islamisation. Indeed, Hijazification should be seen as one form of the widespread 'democratic' assertion of Islamic identities. Political elites across the Arab world, having passed through a phase in which they were relatively uncritical in their adoption of activities and lifestyles coming from other, largely Western, cultures, were forced to confront popular opinion.[3] It became a hallmark of popular sentiment that Saudi Arabia's essential moral values were under threat. In a context in which claims about political and religious authority came under popular criticism, the Hijazi elite turned to the 'romantic Hijaz' and the 'cradle of Islam' for inspiration, and sought to secure a relatively autonomous form of leadership by reshaping social relations and redefining Hijazis' place in the world.

The new terms which the Hijazi elite developed to judge themselves and others are regarded as long-cultivated urban manners, styles of dress and speech and, of course, Sunni (Shafi'i, Hanafi and Maliki) religious rituals. Unable to engage in overtly political competition they have chosen to emphasise, even exaggerate, the ideas and practices of Hijazi culture: *usul* (propriety), *'adat* (customs), *tagalid* (traditions), and *tagwa* (piety). They have sought to establish themselves as an autonomous cultural leadership by fashioning their own criteria of judgement, and by establishing themselves as the final arbiters. Their success is confirmed by the aspiration of upwardly mobile non-elite Hijazis to join the ranks of the *'awa'il*. It is also apparent in the growth of cultural concerns, even fears, especially amongst the third generation (those born since 1970), of being submerged in the public movement towards national homogeneity. These Saudis, formally educated under the terms of a national curriculum that stresses 'Saudi' history, dialect and manners, now readily question what it means to be Saudi. Cultural issues have come to the fore and people commonly raise the concern that their 'own' urban and heterogeneous customs and traditions will be absorbed into a uniform national and religious culture defined solely by the ruling elite.

The social relations of the family, communal and public spheres provided the terrain on which the alternative project could be developed. While Najdi dominance of public spaces has fostered Islamisation, Hijazi communal spaces have become increasingly formalised and regulated according to new, specifically Hijazi, rules of conduct. It is here that the revival, modification and reinvention of tradition is on display. The intensive formalisation of the communal sphere has been critical to the development of the new Hijazi culture and identity, and the preservation and defence of group cohesion.

The revival of tradition and the 'return' to how their grandparents lived offers a great deal to the *'awa'il*. It provides an urgently desired sense of continuity in a situation of rapid economic, political and social change, as well as a means of coping with the increased social mobility resulting from economic distribution based on official patronage. This system of distribution gives rise to fierce competition between rival elite patronymic groups in the region, but the observance of 'tradition' also offers these groups both a sense of non-competitive identification with the local elite groups and an identification with their regional culture. The modification or the invention of tradition fosters a more corporate sense of Hijazi elite status and symbolises aspirations to the cohesion of the Hijaz as a cultural entity with the *'awa'il* as its leader. It also assists in regulating entry to the elite by making emulation of the details of cultural practices exceedingly difficult.

◆ FROM RULES TO BOUNDARIES

The formal regulation of the communal sphere prevents it from being a site of explicit competition, innovation or critical judgement. During the oil boom, particularly in 1979, everyone among the *'awa'il* as well as the other Najdi elites and those considered *nouveau riche*, had access to wealth. Since then, the *'awa'il* has resorted to other means to distinguish their social status. The harnessing of tradition to conspicuous consumption is recorded throughout the ethnography. However, the role of conspicuous consumption has changed from one that is essential to formal activities or events to one that merely 'supports' or 'gives effect to' traditional ceremonies: it has become a means rather than an end. During the 1970s money was perhaps a social leveller. But this situation was only temporary, obtaining while social mobility based on economic power was at its greatest. Other criteria have since been superimposed on those of economic wealth.

Communal gatherings now display a more complex notion of status whose overarching concern is to keep up appearances according to the new criteria that have come to embody social (or behavioural) norms rather than material position. This is because social norms are less tangible and harder to imitate, hence more amenable to regulating the entry of newcomers. While competition continues, the emphasis in communal spaces is on the purity of ideas as expressed, for example, by the ethnic evenings, 'Meccan nights' or traditional rituals such ceremonies as the *ghumra*, and on group solidarity, expressed in the *mawlids* and the *majlis*.

The effects of this are nowhere clearer than in the case of weddings, in which these new communally shared criteria of judgement determine the answer to the fundamental question of whether or not marriage ties can be established between families. The patterns of marriage reflect the incorporation of newly acquired wealth into the Hijazi elite on terms that help to sustain the status of elite families. The internal alliance structure of the *'awa'il* has been built up around these ties, leading to an increasingly integrated cultural elite capable of playing a leading role in the pattern of cultural development.

Hijazification is, in this sense, a hegemonic project, albeit one that is locally confined. It is also one that is not immediately dependent on the formal political institutions of the state but rather is based on the informal institutions of the family and communal sphere. Since the formalised character of communal spaces prevents them from being places of overt innovation and scrutiny these have occurred in family spaces. The examination of food in particular shows how the protection afforded to the family sphere enables a cycle of display and judgement to take place between it and the communal sphere. The family sphere is where innovations are made before being introduced into the communal sphere, and it is in the family sphere that judgements about such innovations are made.

The various influences of the public sphere, be they through direct participation in the economy or religious events, or through the ever-growing media, have their impact on individual families. The privacy of family spaces provides arenas within which responses to these influences can be developed and then introduced into the communal sphere and subjected to wider judgement. The chapter on clothing, for instance, also brought out how these cycles of influence, innovation and judgement are often complex, with influences of different kinds combining over periods of time to produce sometimes surprising results. The history of the *thob*, moving from the *souk* to Western markets, and from there back into the homes of the *'awa'il*, attests to this.

◆ THE FUTURE OF THE HIJAZ

How these patterns will play out in the future cannot be predicted with any certainty, but the general tendencies that can reasonably be expected to be at work in the medium term are fairly clear. The overall patterns of integration and differentiation will persist, as will the basic differentiations of *'awa'il* life, those between the family, communal and public spheres. As before, it will most likely be the patterns of interaction that are subject to change. Moreover, while all the pressures towards integration will continue at the international, regional, national and local levels, the pressures towards differentiation will be most keenly felt locally and nationally.

National, regional and international integration will be most apparent in ways affected by trade, business and communications. Intensifying global economic integration will see the continuation of tendencies towards homogeneous institutions and working practices, and will increase the pressures for acquiring appropriate professional and educational qualifications. The likely result of this for the *'awa'il* is that educational status will grow in significance as a criterion for determining the suitability of Hijazi elite status. On the other hand, local integration is the process of Hijazification itself. As this process persists and draws more people into its ambit it will face greater contestation. The chapter on death rituals, in particular, draws attention to the range of Hijazi interpretations of Islam, ranging from liberal to conservative. These differences are a source of potential difficulty as the social base expands, one that threatens the ability to maintain a clearly defined and widely shared conception of communal life. Unlike the Najdi, the *'awa'il* do not possess political institutions over which they exercise a monopoly of control and through which they can exercise their authority. The price of success in establishing new terms for communal identification is that they become democratised.

National and regional tendencies are closely connected. Despite their differences, the *'awa'il* remain dependent on more or less direct ties to state officials for access to economic goods and political influence. They also have a profound interest in the maintenance of social and political stability. So long as the Saudi state retains its capacity to provide this, the Hijazi *'awa'il* will share vital common interests with it. These interests limit the extent to which the *'awa'il* are likely to distance themselves from the state.

There is, however, a significant tendency towards regional integration and wider cultural identification with Arabs across the Gulf. Increased travel and more sophisticated low-cost telecommunications only serve to reinforce this tendency, while deepening business and other institutional ties also continue to push in this direction. Unresolved political issues affecting the region, such as the issue of Palestine, are sources of potential political difficulties for the Saudi state and could give rise to further tensions between factions making up its elite. All in all, globalisation creates links between different localities and can mean that identity formation elsewhere in the region might yet have considerable bearing on the Hijaz.

These latter considerations are of course more speculative than those relating to economic integration and its likely consequences on the criteria of *'awa'il* membership. So the final pages of this study will return to the theme with which it began, by considering the implications of economic developments for the evolution of criteria of social status within the Hijazi elite.

◆ THE NEXT *'AWA'IL*

At present, status amongst the *'awa'il* is judged according to a complex set of criteria, which are dynamic in various ways. As they are used to accommodate innovations and as they are adapted to changing circumstances their meaning is subject to persistent alteration. Their relative significance also changes. The criteria of social status in the Hijaz during the 1980s and 1990s offered by informants were all related to the status of family and tribe and to its improvement. They were as follows (in descending order of importance): lineage and depth of lineage; reputation; wealth; adherence to 'propriety' and 'tradition'; religious observance; size of patronymic group and the love its members show one another; connections with the royal family; education; and 'good marriages'.

It is highly likely that, during the first decades of the twenty-first century, rituals and traditions will continue to rank high in relation to the other criteria of social status, in order to maintain and define cultural distinctiveness. That is to say, collective identity vis-à-vis the Najdis will continue to be expressed in 'traditional' terms. However, for the purpose of maintaining social elite status *within* the Hijaz, the relative emphasis on 'tradition' and 'propriety' in connection with social status will probably decline and the Hijazi elite will increasingly draw on more individualistic criteria of social status.

Since the recession of 1983 and further economic decline during the 1990s, the possibility of social mobility based purely on money (or economic patronage) has diminished somewhat, so competition amongst the high-status Hijazi patronymic groups will continue to take on non-material forms. As the decades pass, the *'awa'il's* emphasis (or rather overemphasis) on rituals and ceremonies will filter throughout Hijazi society. The ritualised practices of the communal sphere will become 'democratised', i.e. more widely practised and understood, while the group of people able to lay claim to significant lineages will expand, through marriages. The expansion of the tribe will dilute the significance of membership and will encourage other forms of competition. Religion and employment are likely to provide the resources on which such competition will draw.

In this dynamic situation, and confronted with the increasingly demanding requirements of the global economy, it would be reasonable to expect education, as a status criterion, to assume a greater relative importance. This will affect both men and women as the circles of competition widen.[4] High-status patronymic groups will have to achieve the professional education that will enable them to operate in both international and local contexts, though they will still have to combine this with established wealth as well as other criteria, such as lineage and piety. As technical and professional skills become of greater significance patronage is more likely to be granted to those who have them, where previously (especially during the 1970s) it was conveyed largely on the basis of social contacts, possession of wealth and sheer luck.

The Hijazis are well placed to benefit from this change because they can lay claim to a tradition of cosmopolitan education since the beginning of the twentieth century, surpassing others in the Peninsula. As education becomes a more significant status criteria, its quality will improve. The *'awa'il* already send their children, albeit mostly males, to study in the West whenever they feel that local national schools lack the necessary requirements for advancement and professionalism. Others have opted to educate their children in private, more modern schools in Jeddah.[5] The type of education that will be sought would naturally be blended with the prevailing trends, i.e. the observance of tradition, of piety and propriety. There will still be an emphasis on local, rather than foreign, cultural belonging, even for those sent to study at universities abroad. However, the preference in Hijazi education will be for professional qualifications in order to enable the formation of a managerial elite. Members of the Hijazi elite will increasingly seek to acquire expertise as architects, engineers, computer analysts, lawyers, bankers, medical doctors and so on.

The acquisition of education might also develop as a form of competition between the Hijaz and the Najd; until the 1970s a major difference between Hijazis and Najdis was education. Some Najdis still believe that, despite the fact that many Saudis from all regions were enrolled at the local universities and were offered scholarships to study abroad, mainly in the United States, Hijazis continue to hold the lead in education in Saudi Arabia. For their part, Hijazis argue that Najdis may continue to have political power but in the future they will have to depend on the skills that Hijazis are now acquiring in order to run the country. In fact, Hijazis are trying to reopen the 'skills gap' that existed between them and the Najdis in the 1950s and 1960s, a gap that had been closing in the 1970s and the 1980s as Najdis placed increasing emphasis on education.

Until now education has been of a general, liberal arts nature, which has meant Saudi Arabians have held generalist posts, with foreigners occupying all technical and managerial positions. Since the 1980s official policy has been to reduce the number of expatriates employed in Saudi Arabia through Saudiisation. As expatriate workers gradually leave the country, there will be competition for managerial, technical and other professional posts. The *'awa'il*, facing stiffer competition from Najdis and from aspiring Hijazis, will seek to establish themselves as the most suitable candidates to fill these positions.

The relative significance of narrowly economic criteria, then, is likely to increase, but this does not mean that other criteria will simply disappear. In the course of Hijazification the emerging identity of the Hijazi *'awa'il* will continue to develop, but the tensions created by the coexistence of different membership criteria are likely to intensify. Contemporary systems of education originate in the West and are designed to meet the demands of forms of economic life dominated by the West. Being drawn more deeply into such a system poses a serious cultural challenge. Exposure to Western cultural values in this way generates pressure towards individualisation, which has enormous implications for all family members, not least for women. Engagement with the new forms of telecommunications and media not only exposes people to foreign cultural influences but opens up the range of available information and consumer choices available to people, simultaneously diminishing the effectiveness of restrictions that either states or families can impose. As well as more liberal economic practices and values, a growing emphasis on Western-style education is also likely to encourage liberal and constitutional political values.

Of course, Westernisation is not the only form of cultural change. The *'awa'il* have sought to carve out a cultural 'third way' between the Najdi orthodoxies prevalent within the nation-state on the one hand, and the encroachments and enticements of Western culture on the other. They have created a cultural space of their own that, given their predicament, has served them well. Thus far, they have successfully negotiated the many pitfalls standing in the way of the revivalist project.

As the Hijaz becomes ever more closely integrated into the surrounding world—internationally, within the Gulf and wider Arabic and Muslim regions, and into the Saudi nation-state—the *'awa'il* will have to work harder as they continue to balance contending, and intensifying, pressures. They will be drawn into the economic life of Saudi Arabia, but will continue to contest the terms on which this occurs, just as they will be forced to compete amongst themselves. They will continue to define themselves in terms of Islam, but here too there are grounds for divisions amongst themselves as well as between themselves and others. Their task, like most others in the Gulf and Middle East, is to continue to find ways of minimising the contradictions between the demands of Islamic cultural democratisation and the need to accommodate the cultures and technologies emanating from the West. If this study has shown anything, it is that the Hijazi *'awa'il* will continue to confront this task in their own, highly distinctive, manner.

Appendix A:
Deconstructing the *'awa'il*

The English translation of *'awa'il* (from singular *'a'ila*) is 'families'. The same term is used in several Arab countries to describe people of good social standing. When it is said of a person that she has married *walad 'a'ila* (son of a family) or he has married *bint 'a'ila* (daughter of a family) it is understood that the marriage is to a person from a family of good social standing. Another term, *usar,* literally meaning 'families', is also used in other Arab countries when referring to people of high status, but this term is not used frequently in the Hijaz.

A similar extension of the term *'awa'il* refers to women and children and connotes 'responsibility', even to the extent of implying 'burden'. For example, when referring to a man of limited financial means, *'ala gad halu,* people refer to his being *abu 'a'ila,* (the father of the family). This implies sympathy for his heavy responsibility, for the domestic family for which he is responsible usually includes not only his wife and children, but also other women relatives—widows, unmarried women or divorcees.

Other terms used to refer to people of high status have lost much of their significance in the Hijaz. Such terms include *wujaha,* which literally means 'faces' but can be freely translated as the foremost members of the community. Another is *a'yan,* from *'ayn* meaning eye, i.e. those who see and set an example to the people. In Arabic, words for body parts refer to social structure: *ras* (head), *sadr* (bosom), *wajh* (face), *fakhdh* (thigh), *'ayn* (eye). These are used for both the hierarchical position of people and for the space they occupy in a territory or a room. Practical common usages of these terms are seen in Arabic countries. In Jordan, for instance, the senate is referred to as *majlis al-a'yan*. The expression *ash-shuyukh wal-a'yan*, which is used in most Arab countries, refers to *a'yan* as the secular leaders in society, while *ash-shuyukh* (plural of *shaykh*) are the religious leaders. In the Hijaz both religious and secular leaders are called *a'yan*. An important event is often described as being attended by a large number of *shuyukh* and *a'yan*.

The titles *shaykh* (religious leader), *sayyid* (descendant of the Prophet) and *sharif* (descendant of the Prophet and the former Hashemite ruling family) are now used only in private among the *'awa'il*. Officially, the use of *sharif* is prohibited as an implicit challenge to the Al Saud ruling family. The titles of *shaykh* and *sayyid* lost official recognition during the 1980s to curb their indiscriminate use by those without a proper claim to them.

Appendix B:
A Selection of Polite Phrases

'ayni 'alayki barda	Lit: May my eye fall cold on you! May I not cause the evil eye!	To pay someone a compliment unintentionally attracts the evil eye, *hasad*. Thus a polite, considerate person will preface such a remark with *'ayni 'alayki barda,* but I must compliment you on your house/appearance etc.' Used only among women. (The evil eye is considered to be hot.)
'ayni 'aynak	Lit: My eye, your eye!	Used to accompany the mention of an unconventional act carried out brazenly (like looking society straight in the eye with no sense of shame and attempt to hide the deed).
'ifish/ 'ifisha (adj. m/f)	Rough; the opposite of delicate, refined, gentle	Used of a person who is physically rough or whose conversation is not refined.

al-'itab	A form of social reproach	Used when relations are strained due to lack of contact. *Al-'itab* is used by long-term formal friends, *wifyan*, in order to show a desire to keep up good relations.
abshir/ abshiri (imper. m/f) Derived from good news, *bishara*	Lit: Receive the good news! I'll do my best to help you, i.e. You can count on me	If someone wants a reference for a job application, for example, the person asked for help replies '*abshiri*'.
artafi'/ artafi'i (imper. m/f)	Lit: Elevate yourself!	In the past, when all seating was on cushions (of varying heights) on floor, the expression meant literally, 'Move to a higher (i.e. higher-status) place in the seating arrangement'. Nowadays, though all seats are of the same height, those in the 'bosom of the place' *sadr al-mahal*, are still viewed as 'higher' than the others. Thus *aratafi'/i* is used by a host/ess to invite a guest to a more 'honoured' place.
As hak/hik (imper. m/f) Derived from to wake up, be alert, *saha*	Do not ...! Don't you (dare) do it! I warn you (not to ...)!	Used by an older person to warn somebody younger (usually from the same family) not to say or do something.

astawda 'tak *astawda 'tik* *'ind Allah* (m/f)	Lit: I place/ deposit you in the hands of God, i.e. I entrust God with your safe keeping	A phrase used to say goodbye: an alternative to '(go) with peace', *ma 'a assalama*, or 'in the safe keeping of God', *fi aman Allah*. Usually said by an older woman to a younger one. (It would be presumptuous for the younger woman to deposit her elder anywhere!) The reply is, *gibilt al-wadi 'a* (qv).
astur ma wajaht/asturi ma wajahti (m/f)	Lit: Keep the cover upon what you have encountered	Whatever needs to have the cover kept on it is not up to the expected standard. For if guests turn up suddenly and the hostess isn't properly dressed, or if the host family offers a guest a meal that has been hurriedly prepared they will excuse themselves by saying, *asturi ma wajahti*, i.e. Don't talk about our shortcomings.
ba 'id 'anakum	Lit: (May it remain) far away from you!	Polite phrase used to preface the mention of any unfortunate or undesirable event or action, such as illness, a divorce.
baiyyadt bi-wajhana/ baiyyadti bi-wajhana (m/f)	Lit: You have whit-ened our face (the face of the family)	Said by one family member to another (usually an older to a younger) to compliment good behaviour.
barra wa ba 'id	Lit: Outside and far away	Used after the mention of any major misfortune (e.g. fire or death) to ward off danger. Used only by women. Cf. *fi galb al- 'adu, fi wajh al- 'adu*.

bashush/ *bashusha* (adj. m/f)	Smiling, good-natured, pleasant	Used of someone who's good-natured and smiles a lot (e.g. 'Oh! What a *bashush* face!) Used more often of women than men.
ad-dandana (n.)	Singing with a lute, *'ud,* and tabla accompani-ment	The *dandana* is performed at social gatherings.
ad-dashsh (n.)	Rubbish; nonsense conversa-tion/talk	Implies the opposite of a high-status person or object; or job.
dasturak/ *dasturik* (m/f)	(I ask) your pardon/ forgiveness	At a social gathering, if some-one walks (preferably with no shoes on) in front of another seated person on the floor, the former will say, *dasturak/ik.* The expression is also used when a person has their back to some-one else and turns to ask their pardon. The reply is: *dasturak/ik ma'ak/ma'aki,* i.e. You are pardoned.
fadlat khay-rak/fadlat khayrik (m/f)	Lit: The remmant of your prosperity	The phrase is used to acknowl-edge/show appreciation of someone else's generosity. The meaning is, 'My prosperity is but a small part of yours/as nothing compared to yours'.
al-fakhama (n.)	High-status luxury	Luxury as expressed in a grand house, furniture, clothes, jewel-lery etc.

al-fakhfakha (n.)	The act of displaying wealth. Love of pomp, *ubbaha* (qv) and show; love of false appearances	Using luxury and comforts, on a particular occasion, to indicate that one is well-off.
al-fanna (n.)	Fashion (mainly referring to clothes but also social trends)	This word is mainly used by the older generation of women (younger women have tended to adopt *moda*, from Italian). However, with the return to tradition nowadays, *fanna* is increasingly used by younger-women too.
al-farakha (n.) Derived from chicken, *farkha*	Giggly, lively, high-spirited behaviour	Used for behaviour that is uncontrolled and slightly silly (e.g. it might refer to a group of young women having fun together, giggling, chattering, perhaps smoking etc).
faynak? ma had bi yishufak/ faynik? ma had bi yishu-fik (m/f)	Lit: Where have you been? Nobody's seen you	A sentence commonly used among long-term formal friends, *wifyan*. It implies a mild reproach at the absence of the person addressed, or the fact that she has neglected one of her social duties towards the speaker or speaker's family. Cf. *al-'itab*.

fi galb al-ʿadu	Lit: In the heart of the enemy	Polite term used after the mention of a potentially harmful object (e.g. a knife) to ward off danger. (Used of objects rather than subjects, i.e. not of death or major catastrophes.) Used interchangeably with *fi wajh al-ʿadu* (qv). Cf. *barra wa baʿid*.
fi wajh al-ʿadu	Lit: In the face of the enemy	Used interchangeably with *fi-galb al-ʿadu* (qv).
ghandura (adj. f)	Vivacious, something of a coquette, and a good hostess	Used of women who know how to: receive and wait on her guests; cover socially; make her guests feel welcome.
ghillis/ghilsa (adj. m/f)	Silly, irritating	A person who is *ghilsa* is said to have 'heavy blood'. His/ her jokes fall flat and are badly timed; she says the wrong thing at the wrong time and has no sense of what is appropriate to the occasion, no sense of propriety.
gibilt al-wadiʿa	Lit: I accept the deposit	Used by the younger of two people in reply to *astawdaʿtak ind Allah* (qv).

hallaftik bil-Allah la tigumi	I ask you, by God, not to get up	The expression is used in the following situation: an older woman is sitting down and a younger one comes up to pay her respects; the former attempts to rise and the latter, as a mark of consideration, immediately says, *hallaftik bil-Allah la tigumi*. Generally used by a younger woman to an older (but could also be used by extremely polite, considerate younger women to each other).
al-harj	Chatting	Used of men and women (within their own separate social group, *shilla*, or *bashka*).
al-hawas (n.)	Lit: Senses. Consideration for others, social awareness	Used of someone who is always considerate, who knows what to say at the right moment, who is sensitive to others etc. The word is often used as in, 'She is sitting with her senses, *jalsa bihawasaha*.'
Hishri/hishriyya (adj. m/f) Derived from to stuff oneself in through a tiny crack, *hashara*	Nosey	Used of someone who is always pushing themselves in where they are not wanted, poking their nose into what does not concern them etc.

al-ikhtilat (n.)	Lit: Mixing. (Implies mixing of the sexes.)	Used to refer to mixing of the sexes in a social situation. For example, someone might say, 'So you went to a university abroad. Was there mixing of the sexes? *Kan fi ikhtilat?'*, i.e. Did men and women mix socially?
jaba (n.)	The act of saying, 'Be my guest; (You're) welcome'	In the past, a man sitting outside his front door would invite male passers-by from his quarter, *hara*, to step inside by using the expression *jaba*. Nowadays it is used by a man in a public place (e.g. restaurant, coffee shop) to show that he intends to pay. At one point, *jaba* was forbidden by the authorities and the newspapers condemned it because it led to fights in the cafes.
jamid/jamda (adj. m/f)	Stiff, boring	Used of someone who doesn't have much to say, who isn't lively or interesting company.
jammilha Derived from beauty, *jamal*	Let it pass gracefully, in a beautiful manner	At a social gathering, a person who feels uneasy at the presence of someone who's been insulting might advised by a friend, *'jammilha'*, i.e. don't make a scene!
jifis/jifsa	Aggressive	Used of someone whose way of speaking and general demeanour are aggressive, 'not smooth'; someone who irritates everyone.

al-kalfata (n.)	A thing that is rushed, hurried	Something that is rushed is, by implication, not of good quality or a high standard, it is lacking in precision. Used of a conversation, a dress, meal etc. prepared in a hurry and therefore not well done.
kharrata (v.)	1. To brag (about things or events that are not true) 2. To name-drop 3. To talk nonsense	A person of doubtful social origins who claimed that his grandfather was head of one of the most important families of guides for the pilgrims, *mutawwifin,* would be considered a *kharrat.*
khatawat fi haram al-nabi	Lit: Footsteps in the Mosque of the Prophet	A further elaboration on *khatwa 'aziza* (qv) and used in conjunction with it. Generally used among women.
khatwa 'aziza	Lit: Dear foot-step	Used by a hostess as her guest is leaving (or sometimes entering) the house—an expression of warmth, hospitality and general good feelings. Normally used among women. See also: *khatawat fi haram al-nabi.*
la tuhashuna, la tuhashuna, hayya la tuhashuna	Do not desert us, do not desert us, oh! I urge you not to desert us!	A hostess repeats this set compliment to her long-term formal friends, *wifyan,* as she says goodbye to them in order to express her desire to continue seeing them, i.e. to keep up relations with them. Used only among women.

lattatt/ *lattatta* (adj. m/f)	Socially inept, awkward	Used of a person who does not know how to converse, does not weigh his/her words, repeats things that have already been said or should not be repeated, brings up sensitive topics at inopportune moments etc.
lisanaha zayy al-ʿasal	Lit: Her tongue is like honey	Said of a woman who knows how to pay the right set of compliments on the correct occasions. It implies someone who is skilled at the art of conversation.
madhula (adj. f)	Untidy, sloppy, slovenly	Used only of a woman who does not care about her appearance, clothes, home etc.
al-mahafiz (n. pl.)	Lit: The protected ones; the children	When asking how someone's children are, they should not be mentioned directly for fear of attracting the evil eye. The set formula *al-mahafiz* is used instead. For example: 'And how are the protected ones, *al-mahafiz*?'
marbush/ *marbusha* (adj. m/f)	(Socially) awkward; lacking in poise; always in a rush	Used to describe someone who is undignified, who speaks so fast that they swallow their words. A person who is *marbush/a* is always fidgeting, never staying still; rushed and hurried, and therefore lacking in poise.
masfug/ *masfuga* (adj. m/f)	Impetuous	Used of someone who is always in a hurry, who reacts without thinking.

mi'antaz (adj. m)	Proud, haughty	Used for a man who puts on airs, looks proud, tends to look down on others etc.
mi 'arriga al-middawara	Lit: She has tied her headdress elegantly	Used of all Hijazi women in the past. This expression is nowadays used only of elderly women or when reminiscing about the good old days. (The way in which a woman tied her headdress used to be an important indicator of elegance, neatness, and social status.)
mi 'as 'isa (adj. f) Derived from stick, *'asa*	Bony, skinny; too thin; 'like a stick'	Used of a woman who is too skinny to be attractive.
mibahadal/ mibahdala (adj. m/f) Derived from inelegance, lack of refinement, *bahdala*	In bad taste, unsuitable, unworthy	Used for behaviour or clothes that are not in good taste, unsuitable for someone of high status etc. (the opposite of something that indicates respect).
midaghbaja (adj. m/f)	Fat	Used politely of a woman who is very definitely overweight.
midahmal/ midahmala	Slovenly	Used of someone whose clothes are creased and grubby.

mifas 'an/ *mifas 'ana* (adj. m/f) Derived from sharp tongue, *fas 'ana*	With a sharp tongue	Used to describe someone who is spoilt, casual, disrespectful, sharp-tongued etc but in a witty way. Generally used by women.
milaffag/ *milaffaga* (adj. m/f)	1. Inappropriate, unsuitable, not properly planned or well-thought-out	1. Used for anything that is inappropriate (e.g. a present that is not suitable for the recipient or does not meet the occasion; food that has not been well prepared and is not the right thing to serve at that particular time etc).
	2. Made up, invented	2. Used for a story or an account that is not accurate, not quite the truth.
milaghwas/ *milaghwasa* (adj. m/f)	1. Sloppy, messy, not clean	1. Food that is unattractively, sloppily presented, or a dish that has been picked at or previously eaten from, is *milaghwas*.
	2. Inaccurate, distorted	2. A story or account that is distorted and inaccurate is *milaghwas*.
	3. Corrupt, dishonest, shady	3. A corrupt system official, etc. is *milaghwas*.
	4. Used of someone who is a gossip	4. A person who gossips or tells tales about other people is *milaghwas*.
milatlat/ *milatlata* (adj. m/f)	Not prepared, cooked or done properly	In a society where the ceremony of preparing and serving tea is of particular social significance. Used of food and drink, but particularly tea.

mimayyil al-kufiyya	Lit: He's tilting his *kufiyya*. (The *kuffiya* is the man's head cover, always worn under thehead-scarf, the *sumada*)	Used of a man who has a lot of money and is very pleased about it.
minshakih/ minshakiha (adj. m/f)	Extremely, ecstatically happy	Used of someone who is almost euphoric, bursting with joy. (This is a natural happiness, derived from good feelings, the general atmosphere.)
mirastak/ mirastaka (adj. m/f)	Tidy; well-presented; in good taste; *comme il faut*	Used of both people and objects, and to describe behaviour.
mitabtab/ mitabtaba	Diplomatic; very tactful; never making a *faux pas*	A woman described as *mitabtaba* is calm and does not lose her cool in social situations; she always has a witty ready answer.
mitnaghghis/ mitnaghghisa	Missing someone's presence (at a pleasurable moment)	A person is *mitnaghghis/a* when he/she feels a strong desire or longing that someone they are fond of (but who is not present) might be there to share the enjoyment.

al-mubaraka (n.)	(The act of) congratulating	*Al-mubaraka* is necessary on anything from having a baby, or passing an exam, to moving into a new house etc. Gifts are always given on such occasions.
al-mubashara (n.)	The manner in which a guest is served	The word implies a whole set of social rules that govern the way a guest is welcomed and served, i.e. what food is offered, how it is served, the accompanying expressions etc. People say, '*al-mubashara* is chivalry or honour, *muruwwa*'.
al-mujamala (n.) Derived from beauty, *jamal*	Courteous behaviour	*Mujamala* refers to behaviour when one goes out of one's way to please or impress others. Note that it takes place with formal long-term friends, *wifyan*, and outsiders or foreigners, *ajanib*, it is not used with family.
mustamikh/ mustamikha (adj. m/f) Derived from brain, *mukh*	Excited, exultant, brimming over with happiness	Used to describe someone who is excited, elated, ecstatic, perhaps at a piece of good news.
an-nazaka (n.)	Daintiness, refinement	Mainly used for dress but also comportment, behaviour etc.
nifish/nifsha (adj. m/f)	Fussy, petty, small-minded	The word describes someone who is overly concerned about detail etc.

rad rijul	Lit: To return the legs	The expression refers to a visit which must be returned, for example on the occasion of a birth, a wedding, visiting a sick person, expressing condolences etc.
rayig/rayiga (adj. m/f)	Lit: Pure, clean; serene, poised	The opposite of *marbush* (qv). To say that someone is *rayig/a* is high praise indeed!
rijil m 'allaga	Lit: The leg is suspended	The person to whom the phrase is addressed (or of whom it is used) is under a social obligation to return a visit—only then will her leg be considered as 'back on the ground'.
rizil/razila (adj. m/f)	Silly; stupid	Used of someone who makes stupid jokes and has a silly sense of humour.
saltuh/ saltuha (adj. m/f)	Hanger-on; stupid or naive	Used of a person (more usually a man than a woman) who lacks all dignity and self-respect, has no personality of his own and throws himself at people.
at-ta'azzuz (n.)	Behaviour indicating pride and dignity	The family of a future bride, for example, behaves with *at-ta'azzuz* vis-à-vis the groom's family by constantly putting off the date of the wedding in order to show how dear their daughter is to them. i.e. they are loath to part with her.

at-tajammul (n.) Derived from beauty, *jamal*	Lit: Physical beautifica- tion/ becoming beautiful	In the Hijaz, it has acquired the connotation of seemliness, being presentable or *comme il faut*, adding credit, lustre or honour. It is used of any hon- ourable, seemly behaviour.
at-tasbira (n.) Derived from patience, *sabr*	The appease- ment of hunger; snack	*At-tasbira* is a snack eaten at home before going out to din- ner or a lunch party at someone else's house. This is in order not to appear 'hungry' in front of others—it is not considered becoming for someone to look 'hungry' in public; moreover it might attract the evil eye.
tilim/tilma (adj. m/f)	Stupid, unintelli- gent, 'thick', slow-witted	Used of someone with no social *savoir faire*, who does not get subtle hints.
tinih/tinha (adj. m/f)	Thick- skinned; (someone who is) heavy going	Used of someone who always says the wrong thing and has 'heavy blood', i.e. whose pres- ence is wearing.
at-tu'ma (n.)	Gift of God	The *tu'ma* consists of food sent by a relative or close friend. The rule is that the plate must always be returned full (if not with food, then at least piled high with sugar).

al-ubbaha	Self-conscience, pride, stately bearing	Used of someone who has position, wealth and a stately demeanour and shows it in his bearing. This *ubbaha* is clearly recognised by others (e.g. when the individual comes into a room, everyone makes way). Used when referring to high-status people who are confident of their position in society. Can be used of a group of people or an individual, but in the latter case only a man.
wal-ni 'im	Lit: With satisfaction (derived from prosperity). The equivalent of *enchanté* in French	Used only about (or in the presence of) a respected person of high status, in recognition of individual social standing or that of the family. It implies that the person is important, from a family of good social standing, *sira tayyiba*, and also from 'good soil', *turba tayyiba*
way!	Expression of incredulity at hearing something unexpected	*Way!* is often said with the right hand placed on the chest. Used only by woman. If a man said *way!* he would be considered effeminate.
wuh!	Exclamation to show surprise and disapproval	Used for behaviour and is usually accompanied by a mock beating of the chest.

ya ho Derived from *ya* (an interjection) + *huwa* (he)	Lit: Oh, he! (a term used to avoid addressing someone directly)	In the past, it was considered shameful, *'ayb*, for a husband and wife to address each other by their first names: *ya ho* was used instead (until the birth of the first child, when the woman could be addressed as 'Mother of Ahmad/Zain', *umm ahmad/zain*. Nowadays, *ya ho* is sometimes used as a term of endearment to address a marriage partner, relative or close friend. For example, '*ya ho* where've you been all this time?' The meaning of the expression is indicated by the tone in which it is said, for example implying disbelief.
yifarsi' (v.)	To open one's eyes wide; to stare (as a warning)	Parents will do this to their children for example, in order to behave correctly.
yigta'ni Derived from to cut, *gata'a*	Lit: May (God) cut me off!	A form of apology addressed to a very dear person who has been ignored or offended in some way.
yizargin (v.)	To annoy, irritate (others)	Said of someone who drives others crazy, imposes, too much etc.
yizghur (v.)	To stare (in an unpleasant way)	Used of a person who stares straight into someone else's eyes, but in a way that is intrusive and denotes a lack of respect. It has a connotation of envy, or imposing oneself on someone.

Select Glossary

'adat	customs
'agiga	a sacrifice of a lamb for a birth of a child
al 'ai'la	the family
'ai'la kabira	big family
'ala gad al-hal	living within one's means
'ala gad halu	a man of limited financial means
'alim	singular of *'ulema*
'aqida	ideology
'aqilis	Sharifian soldiers
al 'arda al Najdia	the Najdi sword dance
'awa'il	singular *'a'ila*, 'the families'. A term used to describe people of good social standing. *'Awa'il* also means families in the sense of wives, mothers and children. Hence, in public places such as airports in Saudi Arabia where strict segregation of the sexes is observed there are sections reserved for women and their children signposted *'ailat* (literally meaning 'families'); *'aw'ail* meaning women and children also connotes 'responsibility'.
'awra	a woman's defective parts such as her body or her voice
'aza	the condolence, ceremony
'ibada	worship
'iqal	men's headband

'ulema	religious teachers
'umama	special headdress
a 'yan	those who set an example to the people
abu 'a ila	father of a family
adhan	call to prayer
ajanib	the outsiders
aj-janna tahta agdam al-ummahat	Paradise is under the feet of mothers
ajr	reward from God
al-lahja al-hijaziyya	Hijazi dialect
al-Qibla	direction in which all Muslims pray
al-Yamama	Dove of Good Omen, the first Najdi newspaper
amana	objects of trust
anaga	elegance
arham	affines, or relatives by marriage
asala	purity of blood; roots in the region
Ashraf	the Hijazi rulers prior to Al Saud
asl	origin
awgaf	religious endowments
badu	Bedouin term used for Najdi
bagaya hujjaj	pilgrimage remnants
baraka	blessedness
bid 'a	a dangerous innovation or heresy
bid 'a hasana	laudable innovation
buyut tijariyya	merchant household
daya	traditional native midwife
du 'a	a personal prayer of request
fatiha	the opening sura of the Quran
fatwa	religious decrees
gabili	tribal Najdi
giraya	Quran recitations
hai'at kibar al 'ulema	assembly of senior *'ulema*
hajj	pilgrimage
halagat al-'ilm	circles of knowledge

halagat al-wasl	circular link
halat al-salat	gleam of prayer
hasab	depth in lineage
hasad	the evil eye or the envy of another
hijri	lunar Muslim calendar based on the Prophet's move from Mecca to Medina
Hujjuz	from the tribes, from the nomadic areas of the Hijaz
Hussainiyya	distinctive Shia mosque
iftar	breaking of the fast
ijaza	licence to teach
ikhwan	religious brethren
istigama	good religious behaviour
jamila	a favour
karam	generosity
khadiri	non-tribal or non 'pure blood' person
khawaja	Westerners
khira	divination
kufr	disbelief
majlis	men's formal gathering
mal	wealth
maqamat	stages of the Sufi path
mashayikh	religious learned man (singular: *shaykh*)
mawlid	celebration of the birth of the Prophet
min-awwaltams	newcomers, of the day before yesterday
minnana wa fina	established members of the core
mubaraka	congratulation ceremony
muftis	representatives of the four *madhahib*, Sunni schools of law
mulhi	a distraction from religious duties
munadi	a professional announcer
mutaw'a	members of the Committee for the Propagation of the Good and the Forbidding of the Evil, religious police
mutawwifin	guides to the pilgrims
muzawwir	representative who receives and guides the pilgrims in Medina
nadhr	vows to God

naqabat	a guild of camel drivers
nas afadil	eminent or distinguished people
nas kubar	big people
nasab	lineage
nazaka	refinement
Rabi' al-Awwal	the month of the Prophet's birth
rad rijul	returning the legs, i.e. returning a visit
rahmani	ceremony for the Merciful One
ru 'ya	a vision
sabu'	ceremony for naming a child on the seventh day
sadaga	alms giving; alms
safa'	purity
Sawt al Hijaz	The Voice of Hijaz, Hijazi newspaper in the period of the rule of the *Ashraf*
sayyid	descendant of the Prophet
shahada	Muslims' affirmation that there is no God but Allah and that Muhammed is his Prophet.
shari'a	Islamic law
Sharif	descendant of the Prophet and the ruling family of the past
shirk	idolatry
shurug	Najdis, Easterners
sidi	my master
silat ar-rihm	kinship ties
sira	social standing
sira tayyiba	good social standing
sirwal	short trousers worn under men's robes
sum'a	reputation
tagalid	traditions
tagwa	religious observance
tarab	musical enjoyment
tarhib	hospitality
tarigah	Sufi path or method
tarsh al-bahr	the flotsam of the sea
tathir	men's circumcision
tujjar	merchants

Umm al-Qura	the official Hijazi newspaper of the time
usul	propriety
wifyan	faithful ones, long-term friends
wisal	a social tie
wujaha	face of the people or the foremost members of the community
yibayyid bi-wajhahum	whiten their face
yisawwid bi-wajhahum	blacken their face
zakat	tax
zamzam	holy water from the well in Mecca
zawg	good taste

Bibliography and Further Reading

Abbasi, S.M.M., *Islamic Manners*, International Islamic Publishers, Karachi, 1981.

Abir, M., *Saudi Arabia in the Oil Era: Regime and Elites, Conflict and Collaboration*, Croom Helm, London, 1988.

Abu-Lughod, L., *Veiled Sentiments, Honour and Poetry in a Bedouin Society*, University of California Press, Berkeley, 1986.

Albani, M.N., *The Precepts of Funerals and their Heresies* (in Arabic, *ahkam al-janaza wa bida'aha*), al-Maktab al-Islami, Beirut, 1969.

Ali, Y., (trans.) *The Holy Qur'an*, Islamic Foundation, Leicester, 1975.

Alireza, M., *At the Drop of a Veil: The True Story of a California Girl's Years in an Arabian Harem*, Hale, London, 1972.

Almana, M., *Arabia Unified. A Portrait of Ibn Saud*, Hutchinson Benham, London, 1980.

Altorki, S., *Women in Saudi Arabia: Ideology and Behavior among the Elite*, Columbia University Press, New York, 1988.

——and El-Solh, C.F., (eds) *Arab Women in the Field: Studying Your Own Society*, Syracuse University Press, Syracuse, 1988.

Amrou, M.A.A., *Dress and Adornment in the Islamic Shari'a* (in Arabic, *al-libas wal-zinah fil- shari'a al-islamiyya*), Dar al-Furqan, Amman, 1985.

Anderson, B., *Imagined Communities: Reflections on the Origins and Spread of Nationalism*, Verso, London/New York, revised and extended edition, 1991.

Angawi, S.M., 'Makkan Architecture', unpublished PhD thesis, University of London, 1988.

Al-Ansari, A.Q., *The History of the City of Jeddah* (in Arabic, *tarikh madinat jiddah*), Dar Masr lil-Tiba'a, Cairo, 1982.

Antonius, George, *The Arab Awakening*, Librarie du Liban, Beirut, 1969.

Ashour, A.L., *The Certainty of Death by Hafiz al-Jawzi* (in Arabic, *al-thabat' ind al-mamat*), Maktabat al-Quran, Cairo, 1986.

Ayub, H., *The Jurisprudence of Worship* (in Arabic, *fiqh al-'ibadat*), Dar al-Nahda al-Jadida, Beirut, 1986.

Al-Bahiqi, A.B., *The Proof of the Torture of the Grave and the Questioning of the Two Angels* (in Arabic, *ithbat 'adhab al-qabr wasu' al al-malakayn*), Dar al-Jil, Beirut, 1987.

Baker, Randall, *King Husain and the Kingdom of Hejaz*, Oleander, Cambridge, 1979.

Barley, B., *The Innocent Anthropologist: Notes from a Mud Hut*, British Museum, London, 1983.

Berger, P.L., and Luckmann, T., *The Social Construction of Reality: Treatise in the Sociology of Knowledge*, Penguin, Harmondsworth, 1979.

Berry, B., *Shakespeare's Comic Rites*, Cambridge University Press, Cambridge, 1984.

Binzagr, S., *Saudi Arabia: An Artist's View of the Past*, Three Continents, Lausanne, 1979.

Bottomore, T.B., *Elites and Society*, Penguin, Harmondsworth, 1964.

Buckle, R., (ed.) *U and Non-U Revisited*, Debrett's Peerage, London, 1978.

Burton, R.F., *Personal Narrative of a Pilgrimage to El-medinah and Meccah*, Vol. I, *El-Misr*; Vol. II, *El-Medinah*; Vol. III, *Meccah*, Green & Longman, London, 1855.

Campbell, J.K., *Honour, Family and Patronage: A Study of Institutions and Moral Values in a Greek Mountain Community*, Oxford University Press, Oxford, 1964.

Cleveland, W.L., *Islam Against the West*, al-Saqi, London, 1985.

Cohen, A.P., (ed.) *Belonging: Identity and Social Organisation in British Rural Cultures*, Manchester University Press, Manchester, 1982.

——, *Symbolic Construction of Community*, Ellis Horwood, Chichester, 1985.

——, (ed.) *Symbolizing Boundaries: Identity and Diversity in British Culture*, Manchester University Press, Manchester, 1986.

Coleridge, N., *The Fashion Conspiracy. A Remarkable Journey through the Empires of Fashion*, Heinemann, London, 1988.

Crisp, Q., *Manners from Heaven: A Divine Guide to Good Behaviour*, Hutchinson, London, 1984.

Cudsi, A.S., and Hillal Dessouki, A.E., (eds) *Islam and Power*, Croom Helm, London, 1981.

Cunnison, I., *Bagara Arabs: Power and Lineage in a Sudanese Nomad Tribe*, Clarendon Press, Oxford, 1966.

Dazi-Heni, Fatiha, *La diwaniyya, Entre changement social et recompositions politiques au Koweit au cours de la decennie 1981–1992*, De l'Institut d'Etudes Politiques de Paris, Paris, 1995.

Daghustani, A.M., *Kingdom of Saudi Arabia: A Century of Progress*, Ministry of Information, Maktab al-Watan, Riyadh, 1983.

Derraugh, P., and Deraugh, W., *Wedding Etiquette for all Denominations*, Foulsham, Slough, 1983.

Didier, C., *Sojourn with the Grand Sharif of Makkah*, trans. R. Boulind, Oleander, Cambridge, 1985.

Al-Dimashqi, H., *The Horrors of the Graves* (in Arabic, *ahwal al-qubur*), Dar al-Hijra, Cairo, 1987.

Doughty, C., *Travels in Arabia Deserta*, vols I–II, Cambridge University Press, Cambridge, 1888.

Edwards, A.T., *Good and Bad Manners in Architecture*, Philip Allan, London, 1924.

Elias, N., *The History of Manners*, trans. E. Jephcott, Blackwell, Oxford, 1978.

Farsi, M.S., 'Architecture and Urban Pattern of the Pilgrimage Cities in Saudi Arabia' (in Arabic), unpublished MSc thesis, Alexandria University, 1982.

Al-Farsy, F., *Saudi Arabia: A Case Study in Development*, Kegan Paul International, London, 1982.

Field, M., *The Merchants. The Big Business Families of Arabia*, John Murray, London, 1984.

Fitzsimmons, T., (ed.) *Saudi Arabia: Its Peoples, Its Society, Its Culture*, in *Survey of World Cultures*, HRAF, New Haven, CT, 1959.

Geertz, C., *The Interpretation of Cultures*, Basic Books, New York, 1973.

van Gennep, A., *The Rites of Passage*, trans. M.B. Vizedom and G.L. Caffe, University of Chicago Press, Chicago, 1961.

Al-Ghamdi, S.F., *Folk Heritage in the Village and the Town in the Baha Region – the City of Jeddah* (in Arabic, *al-turath al-sha'bi fil qariyya wal madina, mantiqat al-baha madinat jiddah*), Dar al-'Ilm lil-Tiba'a wal Nashr, Jeddah, 1985.

Gill, E., *Clothes*, Cape, London, 1931.

Gluckman, M., *Essays on the Ritual of Social Relations*, Manchester University Press, Manchester, 1962.

Gulick, J., *The Middle East: An Anthropological Perspective*, Good Year, Santa Monica, CA, 1976.

Habib, J.S., *Ibn Sa'uds's warriors of Islam. The Ikhwan of Najd and their Role in the creation of the Sa'udi Kingdom, 1910–1930*, E.J. Brill, Leiden, 1978.

Halliday, Fred, *Arabia Without Sultans*, Penguin Books, London, 1974.

Hertz, R., *Death and the Right Hand*, trans. R. and C. Needham, intro. E.E. Evans-Pritchard, Free Press, New York, 1960.

Hobsbawm, E., and Ranger, T., (eds) *The Invention of Tradition*, Cambridge University Press, Cambridge, 1983.

Hogarth, D.G., *Hejaz before World War I*, Falcon-Oleander, Cambridge, 1978.

Holden, D., and Johns, R., *The House of Saud*, Sidgwick & Jackson, London, 1981.

Hopwood, D., (ed.) *The Arabian Peninsula: Society and Politics*, Allen & Unwin, London, 1972.

Huntington, R., and Metcalf, P., *Celebrations of Death: The Anthropology of Mortuary Ritual*, Cambridge University Press, Cambridge, 1979.

Hurgronje, C.S., (ed.) *Mekkanische Sprichworter und Reden-sarten (Meccan Sayings and Expressions*, collected 1885, Mecca), Internationale Orientalistecongresse, The Hague, 1886.

——, *Mekka in the Latter Part of the 19th Century*, Brill, Leiden, 1970.

Al-Istambouli, M.M., *The Gift of the Bride* (in Arabic, *tuhfat al-'arus*), Dar al-Fikr, Amman, 1985.

Jabar, A., *Wedding Customs and Traditions in the Western Region of the Kingdom of Saudi Arabia: A Modern Anthropological Study* (in Arabic, *'adat wa taqalid al-Zawaj bil-mantiqa al-gharbia min al-mamlaka al-'arabiyya al-sau'dia*), Tihama, Jeddah, 1983.

Al-Jawzia, S.A., *The Soul by Ibn al-Qaim: About the Souls of the Dead and the Living* (in Arabic, *al-ruh li Ibn al-Qaim: fil kalam 'ala arwah al-amwat wa al-ahya*), Dar al-Qalam, Beirut, 1983.

Johnson, R.B., *Manners Makyth Man*, Stanhope Press, Rochester, n.d.

Kapiszewski, A., *Native Arab Population and Foreign Workers in the Gulf States*, Universitas Krakow, Cracow, 1999.

Kapstein, N., 'Materials for the History of the Prophet Muhammad's Birthday Celebration in Mecca', *Der Islam*, 69, 2, 1992.

Katakura, M., *Bedouin Village: A Study of a Saudi Arabian People In Transition*, University. of Tokyo Press, Tokyo, 1977.

Kanafani, A.S., *Aesthetics and Ritual in the United Arab Emirates*, American University of Beirut, 1983.

Khan, M.M., *The Translation of the Meanings of Sahih al-Bukhari*, Islamic University, Medina al-Munawara, Saudi Arabia, 1981.

King, G., *The Traditional Architecture of Saudi Arabia*, I.B. Tauris, London, 1998.

Kingdom of Saudi Arabia, Stacey International, London, 6th revised edition, 1983.

Kostiner, J., and Khoury, P., (eds) *Tribes and State Formation in the Middle East*, I.B. Tauris, London, 1992.

——, *The Making of Saudi Arabia, 1916–1936: From Chieftaincy to Monarchical State*, Oxford University Press, Oxford, 1993.

Lane, E.W., *Arabian Society in the Middle Ages: Studies from the Thousand and One Nights*, ed. S. Lane-Poole, Curzon, London, 1987.

Lienhardt, G., *Divinity and Experience, the Religion of the Dinka*, Clarendon Press, Oxford, 1961.

Lienhardt, P.A., 'The Interpretation of Rumour', in *Studies in Social Anthropology. Essays in Memory of E.E. Evans-Pritchard and by his Former Colleagues*, Oxford University Press, Oxford, 1975.

De Long-Bas, N., *Wahhabi Islam: From Revival and Reform to Global Jihad*, I.B.Tauris, London, 2004.

Lurie, A., *The Language of Clothes*, Heinemann, London, 1981.

MacEoin, D., and Al-Shahi, A., (eds) *Islam in the Modern World*, Croom Helm, London, 1983.

Maghrebi, M.A., *Features of Social Life in the Hejaz in the 14th Century Hijrat* (in Arabic, *malamih al-hayat al-ijtima'iyya fil-hijaz*), Tihama, Jeddah, 1982.

Mauger, T., *Flowered Men and Green Slopes of Arabia*, Souffles, Paris, 1988.

van der Meulen, D., *The Wells of Ibn Saud*, John Murray, London, 1957.

Monroe, E., *Philby of Arabia*, Quartet, London, 1980.

Mukhdir, H.A.A., *Popular Proverbs in Honoured Mecca* (in Arabic, *al-amthila al-'amiyya fi makka al-mukarrama*), Matboughat Nadi Macca al-Thaqafi, Mekka, 1975.

Musil, A., *The Manners and Customs of the Rwala Bedouins*, American Geographical Society, New York, 1928.

Organization of Petroleum Exporting Countries (OPEC), *Annual Statistical Bulletin*, OPEC, Vienna, 1984.

Owen, R., 'The Arab Oil Economy: Present Structure and Future Prospects', in Samih K. Farsoun, (ed.) *Arab Society: Continuity and Change*, Croom Helm, Beckenham, 1985.

Peacock, J.L., *Consciousness and Change*, ed. F.G. Bailey, Blackwell, Oxford, 1979.

Peters, E., 'Aspects of Rank and Status Among Muslims in a Lebanese Village', in J.A. Pitt-Rivers, (ed.) *Mediterranean Countrymen*, Mouton, Paris, 1963.

Philby, H. St. J.B., *Arabia*, Benn, London, 1948.

Piscatori, J.P., (ed.) *Islam in the Political Process*, Cambridge University Press, Cambridge, 1986*a*.

——, *Islam in a World of Nation-states*, Cambridge University Press, Cambridge, 1986*b*.

Pitt-Rivers, J.A., *The People of the Sierra*, University of Chicago Press, Chicago, 1971.

Powdermaker, H., *Stranger and Friend. The Way of an Anthropologist*, Norton, New York, 1966.

Al-Qadi, I.A., *Islamic Book of the Dead, a Collection of Hadiths on the Fire and the Garden*, Diwan, Norwich, 1977.

Al-Qasimi, D., *Social Life among the Arabs* (in Arabic, *al-hayat al-ijtima'iyya 'ind al-'arab*), Dar al-Nafa is, Beirut, 1978.

Rabinow, P., *Reflections of Fieldwork in Morocco*, University of California Press, Berkeley, 1977.

Rafi, M.U., *In the Region of Asir* (in Arabic, *fi rubu' 'asir*), Dar al-Ahd al-Jadid, Cairo, 1954.

Al-Rasheed, Madawi, *A History of Saudi Arabia*, Cambridge University Press, Cambridge, 2002.

Rentz, G., 'Wahhabism and Saudi Arabia', in Derek Hopwood, (ed.) *The Arabian Peninsula: Society and Politics*, Allen & Unwin, London, 1972.

Al-Rihani, Amin, *Tarikh Najd wa-Mulhaqatiha*, Dar al-Kitab al-'Arabi, Beirut, 1981.

Ross, H.C., *The Art of Arabian Costume: A Saudi Arabian Profile*, Arabesque, Fribourg, 1981.

Sabini, J., *Armies in the Sand. The Struggle for Mecca and Medina*, Thames & Hudson, London, 1981.

Salim, S.M., *Ech-Chibayish. An Anthropological Study of a Marsh Village in Iraq*, (PhD dissertation, University of London), Al-Ani Press, Baghdad, 2nd edition, 1970.

Sampson, A., *The Seven Sisters. The Great Oil Companies and the World They Shaped*, Viking, New York, 1975.

Sannu, K., *The Best of Language* (in Arabic, *kheir al-kalam*), Dar al-Qibla, Jeddah, 1984.

Sebai, Z.A., *Health in Saudi Arabia*, Vol. I, Tihama, Riyadh, 1985.

Al-Shahi, A., (ed.) *The Diversity of the Muslim Community: Anthropological Essays in Memory of Peter Lienhardt*, Ithaca, London, 1987.

Al-Siba i, A., *My Aunt Kadarjan* (in Arabic, *khalati kadarjan*), Tihama, Jeddah, 1980.

——, *The History of Mecca* (in Arabic, *tarikh makka*), Nadi mecca al-Thaqafi, Mecca, 1984.

Smith, A., *National Identity*, Penguin Books, London, 1991.

Smith, R., *Kinship and Marriage in Early Arabia*, ed. S.A. Cook, Black, London, 1903.

Stowasser, B.P., *Women in the Qur'an, Traditions and Interpretation*, Oxford University Press, New York, 1994.

Tapper, N., and Tapper, R., '"Eat This, It'll Do You a Power of Good": Food and Commensality among Durani Pashtuns', *American Ethnologist*, 1986.

——and ——, 'The Birth of the Prophet: Ritual and Gender in Turkish Islam', *Man*, 22, 1987.

Teitelbaum, Joshua, *The Rise and Fall of the Hashimite Kingdom of Arabia*, Hurst & Company, London, 2001.

Thesiger, W., *Arabian Sands*, Longman, London, 1964.

Thomas, K., 'The Place of Laughter in Tudor and Stuart England', *Times Literary Supplement*, 21 January 1977.

Trimingham, Spencer, *The Sufi Orders in Islam*, Oxford University Press, London, 1971.

Turner, V., *The Forest of Symbols: Aspects of Ndembu Ritual*, Cornell University Press, Ithaca, NY, 1967.

——, *The Ritual Process: Structure and Anti-Structure*, Aldine, Chicago, 1969.

Vassiliev, Alexei, *The History of Saudi Arabia*, Saqi Books, London, 2000.

Yafi, A., *Management of Some Large Scale Logistical Problems of Hajj, (The Muslim Pilgrimage to Makkah and the Holy Areas)*, University of Texas Press, Austin, 1983.

Yamani, M., 'Birth and Behaviour in a Hospital in Saudi Arabia', *British Society for Middle Eastern Studies Bulletin*, 13, 1987*a*.

——, 'Fasting and Feasting: Some Social Aspects of the Observance of Ramadan in Saudi Arabia', in Ahmed Al-Shsi, (ed.) *The Diversity of the Muslim Community: Anthropological Essays in Memory of Peter Lienhardt*, Ithaca, London, 1987*b*.

——, 'Saudi Arabia and Central Asia: The Islamic Connection', in A. Ehteshami, (ed.) *From the Gulf to Central Asia: Players in the New Great Game*, University of Exeter Press, Exeter, 1994*a*.

——, 'You are What You Cook: Cuisine and Class in Mecca', in S. Zubaida and R. Tapper, *Culinary Cultures of the Middle East*, I.B. Tauris, London, 1994*b*.

——, (ed.) *Feminism and Islam: Legal and Literary Perspectives*, Garnet, London, 1996.

——, 'Changing the Habits of a Lifetime: The Adaptation of Hijazi Dress to the New Social Order', in N. Lindisfarne-Tapper and B. Ingham, (eds) *Languages of Dress in the Middle East*, Curzon, Richmond, 1997.

——, *Changed Identities. The Challenge of the New Generation in Saudi Arabia*, RIIA, London, 2000.

Al-Yassani, A., *Religion and State in the Kingdom of Saudi Arabia*, Westview, Boulder, CO, 1985.

Al-Zahawi, Jamal Effendi al-'Iraqi al-Siddiqi, *The Doctrine of Ahl al Sunna Versus the 'Salafi' Movement*, Kazi Publications, Chicago, 1996.

Zahra, N.A., 'Material Power, Honour, Friendship and the Etiquette of Visiting', *Anthropological Quarterly*, 47, 1974.

Zubaida, Sami, *Islam, the People and the State: Political Ideas and Movements in the Middle East*, I.B. Tauris, London, 1993.

Notes

◆ 1. DEFINING THE HIJAZ

1   Kostiner (1993: 100).
2   Vassiliev (2000).
3   See Al-Yassini (1985: 61). See also Field (1984: 23).
4   Teitelbaum (2001: 24).
5   Al-Zahawi (1996).
6   Vassiliev (2000: 100).
7   Antonius (1969: 133).
8   Teitelbaum (2001: 42–5).
9   Al-Rasheed (2002).
10 See Kostiner (1993: 103, 106).
11 Vassiliev (2000: 282).
12 See Field (1984: 30). This stance extends to the ruling families of the other Gulf Co-operation Council member countries—Kuwait, Qatar, Oman, the United Arab Emirates and Bahrain—which similarly base their legitimacy on tribal descent.
13 Cohen (1982: 6).
14 Field (1984).
15 According to Kapiszewski (1999: 52), in 1997, 6 million foreigners lived and worked in Saudi Arabia, according to the same figures the national population was 13.5 million.
16 See Yamani (2000).

♦ 2. THE HIJAZI *'AWA'IL* AND THE PRESERVATION OF HIJAZI IDENTITY

1 See Appendix A and Select Glossary.
2 This is true not only for the Hijazis. The Shia population of Ahsa, for example, may not build their distinctive mosque, the *Hussainiyya*, or hold the annual rite commemorating Hussain's death.
3 The *fatwa*s were issued by the late Binbaz, Grand Mufti of Saudi Arabia in 1993.
4 Abir (1988: 30).
5 There are today individual Hijazi *mutawwifin*, but they are tightly regulated by the Saudi Ministry of Hajj.
6 The Wahhabi *'ulema*, the Al Sheikh, number several thousands and are thoroughly intermarried with the ruling Al Saud family, itself consisting of around 10,000 people.
7 The position of Hijazi billionaires and that of their families is hence entirely dependent upon their relationship to, and identification with, the Al Saud.
8 There are, however, some words that are uniquely Hijazi. Since the beginning of the 1980s, such words and expressions have become increasingly elaborate, almost to the point of exaggeration.
9 See Appendix A.
10 The names of the families cannot be disclosed, as I promised anonymity to all Hijazis who gave me access to their gatherings and openly shared with me their beliefs, opinions and convictions.
11 Indeed, the institutionalisation of a semi-tribal ruling entity has made neo-tribalism an attractive defence strategy for other culturally threatened groups in the Arabian Peninsula.
12 See Campbell (1964) for Greece and Pitt-Rivers (1971) for Spain.
13 There are instances of *sudgan* where private behaviour is shared with friends. However, the explicitly stated norm is that 'privacy' exists only between family members.
14 Hijazis only acknowledge the Hashemite rulers (now in Jordan) as descendants of the Prophet.
15 Quran, *sura* 93, *al-Dhuha* (The Early Hours), verse 2. Trans. Yusuf Ali.

16 Quran, *sura* 3, *al-Imran* (The Family of Imran), verse 37. Trans. Yusuf Ali.

17 *Zakat* is 2.5 per cent of capital and earnings.

18 Quran, *sura* 49, *al-Hujurat* (The Inner Apartments), verse 13. Trans. Yusuf Ali. This verse is often repeated by the *'awa'il* but is not observed in their behaviour.

19 Some Hijazis say, 'What is Saudi Arabia without Mecca and Medina?' Others say that while oil is ephemeral, Islam and its cradle are everlasting.

20 'Thy Lord hath decreed that ye worship none but Him, and that ye be kind to parents.' Quran, *sura* 17, *al-Asra* (The Children of Israel), verse 23. Trans. Yusuf Ali.

21 *Hadith*: 'The prayers of he who does not maintain his kinship ties, *silat ar-rihm*, will not reach Heaven'.

22 Such weekly *majlis* are named in accordance with the day on which they are held. So, for example, a Saturday night gathering is called *sabtiyya*. Salim explains how the *madyaf* among the Echchbayish is an important indicator of social status and prestige (1970: 171).

23 See Dazi-Heni (1995).

24 Music is viewed by the original Wahhabis as an incitement to forgetfulness of God and sin. However, many Sufis in the Hijaz used music as a means to heighten consciousness of God.

◆ 3. THE POLITICAL AWAKENING OF THE HIJAZI *'AWA'IL*

1 Hurgronje (1970). Also see Yamani (1994*a*).

2 Kostiner (1993: 101).

3 See Appendix A and Select Glossary.

4 Baker (1979: 21).

5 It was considered shameful to go out *qidimi*, i.e. with the *'iqal* headdress, for formal occasions.

6 Today the ruling *Ashraf* of the Hashemite Kingdom of Jordan are direct descendants of the Awn branch, from King Hussain of the Hijaz.

7 This has been compared by Jordanian members of the *Ashraf* to the British going to Sandhurst today.

8 The word *mutawwif* is mainly used by Meccans; the equivalent term used by Indonesians was *shaykh*, while the Turks called the guides *dalil* and the Indians referred to them as *mu'allim* (teacher).

9 Hurgronje (1970: 223).

10 Ibid.: 121.

11 Yafi (1983).

12 According to information given by the Hajj Research Centre in Jeddah in 1984, the Great Mosque at Mecca and that at Medina could each hold around 1 million people.

13 However, although descendants of the *mutawwifin* reproach the Najdis for displacing them, many were not prepared to live in Mecca and work as *mutawwifin* year-round.

14 See Al-Yassini (1985: 48).

15 Ibid.; Najdi *'ulema* were sustained by monies set aside from *zakat* (donations) and *bait al mal* (money raised from organised raids).

16 Al-Rihani (1981: 323).

17 Kostiner (1993: 104).

18 He did this primarily by appointing non-Al Sheikh family members and even non-'pure-blooded' Najdis. In fact the first was a *khadiri*. By this act he reduced the influence of the *'ulema* generally, and the Al Sheikh in particular. Faisal was in a good position to control the *'ulema* not only because of his strong personality, a reputation for piety and Islamic austerity, but also because his mother was from the Al Sheikh.

19 During the reign of King Faisal one Hijazi *'alim* was appointed to the sixteen-member assembly.

20 Al-Yassini (1985).

21 Such as cotton and silk, see Maghrebi (1982: 141).

22 Ibid.: 146.

23 Sabini (1981: 37).

24 Maghrebi (1982: 29).

25 Field (1984: 29).

26 See Maghrebi (1982: 161–2).

27 Many Hijazis felt that the smuggling of gold was justified, believing that it benefited the country. A Hijazi man said: 'We exported gold and brought a livelihood for the people. Instead of bringing in one bag of rice we brought two'.

28 The first oil concession was signed by King Abdul Aziz in 1933 with the American oil companies Socal and Texaco (Ibn Saud was in desperate need of money). Sampson (1975: 109).

29 For example, Harry St John Philby obtained from King Abdul Aziz the exclusive agency rights for Ford cars and tyres. Maghrebi (1982: 142).

30 Field (1984: 20, 29, 30).

31 Ibid.

32 See Al-Yassini (1985: 62).

33 OPEC (1984).

34 See Abir (1988).

35 Ibid.: 185.

36 Ibid.: 203.

◆ 4. THE RITES OF PASSAGE I

1 The criteria for internal competition for social status have different relative importance at each ritual in the life-cycle. For example, as will be seen later, at death 'piety' and 'propriety' are the most prominent criteria.

2 The size of a patronymic group is determined by the number of male and female agnates who share a common surname.

3 This *hadith* is often repeated by Hijazis and other Arabs. Another *hadith*, for which I have not found a written source, quotes the Prophet, who replied to the question, 'Who is the closest person to one?' by saying, 'Your mother, then your mother, then your mother and then your father'.

4 See Berry (1984: 8) on Radcliffe-Brown's idea that rituals express and thereby perpetuate the basic values of society.

5 Al-Ghamdi (1985: 376).

6 See Yamani (1987).

7 See Appendix A and Select Glossary.

8 Carter notes that, 'the government has recently put a ban on the erection of private hospitals of this [luxurious] sort as there are now enough of them to serve the present community.' Carter (1979: 46).

9   All ceremonies relating to the birth event are normally held separately for men and for women. However, as will be seen, most events celebrating birth are women's parties.

10 The *wifyan* are nearly always Hijazi; they are always women. Men have *sudgan* (friends), but the fact that these relationships arise from work implies that the friends will come from different regional and socio-economic backgrounds.

11 Quran, *sura* 19, *Maryam*, and *sura* 36, *Yassin*.

12 Kanafani (1983: 92).

13 Hurgronje (1970: 113–14, 228). Girls were not circumcised in the Hijaz, nor in other parts of Saudi Arabia.

14 The first male born is usually named after the paternal grandfather, and the second after the maternal grandfather.

15 The word *sabu'* is derived from the root of *sabb'a*, seven.

16 This is a common practice in many Muslim countries.

17 The containers' design has as its theme something pure and promising such as a bird or a crescent in metal or in fabric, or may be a simple plate of silver upon which the sweets are served.

18 The *mawlid* is an especially Sufi practice. See Al Shahi (1987: 61).

19 See Kapstein (1992).

20 This is reminiscent of other Muslim countries where the state controls and limits traditional religious expression. Nancy and Richard Tapper note that in Turkey 'the *meylud* recitals have been redefined in secular terms as "ignorant superstitions" antipathetic to the state-controlled religious orthodoxies'. Those who are to participate fully in the modern state are expected to shed such 'superstitions'. Tapper and Tapper (1987: 83).

21 Indeed, I have heard a prominent male member of the *'awa'il* proclaim with some satisfaction that he had just returned from committing a *bid'a* (heresy), i.e. attending a *mawlid*.

22 In some Muslim countries, such as Malaysia, women are accepted for training as Quran reciters.

23 These traditional dishes are meat-filled pastries, *sambusak*, cucumber in a sesame sauce, *salatat tahina*, and a dessert made of flour and egg dipped in honey, *turumba*. The food,

which must exceed the quantity required to feed the numbers gathered, is offered in alms, *sadaga*.

◆ 5. THE RITES OF PASSAGE II

1 See Appendix A and Select Glossary
2 Quran, *sura* 49, *al-Hujurat* (The Inner Apartments), verse 13. Trans. Yusuf Ali. It is interesting that this verse, which is honoured more in the breach than in the observance, is well-known and repeated by the *'awa'il* as well as being printed on the right-hand side of wedding invitation card.
3 Quran, *sura* 5, *al-ma'ida* (The Table Spread), verse 6. Trans. Yusuf Ali.
4 However, the concept of *kafa'a* itself has been debated by the different *madhahib* (schools of Islamic thought), especially the Hanafi school, and is considered by some not to be Islamic since it is not mentioned in the Quran.
5 There are various other synonyms for honour. For instance, *sharaf* refers to honourable conduct in business affairs. All the terms implying honour have become more common during the 1980s as consciousness of cultural distinctiveness became acute.
6 Khan (1981: Vol. VII, 51). In the Hijaz, the bride consents before her father or guardian and two male witnesses. Silence means approval, for it is considered impolite for the bride to say 'yes'. By this point the bride's mother will have already established her approval, thereby minimising the risk of awkward surprises.
7 Maghrebi (1982: 39).
8 See Hurgronje (1970).
9 Although no law forbids men from marrying Jewish women, the practice appears to be taboo.
10 See *Al Qabs*, 17 August 1999.
11 In Egypt a comparable word is *yisharrif*, from *yizayyin*, to honour. There is an Arabic expression, *tajjamal bis-sabr* ('ennobled by patience').
12 This is similar to other Muslim societies. See Abu-Lughod (1986: 55).
13 See Yamani (1996).

14 Slavery was abolished by the late King Faisal in 1965. According to the Quran, a man may have sexual relations with his slave ('or [a captive] that your right hands possess', but a woman cannot. *Sura* 4, *al-Nissa* (The Women), verse 3. Trans. Yusuf Ali).

15 *Milka* is a particular word for the religious contract used by the Hijazis. It literally means 'ownership'. However, the invitation card uses the more classical term, *'agd al-giran* (contract of association). Another term, *katab al-kitab* (the writing of the book), is used in most other Arab countries.

16 *Dukhla*, which literally means 'entry', is the term for a wedding that is most often used in the Hijaz, with a clear sexual connotation. Another popular term is *farah* (happiness). The invitation card refers to *zifaf*, the word more commonly used in other Arab countries.

17 There is no men's party similar to the *dukhla*, in which the women stay up till dawn. But while the women celebrate at the *dukhla* the men sit in another hall or at home with one or more singers, and smoke a hubble-bubble, or waterpipe, *shisha*.

18 Khan (1981: Vol. IV, 59).

19 Maghrebi (1982: 25).

20 The trousseau is no longer displayed or celebrated as before; it has become a private affair.

21 Henna is said to symbolise fertility and good fortune.

22 Hurgronje (1970: 142).

23 Zubaida (1993: ch. 5).

24 Maghrebi (1982: 20).

25 The bigger the piece the more expensive it is.

26 Visas have to be acquired for the latter. This is a difficult process for foreign women in a closed country like Saudi Arabia.

27 Historically there were differences in the *adhan* (call to prayer) in different cities in the country. Today the Wahhabi *adhan* is less melodious, plainer, and more straightforward than the Meccan and Medinese. It is the only type of *adhan* allowed.

28 The *mumlik* is known as *ma'dhun* in most Arab countries.

29 This is usually her father but, if he is no longer living, the oldest paternal uncle or any close agnatic kinsman.

30 Princes are graded in importance, which corresponds to the closeness of their relationship to the king. The sons of these princes are graded in the same way.

31 Maghrebi (1982: 25).

32 Quran, *sura 30, al-Rum* (The Roman Empire), verse 21. Trans. Yusuf Ali.

33 These women are either ex-slaves of the extended families or else those of others 'borrowed' for the occasion, they may also be hired Filipino women. Women at the wedding must be served by other women; they cannot be served by men, for reasons of respectability and for fear of the Wahhabi religious establishment.

34 On such occasions women may issue an invitation saying, 'I have the princess so-and-so for dinner, please come in her honour'.

35 See Elias (1978) on the development in European societies of the concepts of 'shame' and 'delicateness' in association with the use of the knife and fork as opposed to eating with the hand. This practice is not only different from the Najdi but also from neighbouring Gulf Arabs. As Kanafani notes, 'In Arabia it is believed that food must be eaten with the body and for the body without any intermediaries between the body and the food which is the gift of God'. Kanafani (1983: 32).

36 These differences were once readily acknowledged in public. A Hijazi woman has told me that during the first years of unification she was asked when buying a veil in the market which type she wanted, the 'Najdi' or the 'Hijazi'.

◆ 6. THE RITES OF PASSAGE III

1 See Appendix A and Select Glossary.

2 Khan (1981: Vol. II, 225).

3 Amrou (1985: 354).

4 Hurgronje (1970: 148) and Maghrebi (1982: 42).

5 'Oh Allah purify him from his sins as a white garment is purified from soil. Oh Allah wash his sins with water, snow and hail.'

6 The instructions are as follows: 'When the angels come to you and ask you who is your God, what is your religion,

who is your Prophet, tell them Allah is my God, Islam is my religion, Muhammed is my Prophet, the Kaaba is my direction, the Quran is my guide and Muslims are my brothers. I die and I live on the testimony that there is no God but Allah and Muhammed is His Prophet. May Allah instruct you in your plea, may Allah guide your stumbling and forgive you your wrong doings and your sins and (may He) overlook your bad deeds, and make you inhabit Paradise with its felicity, with its good worshippers.' Lane (1987: 530). This *talgin* is performed in nearly the same way in Egypt.

7 This meal consisted of rice with chickpeas and meat, a salad made of sesame and cucumber and tripe stew. The tripe was cut very finely and cooked in a Meccan style. Fruit and *turumba* (a pastry dipped in honey) were also served.

8 Hurgronje (1970: 147) This ceremony of the death anniversary is also described by Maghrebi (1982).

9 Huntington and Metcalf (1979: 2).

10 The order in which the criteria of status are cited here is according to what the *'awa'il* appear to emphasise at times of death. Piety comes before money because the issue of death stresses the most important, lasting cultural values, whereas money is transient. At times of marriage, on the other hand, wealth often comes before piety. Hence, the criteria of status change not only with time but also depend on the occasion.

11 Khan (1981: Vol. II, 187).

12 As discussed by Hertz (1960)

13 Quran, *sura* 4, *al Nisa* (The Women), verse 25.

14 Many streets in Jeddah have been named after prominent past members of the *'awa'il* and other merchant families.

15 The term 'house of condolence' is specific to the Hijazis. It is no longer the 'house of so-and-so' but the 'house of death'. This is usually the house where the deceased lived and died, unless the house is not large enough and a close male relative wishes to hold the condolence ceremony at his own house.

16 People may sometimes light up a house for a birth (a naming ceremony) but always for a marriage, to make it festive, and for a death. Lighting up is associated with celebration, and in the event of death it signifies a celebration of the life

that has been lived and the continuity of the life of the patronymic group. The celebration is not of feasting or
rejoicing but of honouring and proclamation.

17 There is a popular saying, in the Hijaz, '*jariyat al-gadi matat*'
('The slave of the judge has died'), which means that the
degree of emotion stirred by a death—and the social significance of that emotion—rests not with the deceased but with
whom he or she is associated. The slave on her own stands
for little, but because she is identified with an important
person—the judge—a large condolence ceremony is held
for her, because the one receiving the condolence is the
judge. If the important person was known to be particularly
attached to the deceased person, then the ceremony is often
bigger.

18 This saying is very much part of the oral tradition; indeed,
there are no written sources for it.

19 See Altorki (1988: 82–94).

20 The following *hadith* is often repeated by Hijazis: 'Speak of
the good conduct of your deceased'. This is but one of many
*hadith*s that are popular amongst the Hijazi but which are
not recognised by the conservative Najdis.

21 The grave is only opened to put in another body of the family since some of the '*awa'il* were, until the 1970s, interred in
their own patronymic group's burial ground.

22 Al-Jawzia (1983: 47–51).

23 The source of the word *mifawala* is the classical Arabic *fal*
(good omen). The '*awa'il* say that thinking in a pessimistic
manner could trigger a bad omen. This belief is partly based
on the *hadith*: 'Be optimistic, you will find the good'.

24 Acceptable reasons for lateness are absence from the country, serious illness and childbirth (for which there is a 40-
day recovery period).

25 *Hawl* means one year. The death anniversary is called *sani-
yya* in Egypt, *sana* in Iraq and *hawliyya* in the Sudan. The
three terms also mean, annual, one year and yearly.

26 The exception to this rule is a wife, who is allowed to mourn
for longer than three days for her husband. Khan (1981: Vol.
II, 206).

27 Hired Quran reciters are Hijazis of Malaysian, Indonesian
or Egyptian origin. Some members of the '*awa'il* have their
own Quran reciters whom they call on occasions such as the

mawlid, paying them either in cash or with gifts such as Swiss watches.

28 See Tapper and Tapper (1987).

29 At every *mawlid* the oral ceremony is recorded on tapes. These are listened to whenever men or women feel the desire to hear the pious recitation, or they are given to others who are known to have particularly loved the deceased and love the Prophet Muhammed.

30 Quran, *sura* 89, *al-Fajr* (The Break of Day), verses 27–30. Trans. Yusuf Ali.

31 Khan (1981: Vol. II, 213).

32 Ibid.: 214.

33 Whenever and wherever the Quran is recited aloud, Islam obliges those present to listen to it quietly. Those attending are handed sections of the Quran to read, and what is read of it is offered to the soul of the deceased.

34 The Wahhabi fundamentalists wear their garments above the ankle and their beards long in emulation of the Prophet. Amrou (1985: 70).

35 Lane (1987: 532).

36 Urban Hijazi women are distinguished from tribal Bedouin women in that they have always participated at prayers in the mosques, albeit in the special areas reserved to them by the authorities.

37 This is described in detail in Hurgronje (1970).

◆ 7. CULTIVATING THE SOCIAL ARTS I

1 See Appendix A and Select Glossary.

2 Quran, *sura* 49, *al-Hujurat* (The Inner Apartments), verse 12.

◆ 8. CULTIVATING THE SOCIAL ARTS II

1 See Appendix A and Select Glossary.

2 See Yamani (1994).

3 *Dubyaza* in the Indian subcontinent means 'twice onions' and is usually a meat stew which fried onions are put into

twice. It is interesting how in the Hijaz the same name was given to an entirely different sweet dish.

4 Quran, *sura* 33, *al-Ahzab* (The Confederates), verse 53.

5 Quran *sura* 113, *al-Falaq* (The Dawn).

6 The first Saudi cookbook was published in Saudi Arabia in 1984, written jointly by six Saudi women from high-status patronymic groups from different parts of the country. The recipes are from various cities and regions, but these are not identified in the text, in accordance with the authorities' aim of promoting national homogeneity.

◆ 9. CULTIVATING THE SOCIAL ARTS III

1 See Appendix A and Select Glossary.

2 See Mauger (1988).

3 See Hurgronje (1970).

4 See Maghrebi (1982).

5 See illustrations of this dress in Binzagr (1979).

6 Women still wear their hair long; indeed, until the 1950s it was considered shameful to cut one's hair.

7 See Baker (1979) and Hogarth (1978).

8 See Al-Yassini (1985).

9 See Yamani (1996: 278).

10 Coleridge (1988: 197).

11 See Lurie (1981: 49).

12 See the illustrations in Binzagr (1979) and more descriptions of brides' dresses in Hurgronje (1970).

13 In Jeddah and Mecca winter is not as cold as in the north—Medina, Riyadh etc. Hence white *thiyab* (singular: *thob*) are worn.

14 According to Abu Daoud: cited in Amrou (1985: 214).

15 It has taken not only the shape of the garment but also the name. However it is thought of as a woman's dress, not a man's, for the attempt by women to resemble men in dress is disapproved of by the Prophet. According to Al-Bukhari, 'the Prophet cursed women who take the appearance of men, and men who take the appearance of women'. Cited in Amrou (1985: 323).

◆ 10. CONCLUSION

1 See Appendix A and Select Glossary.
2 Externally, Iran's Islamic revolution with its influence on other neighbouring Islamic countries; and internally, the raid on the Great Mosque in Mecca by Juhaiman and his group.
3 See, for example, Piscatori (1986) and Hourani (1983).
4 See Yamani (2000) Many among the new generation of women who have been educated aspire to join the ranks of the professions rather than be housewives like their mothers.
5 National schools supervised by the religious *'ulema* are seen to lack the ability to provide students with proficiency in English and the means to meet the realities of the outside world. By contrast, some of the new private schools have adopted American models.